Psychological Research in Prisons

Kids Company

The author has donated his royalties for this book to Kids Company, a registered charity.

Statement from the Director of Kids Company

In 2005 through our therapeutic programmes we supported some 4,500 clients, of whom approximately 300 were adults (patients/carers and teachers). As a charity we aim to reach communities of children who present with complex emotional and practical needs.

In excess of 95% of the children refer themselves to our services, hearing about us through word-of-mouth on the streets and in their schools. They are young people who love their parents but often live with worry for their well-being. Children as young as four years are left to survive their experiences of violence and neglect, and to meet their own basic needs. Many children aged ten and eleven years old turn to crime in order to feed and clothe themselves. These 'lone children' live in local authorities where social work departments are at breaking point. Often there are no spaces in schools or mental health clinics to accommodate their needs.

The absence of a functioning adult in their lives results in these children having an invisible citizenship. Kids Company advocates on their behalf, often helps them access statutory resources, where possible, and problem-solves their lives in the hope of restoring some consistency and reducing their sense of terror. We aim to return their childhood.

Camila Batmanghelidjh
Director
Kids Company
1 Kenbury Street
London SE5 9BS
Tel: 0845 644 6836

Psychological Research in Prisons

Edited by

Graham J. Towl
Ministry of Justice

The British Psychological Society

BPS Blackwell

BLACKWELL PUBLISHING
350 Main Street, Malden, MA 02148-5020, USA
9600 Garsington Road, Oxford OX4 2DQ, UK
550 Swanston Street, Carlton, Victoria 3053, Australia

First published 2006 by The British Psychological Society and Blackwell Publishing Ltd

3   2008

Library of Congress Cataloging-in-Publication Data

Psychological research in prisons/edited by Graham J. Towl.
    p. cm.
  Includes bibliographical references and index.
  ISBN: 978-1-4051-3314-2 (pbk.: alk. paper)
    1. Correctional psychology – Research. 2. Prisoners–Mental health
services. 3. Offenders with mental disabilities–Rehabilitation.
4. Prison psychology–Research   I. Towl, Graham J.
HV6089.P795 2006
365′.66–dc22

                                        2006001710

A catalogue record for this title is available from the British Library.

Set in 10/12.5 pt Photina
by Newgen Imaging Systems (P) Ltd., Chennai, India
Printed and bound in Singapore
by COS Printers Pte Ltd

The publisher's policy is to use permanent paper from mills that operate a sustainable forestry
policy, and which has been manufactured from pulp processed using acid-free and elementary
chlorine-free practices. Furthermore, the publisher ensures that the text paper and cover board
used have met acceptable environmental accreditation standards.

For further information on
Blackwell Publishing, visit our website:
www.blackwellpublishing.com

The British Psychological Society's free Research Digest e-mail service rounds up the latest
research and relates it to your syllabus in a user-friendly way. To subscribe go to
www.researchdigest.org.uk or send a blank e-mail to subscribe-rd@lists.bps.org.uk

Contents

Foreword

David Faulkner

Most of the chapters in this volume provide descriptions of evidence-based psychological studies undertaken by applied forensic psychologists working with prisoners. They illuminate important aspects of prisoners' behaviour and management and the nature of the institutions in which they are detained. They will be of value to managers and practitioners who have responsibility for prisons, and also to other researchers, including criminologists, whose interests are in similar areas of work. The chapters have an immediate application to subjects such as suicides and self-injury, bullying, the misuse of drugs and the treatment of special groups of prisoners such as young offenders, sexual offenders and those serving life sentences. All of those are matters of serious concern in today's prison system.

The volume is however much more than a description of a selection of academic studies. The chapters raise questions about the role and contribution of psychologists working in a prison setting, and about the wider intellectual, political and moral context in which a modern penal system has to operate. In his introduction, Graham J. Towl states that 'historically the generic graduate skills of psychological staff have perhaps been a key driver in their recruitment [in] . . . an organisation which, on the whole, has often found it difficult to recruit sufficient high quality graduates'. That was the reason for which Arthur (later Sir Arthur) Peterson introduced the first psychologists to the Prison Commission almost 50 years ago.

Since then, psychologists have not only applied their skills in forensic psychology to the treatment (or it would now be said management) of prisoners. They have also helped to promote a spirit of intellectual inquiry and rigorous analysis which has added to the professional competence and standing of the service as a whole. Early examples from the present writers' own experience included their contribution over many years to staff training at Wakefield, Leyhill and Newbold Revel; the exposure in the early 1970s of some of the myths which had become attached to borstal training, and the part which psychologists played in its modernisation; and the first recognition in the late

1970s of racial discrimination and prejudice (to the disbelief of many of their colleagues at the time).

The same spirit of inquiry and analysis is needed just as urgently today. Lessons which emerge from the present selection of studies include the limitations and the potentially distorting effect of regarding rates of reconviction as the only measure of success; the importance of treating prisoners (and other offenders) 'holistically' as living persons, taking account of their whole situation in and out of prison; and the need to consider and, if necessary, to change the character and dynamics of the whole institution (e.g., when dealing with bullying or drugs). Looking ahead, the creation of the National Offender Management Service (NOMS) will need to be accompanied by the development of a professional culture which is able to handle the increasingly demanding political and managerial context, including the new procedures for 'contestability', while challenging dubious assumptions and maintaining the highest standards of integrity and respect for human rights. Ministers have already spoken about the need for a change of culture, but mostly in the narrow context of contestability, and they have said nothing about the implications for recruitment, training, careers and leadership. Their silence is in sharp contrast to the attention which those subjects are receiving in connection with the police.

The book shows instances where the service might be – perhaps already is being – put to the test. One example is the theory and practice of risk assessment, and the ethical and empirical considerations which arise from them. Another is judgements about 'what works?' (with or without a question mark), the evidence on which they are made, and the consequences of applying them too rigidly in practice. A third is the thoughtless and potentially misleading use of language. There is no lack of public criticism of the jargon and clichés which are so often used in government publications and internal documents. But the issue is not just a matter of style. Unsuitable language – for example when words or images are transferred from one context to another – can distort thinking and create misunderstandings. Various contributors draw attention to the danger in expressions such as 'criminogenic need', 'high dosage' and 'treatment integrity', and the spurious impression of scientific authority which such 'pseudo-labelling' is intended to create. A fourth example is the 'manualised' approach to penal treatment where the practitioner's task is to follow procedure as set out in the manual of instructions and to avoid making judgements of their own – not least for their own protection in what has increasingly become a managerial culture of blame.

All that should be seen against a wider background of government thinking and writing which persists in portraying public service as a commercial enterprise marketing a service or product. The analogy can be, and often has been, useful to make a point. But the comparison breaks down when the complexity of services such as health, education and criminal justice is taken into account, and it becomes positively dangerous when it comes to dominate the whole mentality of government and public service. It is especially dangerous in criminal justice, where the 'business' is not one of production, distribution and sale but of upholding values and building and sustaining relationships, and where under NOMS the only 'purchaser' is the government itself. Some of the chapters in this volume suggest that the 'market' model of criminal justice may now be coming to the end of its useful life, as the 'medical' and 'justice' models did in the past.

It is not yet clear how NOMS will work or what impact its creation will have on reoffending or on the character of English justice, or how it will interact with English society more generally (Scotland and Northern Ireland are not involved, and there may not be much effect in Wales). Its vision of offender management may contribute to a more inclusive, responsive and responsible system of justice, and through that to similar changes in society as a whole. Its notion of contestability may help to support that contribution, for example if it is used in conjunction with offender management to create partnerships, relationships and responsibilities as proposed in the recent Green Paper *Reducing Re-Offending Through Skills and Employment* (Department for Education and Skills 2005, CM 6702). Or the ideas could be applied in a way which deepens social divisions, creates new administrative 'silos', increases fragmentation and recriminations, and re-enforces a culture of 'manualised' working.

Psychologists (and philosophers) should be especially well qualified to recognise the dangers and help the service to overcome them. This volume points to some of the ways in which they should be able to do so.

David Faulkner is a Senior Research Associate at the University of Oxford Centre for Criminology and was a Fellow of St John's College from 1992 to 1999. His main career was in the Home Office, where he served in the Prison Department (as it then was) from 1963 to 1966, 1970 to 1974 and as Director of Operational Policy from 1980 to 1982. He became Deputy Secretary in charge of the Criminal and Research and Statistics Departments in 1982 and Principal Establishment Officer in 1990.

Notes on Contributors

Editor

Graham J. Towl is Chief Psychologist based at the Ministry of Justice. He also holds visiting chairs at the universities of Birmingham and Portsmouth. Previously he was Head of Psychological Services in the Prison and Probation Services, where he led a strategic approach to the organisation and delivery of psychological services over a five-year period. He was the recipient of the British Psychological Society (BPS) award for distinguished contributions to professional psychology in 2003. He has published extensively in the forensic mental health field. He is a previous chair and treasurer of the BPS Division of Forensic Psychology and was the founding chair of the Board of Examiners in Forensic Psychology in the UK. He is the editor of *Evidence Based Mental Health*, a journal containing high-quality international research abstracts with expert commentaries. He was a founding editor of the multidisciplinary *British Journal of Forensic Practice* and also is founding editor of the *British Journal of Leadership in Public Services*. Currently he is an external examiner for the MPhil in Criminology at the University of Cambridge.

Contributors

Derval Ambrose is a Principal Psychologist in the Applied Psychology Group, Health and Offender Partnerships, Home Office/Department of Health. Her research interests include work with young offenders and the use of psychotherapy in prisons.

Jo Bailey is the Area Psychologist for the Eastern Area, HM Prison Service and Visiting Senior Lecturer at the University of East Anglia. Her research interests include life sentence prisoners.

David A. Crighton is Deputy Head of Psychology, Health and Offender Partnerships, Home Office/Department of Health, and Visiting Professor of

Psychology at London Metropolitan University. His research interests include risk assessment, the development of mental health services and sexual offenders.

David P. Farrington is Professor of Criminological Psychology at the University of Cambridge Institute of Criminology and is Director of the Cambridge Study into Delinquent Development. His research interests and prolific output include the development of criminal behaviour in childhood and the evaluation of interventions to reduce offending.

Jane L. Ireland is a Consultant in Forensic Psychology at Ashworth Hospital and Reader in Psychology at the University of Central Lancashire. Her research interests include bullying in secure environments.

Darrick Joliffe is a Lecturer at the University of Cambridge Institute of Criminology. His research interests include methods for evaluating interventions to reduce offending.

Kate A. Painter is a Senior Research Associate at the University of Cambridge Institute of Criminology. Her research interests include approaches to crime reductions and gender issues in crime.

Louisa Snow is Principal Research Officer with the Women's Policy Unit. Her research interests include women offenders and the assessment and intervention in self-injury.

Brian A. Thomas-Peter is Director of Psychological Services at Reaside Clinic and Visiting Professor of Psychology at the University of Birmingham. His research interests include personality disorder and the treatment of sexual offenders.

Introduction

Graham J. Towl

This is a book about evidence-based psychological approaches to working with prisoners. Psychologists do not have an exclusive claim on psychology. Most, but not all, of the contributors to this volume are psychologists, but all have something important to contribute on psychology. The research-based approach which underpins the chapters reflects a broader commitment to evidence-based practice which is both eclectic and reflective. This perhaps contrasts with much of the literature on working with offenders in recent years, which has often been constrained under the conceptually limited and increasingly unhelpful rubric of 'what works'. As one contributor to this volume points out, the term 'what works' used to include a question mark. Subsequently this appears to have been dispensed with. Readers may wish to reflect upon what such a transition in nomenclature means. Indeed, there is perhaps a need to move on from such a potentially dichotomous – it works or it doesn't – distinction. More recent attempts have been made to look at what is effective with whom and so on. However, the language used to frame the work seems to run counter to an understanding of the nature of evidence. It is not that something works or doesn't, rather the debate could perhaps more productively be about the types and levels of evidence in support of particular approaches. This may well result in a more diverse and effective range of responses in meeting needs.

Evidence-based practice arguably better affords the opportunity for a two-way engagement with researchers and practitioners about emerging evidence bases. David A. Crighton, in the first chapter of this volume plausibly speculates that there will, in future years, be an increasing closeness and indeed overlap in the work of many psychological researchers and practitioners. There are some professional developments which lend further support to this view. For example, in recent years, psychologists employed by public sector prisons have become more involved in the vetting of research proposals to undertake work with prisoners. At a policy level this development was introduced for two compelling reasons. First, because as graduates in psychology, it was thought that this staff group would be suited to this type of role given their knowledge of research in comparison with other prison staff. Indeed, historically the generic graduate skills of psychological staff have perhaps been a key driver in their recruitment. This is especially so against a backdrop of an organisation which, on the whole, has often found it difficult to recruit sufficient high-quality graduates. Graduate skills have been drawn upon and valued by prison managers, hence sometimes psychological staff have found themselves being involved in much work which would not formally be recognised as 'psychological' in its nature. The importance of the value of generic graduate skills to the organisation is often missed in accounts of the growth in numbers of psychological staff in recent years.

The second reason for the policy development was that it gave legitimacy to psychological staff engaging, or in some cases re-engaging, with research and ideas about research. Again David Crighton eloquently covers this territory in the first chapter of this volume.

Continuing with the theme of the language used in work with prisoners (and offenders more generally) it is perhaps worth looking at this more closely. Terms such as 'criminogenic', 'high dosage' and 'treatment integrity' appear to be commonly used in the literature and in practice. But what do such terms actually mean, and crucially what do they contribute? The term 'criminogenic' is routinely juxtaposed with 'factors' and appears to be used to refer to those 'factors' which are linked to an increased risk of reoffending. Arguably the term could just as well have been 'desistogenic' referring to factors likely to impact on reducing the risk of reoffending. But this would be an equally lugubrious approach. The term 'high dosage' seems to generally refer to the number of sessions of intervention work undertaken. 'Treatment integrity' is commonly used to refer to manual compliance, which is delivering a manualised approach to working with offenders in the way specified in the manual. Brian A. Thomas-Peter expresses his concern (as does David Crighton) about the use of such unhelpful and unnecessary jargon. Both single out 'criminogenic' as an unhelpful term. One essential problem with the term is that it appears to imply a level of compartmentalisation to the human condition which is simply not supported by the evidence. For example, drug misuse may be seen as a 'criminogenic factor', if we further apply this it would presumably also need to be highlighted as a 'healthogenic factor'. There may be an apparent scientific gloss to such terminology but in fact nothing substantive is added. Pseudo-scientific labelling exercises are not 'science', nor indeed for our purposes are they necessarily evidence based. Such language perhaps most plausibly reflects an unduly mechanistic approach which effectively serves to mask the true complexities of understanding criminal behaviour. The term then is, although popular, at best superfluous. Returning to the medicalised term 'high dosage' when referring to the number of intervention sessions, this is surely an example of jargon for its own sake. Although again some might argue that the medicalisation of the term gives a potentially more credible veneer to it. With regard to the term 'treatment integrity' this is potentially unhelpful since the term has largely been used to simply refer to the degree of compliance with a manual-based approach.

This book has as its focus an evidence-based approach. The chapters are split into two main sections. The first section covers the context, both scientific and socio-political, of psychological evidence and practice. The section finishes with a chapter on the needs of prisoners. This is intended to contribute to setting the scene for the second section which has as its focus work undertaken to meet identified needs. The range covered in both sections is not by any means intended to be comprehensive, but rather illustrative. The second section closes with an exploration and examination of the research into work with lifers and sex offenders. Both represent key areas of psychological practice among many psychologists employed by public sector prisons.

David Crighton begins by giving an account of the importance of an appreciation of scientific approaches to our understanding. He links this to a discussion of evidence-based practice. He helpfully illustrates a number of his observations about methodology using two examples of research undertaken by psychologists in prisons. Both studies are the largest of their kind in terms of their sample sizes, on suicide and lifers respectively. Good research needs to be based upon a sound ethical framework. Refreshingly Crighton addresses the importance of ethical issues in both research and practice. This may sometimes mean questioning received or rarely questioned apparent wisdoms. To do this most effectively requires an understanding of the broader context of our work. This is the topic of the chapter which follows by Brian Thomas-Peter. While acknowledging some of the positive progress in psychological approaches to working with offenders Thomas-Peter also provides a useful critique of the modern context of such work. His concerns about the 'new empirical orthodoxy' are outlined, and he also helpfully exposes the decidedly weak nature of some of the evidence which has sometimes been used in support of arguments to exclude some prisoners from treatment interventions. This more broadly touches upon a pervasive theme in this volume which is about the importance of being ethical and accountable for the choices we exercise as professionals.

Rounding off the first section of the book, Thomas-Peter addresses the fundamental area of consideration of the needs of offenders with an emphasis on the psychological processes of change. He begins by making the point that needs involve more than simply what have become known as 'criminogenic needs'. He convincingly argues that we need to carefully consider issues about both group dynamics and 'readiness to change' when providing interventions such as structured group work with offenders. He also shares an example to illustrate some of the potential hazards of not giving sufficient consideration to such factors. For example, a prisoner with a sadistic interest in their sexual offending may not benefit from empathy training. Indeed Thomas-Peter further argues that a failure to be 'case sensitive' may potentially worsen offence-related factors. He also calls into question the therapeutic impact of 'confrontation' with an informed critique of the clinical territory.

The second section of the book has a shift of focus from the context and needs of offenders to addressing these needs. In much of the work undertaken by psychologists directly employed within public sector prisons there has been a particular, and understandable, focus on the forensic aspects of applied psychology. Much of the work has been about risk assessment, management and interventions to reduce the risk of reoffending. However, other areas have tended to be neglected.[1] As health professionals, psychologists, from whatever specialism of applied psychology, have an obligation when working with offenders to bring with them a holistic understanding of the person. Evidence and arguments in support of this approach are further built upon in the second section of this volume.

Suicides in prisons are a matter of significant concern. Psychologists have not perhaps been as focussed on this as they should have in prisons. This is regrettable because psychological models of conceptualising and intervening to reduce the risk of suicides potentially have much to offer. However, in recent years some psychologists have become more involved in the challenging area of suicide prevention. Some contributions have been practice focussed whereas others have involved research. David Crighton undertook research into suicides in prisons drawing from a public health framework. This is the subject of his chapter which includes a pithy review of this important area of research.

Next Louisa Snow covers the research into self-injury and attempted suicide in prisons. She includes her own research into this often little understood area. A particular strength of her study was in the examination of the motivational and emotional antecedents to both attempted suicide and self-injury. The policy and practice implications of her work have already started to have influence and impact.

Bullying in prisons has until comparatively recently been an under-researched area. Jane Ireland has been extensively involved in researching this emerging area. Ireland takes an evidence-based approach in her chapter, which hopefully will provide a useful reference point for those designing and developing interventions to reduce bullying in prisons.

Chapter 7 includes a review of some of the promising evidence into the effectiveness of drug-misuse interventions in prisons. Studies on the efficacy of drug-misuse interventions have tended, understandably, to focus primarily upon improved health outcomes. More recently there has been an increase in evaluative work with reconviction levels as a measure of success. One key area of learning methodologically, which may have application elsewhere, is the importance of having a range of measures to assess 'success'. Without appropriately sensitive measures, sometimes potentially discernable changes may be missed. Drug-misuse interventions provide perhaps a good example of where both issues of improved health and reducing the risk of reoffending may be addressed together.

The next two chapters are about regime-based interventions with young people in prisons. It is probably axiomatic to state that the impact of effective work with young people in prisons may well have greater absolute health and crime-reduction benefits. Derval Ambrose describes and reflects upon research on the high-intensity training (HIT) intervention in the 1990s and also touches upon the work at the Military Corrective Training Centre (MCTC) at Colchester. This is followed with a chapter by David Farrington, Kate Painter and Derek Joliffe on the four-year follow-up (quantitative and qualitative) data from the MCTC. Disappointingly there was no evidence in support of the efficacy of the approach as a means of reducing the risk of reconviction. However, in terms of developing the evidence base, it is important to report such findings. Failure to do so can result in skewed data which may result in a misplaced optimism based on published 'successful' evidence.

The final part of the second section of this volume has as its focus two areas of significant activity among many psychologists working in prisons: lifers and sex offenders. David Crighton and Jo Bailey describe the policy and practice context of work with lifers. They go on to report the findings from research by Jo Bailey which, as alluded to earlier, is the most comprehensive of its kind relating to released and recalled lifers in England and Wales. They provide insights from this rich and extensive evidence particularly in relation to risk assessment and management.

The volume ends with a chapter by David Crighton on psychological research on sex offenders. Crighton makes the important, but often overlooked, point that what we appear to 'know' about sex offenders is confined to a sample who are unlikely to be representative of the population of sex offenders. Despite much research and practice in this challenging area, disappointingly little headway has been made in terms of being able to demonstrate a reduction in reconviction levels for those participating in such structured interventions in prisons. It should of course be acknowledged that it is genuinely difficult, partly because of issues of base rates, to demonstrate change in reduced reconviction rates. However, after over a decade of manualised approaches to working with sex offenders in prisons in England and Wales, no studies appear to report a statistically significant reduction in sexual reconvictions. As touched upon earlier, particularly in the chapter by Brian Thomas-Peter, perhaps there is more that we could do to enhance the possibility of having a greater treatment impact.

This collection of chapters is intended to contribute to the growing field of evidence-based approaches drawing from psychological perspectives in the challenging field of prison research. There are no signs of a reduction of interest in psychological perspectives, indeed much of what psychology has to offer can often be delivered by staff from backgrounds other than that of professional psychology. Indeed in terms of improving the services provided our challenge for the future seems two-fold; first to ensure that psychological approaches are drawn from a firm and eclectic evidence base; second to ensure that evidence-based psychological interventions are available and accessible to those who may benefit from them.

I hope that readers will find food for thought in the chapters that follow.

Notes

1. Towl, G.J. (2005). National Offender Management Service: Implications for applied psychologists in probation and prisons. *Forensic Update* **81**: 22–26.

Chapter 1

Methodological Issues in Psychological Research in Prisons

David A. Crighton

Introduction

Prisons provide both a wealth of challenges and a wealth of opportunities for psychological research. One of the most visible for psychologists, and also for other health care practitioners, is the development of evidence-based practice (EBP). This approach aims to ensure that practitioners work is increasingly grounded in 'scientific' research and, reciprocally, that practice concerns have a greater influence on research.

In order to understand better the implications of this change, the nature of EBP and scientific method is outlined in greater detail below, with particular reference to the philosophical and ethical bases. The ethical issues raised by psychological research in prisons are very similar to those raised in other areas of research, however it has been cogently argued that they are often brought into sharper relief in forensic settings (Towl, 1994a). The most striking ethical issue and one often overlooked is the need for clarity of precise aims in research. Research which simply serves to do little more than progress the careers of researchers, with no wider positive effects, seems wholly inadequate to justify often very intrusive studies. Within this framework it is also perhaps worth noting the issue of language. As an example, a number of researchers still routinely use terms such as 'criminogenic'. Despite the pseudo-scientific sound of such terms, they add nothing at all to our understanding of criminal behaviour and may suggest a level of precision in our understanding which is simply not supported in the evidence base (Towl, 2004a). Across psychological research such ethical issues have come increasingly to the fore and this trend seems set to continue.

Examples of good psychological research in prisons are important markers for practitioners, policy makers and researchers. They show potential avenues for development and demonstrate effective methodologies that can be used. Two examples of such research are outlined, although there are numerous of such examples of good-quality research and indeed examples of poor quality research. These examples have been chosen to show what can be achieved effectively and efficiently in two areas of pressing concern within prisons.

Perhaps the single largest area of growth in research efforts over the last decade has been in attempting to establish whether or not particular psychological interventions have an impact on levels of reoffending (Farrington *et al.*, 2000; Harper and Chitty, 2004; Tong and Farrington, 2004). It seems clear from the current evidence base that randomised control trials (RCTs) will be of growing importance in providing good-quality evidence here (Farrington and Jolliffe, 2002; Farrington, 2003). It also seems evident that an understanding of the economics of criminal justice will be ever more central as researchers draw more effectively from current criminology discourses (Cohen, 1998).

The practicalities of doing research in prisons are in a number of respects qualitatively different from other settings. Of course there are likely to be significant areas of overlap that will be familiar to would-be researchers, and a good research design outside a prison will often be a good research design within a prison. The key differences tend to follow on from some of the specific legal duties of senior managers in prisons to ensure the security and safety of the institution.[1] Such considerations influence research from the point of first request to post publication of results; the main issues are outlined and discussed, since these may often be novel to external researchers.

The future direction of psychological research within prisons seems both an important and interesting area to address. Of course, seeking to predict the future is a fraught and notoriously inaccurate business but some key trends do seem discernible and are outlined below.

The Basis of Psychological Research in Prisons

Philosophical issues

EBP is very much part of current attempts to improve the delivery and effectiveness of practice. It is therefore worth spending some time looking at the basis for such approaches and, in turn, at how practitioners might contribute most effectively by the development of practice-based evidence.

EBP is essentially the use of scientifically gathered evidence to inform the use of assessments and interventions, for our purposes, in health care. Therefore the philosophical basis of the scientific methods, the impacts of this and some of the criticisms raised are considered below.

The use of what would today be recognised as scientific approaches have a lengthy history. A history of the development of science is, of course, outside the scope of this chapter, however, it is clear that the use of mathematics was well developed in the Arab world and subsequently in Ancient Greece and Rome. The use of hypothesis formulation, experimentation and the recording of empirical data in a recognisably modern manner were seen in the work of Roger Bacon, a thirteenth-century Franciscan Friar and philosopher. Yet it was the European Renaissance of the fifteenth and early-sixteenth centuries that saw the beginnings of the most rapid growth in the use of scientific methods in areas as diverse as human anatomy, art and engineering (DaVinchi, 1998; Henry, 2001).

This scientific method has been described as being based on the hypothetico-deductive method in which hypotheses are generated based on an overall theory. These hypotheses are then tested by the use of carefully designed experiments which allow the initial theory to be revised (Popper, 1968).[2] In this analysis it is the systematic attempts to falsify hypotheses that separate true from pseudo-sciences. This view of science has been subject to a number of criticisms. In particular it has been suggested that it is an idealised view of science (Kuhn, 1996). In his analysis Kuhn saw scientists as holding on, relatively conservatively, to general models and paradigms until evidence built up to an extent that required a paradigm shift, due to the sheer accumulation of problems with a given approach. An example of this in psychology would perhaps be the perseverance of the behaviourist approach in the face of accumulating evidence that it provided on a partial and inadequate theoretical framework (Miller, 1967). It has also been suggested that Popper's view of science underestimated the role of observation in deciding what is, and is not, important to study. It is in this analysis that observation is used to invent theories to test and, as has been demonstrated, is itself a constructive process that is subject to interpretation (Miller, 1967).

The exclusive stress on evidence and empirical testing has also been questioned (Kuhn, 1996). Much of what would be seen as science is not exclusively based on evidence but may be logical, conceptual or mathematical in nature. The oft-quoted example here is the early-twentieth-century theoretical work of Albert Einstein on general relativity. However, the point is equally applicable to much of the developing work with cognitive neuropsychology, which draws on logical, conceptual and mathematical models to seek to account for aspects of thought. The key quality that makes such models scientific is, it is argued, that they are open to test and falsification.[3]

The use of such an approach in the social sciences has also been criticised on both philosophical and pragmatic grounds. It is argued that much of the social sciences have, largely as a result of the complexity of the material being studied, been built on the basis of mathematical correlations between variables, rather than the hypothetico-deductive method common to the natural sciences (Brown *et al.*, 1996).

Philosophical criticisms have portrayed much of the social sciences as 'positivistic', with the work of Durkheim (1953) often being given as an example of this. Yet it is argued that social processes are often more than the sum of their parts. Studying individuals, however carefully, cannot adequately capture emerging phenomena such as social hierarchies, class, health inequalities and so on (Brown *et al.*, 1996). Despite the ability to statistically demonstrate such phenomena, notions such as inequality, it is argued, remain little more than theoretical constructs (Townsend *et al.*, 1990).

More radical criticisms have been raised by those who have been broadly termed post-modernist philosophers, who have argued that there is nothing intrinsically superior about scientific knowledge compared with other knowledge systems, for example Voodoo (Feyerabend, 1999). Such views tend to see science as a powerful rhetorical device that has been more persuasive than other approaches. In many respects such views can be seen to draw from those of Bishop Berkeley (1685–1753) which were that there is no external reality to study and that all our experiences are mental; as such, everyday experience is illusory. Interestingly Popper (1968) shared the view that there is nothing intrinsically special about scientific approaches, suggesting,

> Science is nothing but enlightened and responsible common sense – common sense broadened by imaginative critical thinking.

At a philosophical level Popper also rejected the notion that science could be objective, arguing instead that this meant intersubjectivity, rather than reflecting an incontrovertible state of some external reality. It seems axiomatic that all observation takes place within a set of theoretical assumptions that will influence the observation[4] (Popper, 1968).

It has been argued by 'post-modernist' philosophers that there is a marked incredulity towards 'metanarratives'. These metanarratives are grand large-scale theories and philosophies of the world. For the purposes of this chapter the two most important are history as progress and the 'knowability' of everything by science (Brown *et al.*, 1996). It is argued that these kinds of beliefs are inadequate. The influence of the broad basis of post-modernist philosophical critiques has, it is probably fair to say, been limited within psychology and has often been received with varying degrees of hostility across the broad scientific community. Some points do have a resonance though. For example, the notion of scientific method as a powerful rhetorical device seems to be a fair observation. The suggestion of equality between systems of knowledge or epistemologies though has been fiercely contested on both moral and pragmatic grounds.

Ethical Issues

It is perhaps a helpful and healthy exercise to begin a discussion of research ethics by looking at the Tuskagee Syphilis Study (Brawley, 1999). This study is chosen here because it was one conducted by a range of health care practitioners in the community, rather than being a solely psychological study.[5] It is chosen because it illustrates particularly starkly a number of the key ethical issues. It was conducted in the US and involved studying the progress of syphilis in a group of men. In this study, a treatment that was known to be effective (antibiotics) was withheld from a group of 399 black men, all of low socio-economic status,[6] so that the full disease course could be studied.

This study seems an important and particularly relevant exemplar for a number of reasons. First, the study was targeted at a vulnerable group of participants. All the men studied were African Americans. Most were described as living in varying degrees of poverty. The levels of literacy and numeracy among the group appear to have been very low, making them dependent on professionals to adequately inform them about and explain to them the nature of the research, their treatment options and the likely risks. It is also important to note that this appears to have been adequately designed in terms of areas such as experimental design and mathematical analysis of data. It also took place under the auspices of the US Public Health Service.[7] It involved a range of well-qualified health professionals, many of whom had regular direct contact with the participants. The study ran for about 40 years (from 1932–72). Shockingly, it only came to an end when the study and its unethical methods were described by journalists from the *Washington Star* (Jones, 1993).

This study raises a number of key issues. It is clear that there is nothing intrinsically ethical about the scientific method and scientists and researchers. Despite a presumable commitment to protect participants from harm, across professional groups, large numbers of well-qualified multidisciplinary and professional staff involved in this study behaved in ways which seriously injured vulnerable patients over many years by withholding interventions that were known to be effective. The study was targeted at some of the most vulnerable people in society at that time. Researchers lied to, misled and deceived these vulnerable people in order to ensure data was collected efficiently for the study.

The problems with this study could be multiplied and it is sadly far from being an isolated example. Yet one of the key points in relation to psychological research in prisons is that prisoners, in this respect, are a vulnerable population. The nature of imprisonment means that prisoners are an easily accessible group within a coercive environment. Therefore special care needs to be taken in relation to the ethical safeguards for psychological research and interventions. This would seem particularly apposite where there is a balance between the protection of individual prisoners and the protection of others from the potential actions of prisoners.

A number of implications arise from this. Informed consent is fundamental to any psychological research and this applies equally to all participants. There are no grounds for not addressing issues of consent from prisoners. Likewise it is a general premise of ethical research studies that participants may withdraw at any time without experiencing any adverse impact. This is a fundamental protection for participants since it helps to ensure that their consent is freely given and is ongoing.

Research should not knowingly harm those who participate and the risks of harm should be made clear to participants in the light of current and developing knowledge. When dealing with experimental interventions it is, of course, impossible to give guarantees that no harm will occur. Experimental approaches by their intrinsic nature may have no impact, or may actively harm participants. Researchers in prisons need to make explicit in an honest and forthright way what they believe the risks to be and how likely they feel these are and, additionally, to update participants in the event that these change.[8] This was one of the striking failings in Tuskagee where the ineffectiveness of the interventions used and the increasing risks of not treating syphilis with appropriate antibiotics became more and more clear during the course of the study. Without an understanding of current and developing risks, it is difficult to see how participants' consent can be seen as in any way having validity.[9]

RCTs are seen as one of the more powerful methodologies available to study health care interventions. In essence RCTs involve randomly allocating participants to an experimental treatment condition or, normally, a treatment as usual condition. The power of such studies is increased by ensuring that participants and, importantly, also practitioners, do not know who is allocated to which groups (termed the double-blind methodology). This approach has been used extensively in scientific research to very good effect (Farrington, 2003). It does though raise a number of ethical and practical issues.

It can be argued that it is unethical to deprive anyone of an effective treatment, as happened in Tuskagee. It is therefore important that this methodology is applied in relation to experimental studies in which the outcome of the intervention is not known. The flip side of this argument is clearly that it is similarly unethical to subject people to the risks associated with interventions that may be ineffective or harmful.

While the use of RCTs may seem obviously useful, it is complicated by a number of additional ethical considerations. Where the effects in a trial are not strong (either positively or negatively) there may be a need to replicate studies even though there are emergent known risks for participants. Here the most appropriate ethical course of action would be to share these facts as fully as possible with participants.[10] Similarly in some RCTs powerful findings might emerge during the study, again potentially in positive or negative ways. In both cases it would seem appropriate to stop such studies. The ethical judgement for researchers here will always be when there is enough information to make this decision.

Evidence-Based Practice

The move towards using the scientific research evidence base to inform practice has been subject to a number of criticisms and it is perhaps worth airing some of the more salient ones here.

The first is largely an economic argument which in summary points out that what health care practice delivers accounts for only a small part of the variance in health outcomes (Reinhardt *et al.*, 2003). Less clearly defined areas such as stress levels, environmental exposure to toxins, healthy behaviours and genetic makeup interact to account for by far the largest part of health outcomes. This in turn raises the question of why so much effort is expended on refining health care interventions at all, other than to ensure lucrative employment for professional groups (Reinhardt, 2002). A similar economic argument could be applied across criminal justice settings. There are clear potential merits in such arguments, especially in relation to a shift of focus to reducing the causes of crime by reducing poverty, improving educational opportunity and improving housing, rather than focussing almost exclusively on interventions after the fact. At a fundamental level there is no substantive contradiction between such a shift and the use of EBP. Indeed it seems likely that good-quality EBP may increasingly lead practitioners towards a greater focus on preventative work as being more productive.

EBP has also been subject to criticism from professional bodies which have expressed concerns about the role of EBP in determining clinical practice. In the US this has also taken the form of concerns about the role of managed care organisations (MCOs) in dictating practice and excluding the use of assessments and interventions that have not been empirically validated (Levant, 2004). Such concerns are likely to be overstated though. The current evidence base in most areas is far short of legitimately being able to provide detailed prescription to practitioners.[11] Equally such developments serve to provide protection for people against interventions that are not evidence based and may be expensive and ineffective or indeed actively harmful to them.

More persuasively it has been suggested that there are as yet unresolved difficulties with the generalisability of EBP findings across populations. Findings predominantly based on white middle-class samples may have less relevance to black working-class populations for example (Levant, 2004). In addition it is evident that some approaches are less suited to empirical evaluation than others. For example, short-term protocol-based psychological interventions lend themselves more easily to such evaluation than long-term humanistic psychological therapies. While such criticisms appear to have some salience, it does seem that they are to a large extent concerned with limitations in the research base and research methodologies, rather than being more fundamental critiques of drawing on empirical evidence to guide interventions.

A more fundamental criticism is that health care interventions should be driven by patient preferences rather than outcome data (Stout, 2004). Such an approach though seems to be seriously flawed in a number of respects. It runs the risk of institutionalising what have been termed 'clinical mythologies' (Stout, 2004), subjecting people to interventions that simply do not improve their health.[12] Despite more than 40 years of sophisticated research, a number of examples of such mythologies can be identified that have yielded little empirical support. Looking at the psychological arena, it has been argued that these would include:

- the notion that psychopharmacological approaches are superior in the treatment of emotional complaints;
- the utility of psychiatric diagnoses in selecting treatment and predicting outcomes;
- the superiority of any one therapeutic approach over another[13] (Duncan and Miller, 2000).

Some also fear that the development of EBP will serve to limit and stifle innovation.

Indeed it is worth noting that many of these negative outcomes are possible if EBP is adopted without thoughtful and critical appraisal (Stout, 2004). It is not a panacea but simply to ignore empirical evidence seems to generate far more and greater risks.

Examples of Effective Research

Prisoners are a potentially captive audience for researchers. Yet surprisingly comparatively little of the research done with prisoners has proved to have much utility for prisoners, prisons or the wider society. As noted above, this not only raises a number of significant ethical concerns but it also raises what might be termed practical concerns.

The resources available to prisons are finite and the core activities or functions of prisons are primarily concerned with protecting the public, both by containing prisoners and by contributing to rehabilitation. Much of the history of psychological research in prisons though has contributed little to this goal, being more plausibly linked to developing the personal and professional interests of researchers, or alternatively identifying the need for further funded research. A lack of investment into such research in prisons has been criticised (Gunn, personal communication) but it is clear that significant resources have in the past been spent supporting often unproductive research.

Even so there are examples of effective psychological research taking place in prisons often at modest cost. For the purposes of this chapter two examples have been chosen, both completed as doctoral dissertations: Crighton (2000b) and Bailey (2006). The former was a study of suicide in prisons and the latter a study of life sentence offenders.

Suicides in prisons

In looking at suicides in prisons Crighton (2000b) conducted the largest detailed retrospective analysis to date of reports into 525 self-inflicted deaths in prisons in England and Wales between 1988 and 1998. The study involved both a detailed empirical analysis of these cases and a qualitative analysis. Multiple sources of data were used to provide what has been termed 'triangulation' (Campbell and Fiske, 1959; Good and Watts, 1989). The logic behind such approaches is that if multiple sources of data coincide, then greater confidence can be placed in the conclusions reached.

This study served to challenge a number of erroneous views about such deaths. For example, it demonstrated that over the period studied the rates of self-inflicted deaths for men in prison were higher than for women.[14] One of the most striking findings from this study was the relative level of risk over time. The first day from reception appeared to be a time of exceptional risk. The findings here were particularly striking and if extrapolated across a year would yield a rate of more than 9,000 deaths per year. The first week remained a period of very high risk, with a period of reducing risk up to a plateau at around 31 days post reception (Crighton, 2000b). This arguably appeared to reflect the high levels of anxiety and distress reported by prisoners in adapting to a new environment. Yet interestingly further analysis suggested that the effect was largely independent of experience or absolute time spent in prison custody overall, with transfers between prisons seeming to give rise to similarly increased risk. This finding called into question the practice of transferring prisoners assessed as being at high risk, since the change of environment appeared, all thing being equal, to be of central importance in inflating the level of risk.

The research also demonstrated that remand prisoners were not at exceptional risk compared to sentenced prisoners. This was in fact a popular myth based on the poor use of statistics. Put straightforwardly there are many more remand prisoners passing through prisons than sentenced prisoners but on any given day there will be relatively smaller numbers of remand prisoners. Hence if the rate of self-inflicted deaths is calculated on the basis of the average daily population in prison the rate for remand prisoners will be misleadingly inflated. Thus attempts to focus unduly on remand prisoners were fundamentally misguided.

The research identified very high levels of mental disorder among those who took their own lives, with around 7% being prescribed anti-psychotic medication at the time of their death and 12% on anxiolytic medication. Around 5% were receiving methadone detoxification for opiate addiction but this represented only a small fraction of those with substance abuse problems (Crighton, 2000b). From the analysis of the qualitative data these proxy measures seemed to produce a marked underestimate of the true levels of mental health problems experienced, with relatively poor levels of identification and intervention during the period studied.

Local prisons were found to have the highest rates of suicide, with much lower rates seen in other prisons regardless of security categorisation. This seemed to be linked to the fact that local prisons tend to have the least stable population, with many prisoners being in the prison for short periods of time. They also seemed to face significantly greater challenges in terms of receiving prisoners who needed detoxification from drugs and interventions for untreated mental disorders. Despite this the strategies put in place to prevent suicide did not differentiate at the time between types of prisons.[15]

The study also suggested links between violent offending, length of sentence and self-inflicted deaths. Those convicted of violent offences and facing indeterminate (life) sentences were particularly at risk.

In line with a number of community studies a large proportion of prisoners has clearly expressed their intention to end their lives, with 51% doing so. A large number had previously caused injury to themselves (45%) and 12% had done so during the same period in custody that they killed themselves. In parallel to this, 30% had been identified as at risk at some point in prison and 15% were being monitored at the time of their death. The qualitative data though suggested that the responses used by prison staff, or available to them, were often inadequate. Staff responses to expressions of suicidal intent varied markedly with a majority referring prisoners to the health care centre but with a significant minority (18%) taking no action.

Based on the findings a two-stage theoretical model of suicides in prison was advocated that drew together violence directed towards self and others, based largely on the work of Plutchik (1994). Using this model a public health approach to suicide reduction was advocated which sought to address suicide risk at multiple points (Crighton, 2004).

A number of criticisms of this study can be raised. Most obviously the study was retrospective and based on written records. The retrospective nature of many studies into suicide raises the question of whether such findings are still germane. It is, for example, possible that new factors have emerged that impact on suicide. An example of this might be the growth in illicit drug abuse. In early studies this was seldom noted but has now become a highly salient and potentially very significant factor.

The use of retrospective analyses in suicide is, in one sense, unavoidable. It is of course possible to look at analogous conditions such as self-injury, in the hope that these can tell us something about self-inflicted deaths. Yet it remains likely that, as has been convincingly argued elsewhere, as a group, such people will differ from those who go on to complete suicide (Towl *et al.*, 2000), hence recourse to study the available materials relating to the persons death retrospectively.

Life sentence offenders

The most extensive study of the characteristics of those subject to life sentences is the study by Bailey (2006) which analysed a sample of 6,191 life sentence offenders on whom the Home Office had recorded information. Of this sample 3,054 were offenders who had been a liberty in the community under life licence. Like the study by Crighton (2000b), this study comprised both quant- itative and qualitative analyses and a triangulation of the research data in an effort to improve confidence in the findings.

In line with the prison population more generally it was found that the vast majority of this group were men, with 269 (4%) of the sample being women. Women appeared less likely to be recalled to prison when on life licence with only one woman being subject to such a process.

A detailed study of life sentence prisoners who had been released from prison was undertaken. Just over 5% of these had been subject to a recall to prison. On the surface this might appear a relatively good performance in terms of pre- dicting future offending. However, Bailey suggests that it was in fact relatively poor, because just over half the life sentence population of 6,191 studied (pre- sumably including those felt to be the highest risk) had not been released at all. Wide variations were noted in the work undertaken with life sentence prisoners to prepare them for release and also in the quality of risk-assessment work.

This research also looked in detail at the nature of supervision and the process of recall under licence (Bailey, 2006). Wide variations were found in the quantity, nature and quality of supervision of offenders by probation officers. There appeared to be little consensus between probation officers about the nature of their role with a range of approaches seen. Some supervisors appeared to see their role as one of routine monitoring through formal office- based appointments. Others seemed to see their role as providing practical social work support with little in the way of monitoring. The most effective approach seemed to be a mix of monitoring and support but this seemed relat- ively rare. From the data gathered it seems clear that a number of life sentence offenders on licence may have been engaged in high-risk behaviour but have simply not been recalled due to poor supervision and recall practices.

The research found a statistically significant correlation of +0.25 between date of birth and date of discharge from prison. This suggests that, not unex- pectedly, older prisoners were more likely to be discharged. The extent of this correlation though could be seen as surprisingly low given the fact that risk of many forms of offending decreases with age (Towl and Crighton, 1996; Crighton, 2004). This finding was to some extent confirmed by Bailey's finding of a statistically significant negative correlation (-0.22) between recalls and age, suggesting that younger offenders were more likely to be recalled under licence. Those detained at Her Majesty's Pleasure are significantly over-represented among recalls to prison, comprising 12% of recalls against 7% of the life sentence population. In contrast those convicted as adults were under-represented. This difference was found to be statistically significant at the 5% level of probability ($\chi^2 = 4.941 \, p > 0.05$ d.f. 1). A number of possible explanations are suggested for this finding. These would include the possibility that those convicted at a younger age tend to be released at a younger age. It is also possible that those convicted of such serious offences as children may represent a group with more serious psychological and social difficulties.

The rates of recalled offenders by country of birth was also analysed with one striking finding emerging. An over-representation of offenders born in Jamaica (5.7% compared to 1.7% of the life sentence population) was found. The sample size was too small to look at other Caribbean islands and the small numbers involved mean that any conclusions are tentative. However, there are a number of possible suggested explanations for this finding. First, Bailey (2006) suggests that this predominantly black group of offenders may be subject to a range of social and economic factors that make them more likely to reoffend and/or breach their licence conditions. For example, they may be more likely to be unemployed, live in poor housing areas, mix with anti-social groups and so on. However, it does seem likely that offenders born in Asia and Africa would be subject to similar levels of social exclusion. It is also possible that Jamaican offenders may be subject to biases in the recall process itself, they may have been subject to less effective assessment and intervention work in custody, or they may engage in behaviours that make recall more likely. Or it may be to some degree a product of racism, whether institutionalised or otherwise.

Again a number of criticisms of this study can be raised. As with the Crighton (2000b) study a retrospective analysis was used based on existing computer and written records. Again this raises the question of how relevant the historical snapshot is to current practice, in the face of organisational and social changes.

Equally though criticisms can be raised about prospective studies which potentially raise the concern of influencing what is being studied. Such prospective studies are also subject to social and organisational changes as they progress since it is not possible to control such factors. Unlike studies of suicide, however, it is of course possible to talk directly to life sentence prisoners about their experiences as they are happening.

Practical Issues

In order to address some of the concerns about the involvement of prisoners in research, prisons have radically revised their approach to approving external research (HM Prison Service, 2004b; 2005). There are essentially two aims here: (1) to protect prisoners and (2) to ensure that prison resources are used to best effect.

In order to ensure this, external researchers are required to submit formal applications to conduct research. These are subject to differing levels of assessment depending on the scale and nature of the proposed research summarised in Table 1.1.

Applications are assessed against a number of key criteria.

1   The research must be ethically sound.
2   The research must be methodologically sound.
3   The research must be of potential value to the Prison Service or Home Office National Offender Management Service.

Any application that cannot demonstrate all three of these is likely to be rejected and any that does not meet the first two should always be rejected. A number of additional criteria are also used to assess applications for external research which are generally practical in nature and concern whether the resources (time, staff, information) needed to support the research are likely to be available and in proportion to any potential benefits of the research. Similarly issues of security are involved in any assessment along with consideration of whether the research is potentially sensitive.

Where the research involves children under 16 or vulnerable groups researchers will need to demonstrate that they have adequately addressed any ethical issues. Similarly researchers will need to demonstrate that they

Table 1.1   Levels of assessment depending on the scale and nature of the proposed research

Where the research is taking place	Who should review the application
One prison	Prison governor/Research contact
A number of prisons in one Prison Service area	Area psychologist
A number of prisons in more than one Prison Service area	Planning Group HM Prison Service
National strategic research – including research to be published by the Home Office or sent to ministers, research that will cost more than £10K or more than 30 days' staff time	Research, development and statistics – NOMS

have taken adequate steps to address any negative results from research. For example, a study of levels of sexual abuse is likely to generate concerns, anxiety and potentially distress among participants and responses of such effects need to form part of a research proposal.

Where research proposals raise specific ethical issues the application may simply be rejected or, alternatively, may be discussed directly with the researcher. Specialist advice on such issues is via the area psychologist. Where the area psychologist cannot provide advice they must refer the query to Planning Group at Prison Service Headquarters, who will convene a meeting of the Ethics Panel. This panel will review the research application and provide written guidance to the research contact/prison governor/area psychologist who originated the ethical query. This decision of the Ethics Panel can only be overruled by the Director General of the Prison Service, or their nominated representative.[16]

Research relating solely to health care should go through the recognised National Health Service (NHS) ethical procedures, Multi-Centre Research Ethics Committees (MRECs) or Local Research Ethics Committees (LRECs). These are expert bodies concerned with and accountable for ethical approval of health research. As such applications do not require additional ethical authority.

Models for Future Research

As alluded to earlier in this chapter, making predictions about the future is a potentially fraught exercise. However, a number of key themes are evident and seem likely to influence developments.

These would include an ongoing focus on ethical practice. Recent scandals across health care, often involving people at vulnerable stages of their lives, make it essential that psychological research in prisons is conducted to high ethical standards.

With the likely advent of statutory registration for psychologists, it seems likely that a significant impetus for improving standards will be created particularly for psychological research undertaken by psychologists. Such standards will, of course, need to apply equally to both internal and external research involving prisoners.

Within such parameters it also seems evident that research will increasingly need to be seen as useful. Part of this of course involves research being methodologically adequate for its purpose but it also involves a shift towards increasingly applied research in prison settings. The role of EBP seems set to grow significantly in coming years and research will be needed to fill the gaps in the existing knowledge base. As part of this trend it seems likely practitioners will need to become increasingly active in influencing the strategic direction of research at local, regional and national levels. Traditional distinctions between 'researchers' and 'practitioners' and between 'academic' and 'practice' settings will need to be increasingly bridged if research is to be relevant and practitioners are to base their work more firmly on empirical research.

At several points throughout this book it is noted that offenders themselves have a great deal to tell us about what interventions are likely to be helpful and effective. Even so it is clear that some practitioners and policy makers have reservations about this. At times it seems that interventions need to be framed as additional punishments, an approach which is often supported by a framework of pseudo-scientific jargon referred to previously, such as talking about 'criminogenic' factors (based on the illusion that these can be somehow isolated independently) and 'dosage' (rather than number of sessions!) in relation to psychological therapies. We need to put aside the absurdities of such potentially misleading and damaging linguistic practices and focus upon both a theoretical and practical understanding of how we can help to enable positive change. As noted in an excellent review for the Scottish Executive psychological interventions do not work in such a simple and mechanistic manner (McNeill *et al.*, 2005). Effective approaches are highly dependent on practitioners being able to develop an effective and flexible working alliance with those they work with and their developing a collaborative and client-driven approach. It seems likely therefore that research will need to increasingly focus on how to deliver interventions in the prison context, if they are to contribute to reducing future offending.

As noted above many of the pressing research questions can be addressed by high-quality research studies and many of these do not require lavish research funding. The studies by Crighton (2000b) and Bailey (2006) provide examples of this. In developing links with local universities, prisons have the potential to tap into considerable research expertise as part of a mutually beneficial partnership working.

The experimental nature of many of the psychological interventions used in prisons makes them particularly suited to the use of RCT methodologies. Given the power of such methodologies it would be a missed opportunity if one or more areas were not subjected to this form of testing.

The advent of the National Offender Management Service at the Home Office has led to a clearer focus on the distinction of commissioners and service delivery. The impact of this on psychological research is likely to be similar to other areas of work, with an increasing number of potential suppliers able to compete for such research work. In the future it seems likely that there will be a shift with less work being directly done 'in-house' and more being done by other potentially more cost-effective 'suppliers'. The role of commissioners of psychological research will increasingly become one of specifying policy on what needs to be researched and effective contract management.

It is a time of rapid change in research and criminal justice policy and practice. It is though undoubtedly an exciting time to be involved in psychological research in prisons and more generally across offender management services. Research has never been healthier, in terms of both quality and quantity. The growth of EBP seems set to fuel the need for effective psychological research and better joint working between research and applied settings, with great potential benefits for both. It is to be hoped that practitioners, researchers and policy makers will grasp these opportunities fully.

Notes

1. This is in a number of respects different from other applied research settings such as, for example, hospitals and schools. In these, senior managers have a clear duty of care to patients and children within their institutions. They have a significantly less defined duty to ensure the security of the institutions, both in terms of access and also what materials and information may move within the institution.
2. It is often incorrectly suggested that the use of such methods to study human behaviour is a recent development. In fact examples of such approaches date back at least to the Renaissance. For example the Dutch physician Johan Weyer undertook work that looked very much like modern experimental applied psychology to test cases of demonic possession by careful observation. His findings and views on witchcraft were published in *De Praestigiis Daemonum et Incantatiponibus ac Venificiis* (On the Illusions of the Demons and on Spells and Poisons, 1563) and he is often credited as the first person to coin the term 'mentally ill' to describe many people accused of witchcraft.
3. Although not considered here this is often at the heart of questions about whether mathematics is in fact a science. Similar questions arise in relation to theories in areas in theoretical physics such as quantum mechanics and string theory, where it is currently difficult to see ways to test explanatory models, raising the question of whether these are science or metaphysics.
4. Interestingly scientists historically seem to have been far less focussed in the areas they would seek to observe. Roger Bacon's credulity in the areas he was prepared to explore was noted during his lifetime. Isaac Newton was known for studying alchemy and the occult, alongside his studies of optics and gravity. Johan Weyer, as well as identifying the basis of witchcraft in mental disorder, wrote a typology of demons and suggested positive ways of invoking them (although it seems likely that much or all of this was mockingly written).
5. There are unfortunately a number of examples of unethical conduct in psychological research but no single study appeared to illustrate the range of ethical and professional failings analysed so fully in the Tuskagee study.
6. This term in many ways seems inadequate to capture the conditions that the study participants lived in. Many of the group lived in conditions of profound poverty and social deprivation.
7. There is an extensive psychological research literature on the area of compliance which suggests higher levels of compliance to high-status individuals or institutions. The involvement of a federal US health agency may therefore have

been a factor influencing (though not excusing) the very high levels of professional misconduct among staff on the study.

8. While there is a primary duty towards participants in any study, it can be argued that there is an additional duty towards policy makers, funding bodies and broader society to include future possible cohorts.

9. Historically a common practice in some health care research has been to obtain written consent. Recent scandals in pathology have shown that many such documents were designed to essentially give an open-ended consent to health professionals to do as they wished, rather than as a way to confirm that informed consent had been given. Again this has been seen as unethical practice since, in these examples, it was evident that relatives had been given a totally inadequate understanding of what they were consenting to, or had been misled. In some cases it appeared that staff had been motivated by concerns about the need to identify the causes of death and the potential prevention and cure of future illness. Such justification was seen as inadequate to justify unethical practices (Hall, 2001).

10. One option here is to use RCTs with a crossover design. Here participants are exposed to both intervention conditions but in differing orders. These designs go some way to mitigating potential negative effects for participants but cannot eliminate them altogether.

11. There are of course managerial reasons why such prescription might appear desirable but in the context of psychological interventions this is likely to undermine what is effective about such approaches, since these depend so heavily upon the ability of practitioners to respond flexibly and empathically to emerging needs.

12. While Stout is critical of such 'mythologies' an even more critical view is given by the health economist Reinhardt (2002), who convincingly argues that such approaches are often designed to maximise the income of health care practitioners at the expense of patients and interventions that may serve to genuinely improve health outcomes.

13. Indeed in looking at the impact of psychological therapies Duncan and Miller concluded that the distribution of effects was as follows: 15% model and technique, 15% hope and expectancy, 30% relationship factors and 40% client factors.

14. The rates for women were subject to marked fluctuations due largely to the relatively small numbers involved. For shorter timeframes the rate may appear higher for women but this appeared to be a sampling effect.

15. This has now changed with a focus of resources on local prisons and the creation of first night induction centres as part of a new approach to preventing such deaths.

16. In late 2005 the Prison Service Order concerning external research and the Ethics Panel was in the process of being revised. The current version of all Prison Service Orders currently in force can be found on the Prison Service website – www.hmprisonservice.gov.uk

Chapter 2

The Modern Context of Psychology in Corrections: Influences, Limitations and Values of 'What Works'

Brian A. Thomas-Peter

Introduction

These are rare times for psychology and applied psychologists within corrections. Never has psychology been more influential. The rolling out of accredited programmes in the UK since 1996 within prisons and probation illustrates this success in very real terms (Blud, 2003). In addition, the contribution psychology has made to the knowledge base of risk assessment, risk management and corrections policy all add up to halcyon days for the discipline and all those who apply it. So substantial has the effort of those in corrections been that there are now reviews of the meta-analytic literature (McGuire, 2002). It is fair to conclude that corrections in the UK, and perhaps elsewhere, have never been so 'psychology minded'. Ogloff and Davies (2004) express hope that this trend continues and caution that the pendulum will swing away from hard won liberal rehabilitation policies back to greater punitiveness if we do not sustain our commitment to the risk–needs model that has driven this success. Two rather sobering and related observations might be made about these circumstances.

This apparent rehabilitation ethos in the UK and elsewhere should not be mistaken for liberal enlightenment. Recent criminological discourses, which collectively have become known as the 'New Punitiveness' (Pratt *et al.*, 2005), make a convincing argument that the last few decades have been a remarkably unenlightened period. In this respect our first argument must be in establishing where the liberal-punitive pendulum really is. Some have argued that psychologists offering cognitive-behavioural therapy (CBT)-based programmes and proclaiming their central place in 'what works' for offenders have provided a 'veil of liberalism' (Moore and Hannah-Moffat, 2005) that masks narrow-mindedness if not blatantly anti-therapeutic attitudes, brutal environments and reactionary political trends. Those who have supported the 'what works' ideology from early days will be dismayed by this, believing as they do in the noble struggle against the pessimism of the era of 'nothing works'. To say this belief has been an illusion would overstate the argument, but psychologists have been insufficiently aware of the extent to which psychology has played a part in holding the pendulum away from enlightenment. To make their impact psychologists have had to accept, work within and support a profoundly reactionary set of values, which has sought to redefine the profession.

The second observation is that the popularity of psychological programmes is unlikely to last. There will be a moment when policy questions are asked about the value of psychology in corrections. The problem of small and short-lived effects (McGuire, 1997), the problem of drop-outs and non-completers of programmes (McMurran and Theodosi, 2005) and studies questioning the value of CBT programmes with sex offenders (Friendship *et al.*, 2003c), anger/violence programmes (Howells *et al.*, 2002) and the effect of 'thinking' programmes (Falshaw *et al.*, 2003b) on recidivism have brought this question closer.

In this chapter, I argue that we must understand the contribution of psychology and CBT in this broad context, if we are to prevent the forces of conservativism, managerialism and empirical orthodoxy consuming all that is positive in psychological therapy within prisons. We must understand the differences between psychology and a host of factors that influence applied psychologists, such as social trend, political fashion, organisational need and programme management. We must also understand what these influences are doing to the definition of psychology and psychologists. Failing to see the context may result in the contribution of psychology being contaminated by factors associated with but not of psychology. It may also mean a diminishing of psychology and psychological interventions.

Critics of correctional treatment might observe that there are very few examples of programmes that successfully engage all of the principles associated with 'what works'. Whether it is the six principles of McGuire (1995), the fourteen principles of Losel (1998) or the eight principles of Latissa *et al.* (2002), most programmes do what they can do within their constraints. This brings problems, not least of which is evaluating psychological programmes without the context and infrastructure that will make them most effective. At one level, this amounts to unconsciously sustaining the illusion of liberal and safe rehabilitation. At another level, we cannot hope to display positive outcomes for narrow interventions that swim against the tide of 'criminogenic' influences outside of programmatic control. At the same time there have been efforts to ensure compliance to the 'what works' doctrine that have brought a different set of problems and risks to the credibility of applied psychology and psychologists.

In the end, by holding and operating under this 'veil of liberalism' we may be at risk of undermining the contribution and credibility of CBT and psychology generally, in part by the very efforts of those who seek to apply it. This chapter hopes to indicate how more value can be extracted from psychological interventions if this context and these influences are understood.

There are three related international influences on psychology in corrections that have emerged since 1990. They include a socio-political trend that may be depicted as a new intolerance of deviance. Others have made similar arguments described as the 'death of liberalism' (Gunn, 2000), or the 'new punitiveness' (Pratt *et al.*, 2005). The second is public sector reform, which in the UK and elsewhere has been characterised as 'new public management' (Hood, 1991). Finally, there has developed a form of empirical orthodoxy in applied forensic psychology that has resulted in great clarity and progress in some respects and some naivety in others. Each of these offers a commentary from which we can see the influences and limits of applied psychology within corrections.

The New Intolerance

There have been numerous challenges to liberal justice in Western democracies. These challenges include 'Three strikes and you are out'; the right to silence; the assumption of innocence; the standards of evidence; the right to remain anonymous; the demise of single jeopardy; detention without trial; return of 'shaming' punishments; and sentence migration whereby determinate sentences become indefinite incarceration.

Each of these brings to mind the changing world we live in and the growing anxiety about our personal safety and national security. Together they reveal a changing attitude towards offenders in which traditional individual liberties are giving way to public protection concerns. Psychologists have contributed to this erosion of liberties with their preoccupation with 'risk' and redefinition of psychological 'need' as that which is desirable for society.

A similar trend is seen in statutory developments within criminal justice and mental health legislation in the UK since 1990. For example, within the criminal justice system there has been, among others, the Criminal Justice Act 1991, the Crime (Sentences) Act 1997, the Sex Offender Act 1997, the Crime and Disorder Act 1998 and the Criminal Justice Act 2003 which required participation of key agencies in the multi-agency public protection arrangements. In mental health there is the current proposed reform of the Mental Health Act that explicitly addresses the issue of risk as a responsibility of health. Between the National Health Service (NHS) and Home Office there has developed the dangerous and severe personality disorder initiative, which is designed to both meet the unmet need of this complicated and ill-defined group and, crucially, to protect the public. There is nothing psychological about these observations but there are implications for the role of psychologists and the application of psychology in this new context.

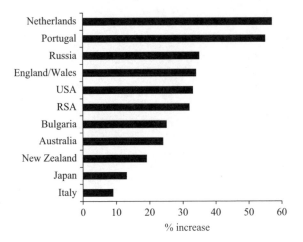

Figure 2.1 Percentage increase in prison population 1992–7 (Home Office Research Findings No. 88)

The size of these social changes can be seen in international observations. In Figure 2.1 the percentage increase in prison population is illustrated in a group of countries taken from East and Western Europe, America, Africa, Australia and Asia, during the middle period of the 1990s. Interestingly, a large percentage increase appears in the Netherlands, traditionally known as a very liberal democracy and noted for its permissiveness and tolerance. It seems that this reputation is no longer warranted, at least as it applies to sentencing policy.

England and Wales are interesting because of the average prison population rising from nearly 50,000 in 1987 to nearly 75,000 in 2003 (ONS Crime and Justice website). For both adult and young offenders, more people are being incarcerated for longer periods, especially for interpersonal crimes and this seems the basis of the percentage rise in the imprisoned population.

If we consider the US in more detail by looking at incarceration in the federal penitentiary system, perhaps a better index of broad social trend than state jurisdictions, we observe clear changes in Figure 2.2. After a 15-year period of relative stability throughout the 1970s and 1980s there is an extraordinary rise in the number imprisoned from the late 1980s through the 1990s and into the following century. Some of this is fuelled by the growth of drug offenders, but not all of it.

If any further evidence is needed to make the point that the world of criminal justice changed in the 1990s a more troubling observation is available from Amnesty International US and is presented in Figure 2.3. It depicts the number of executions in the US over 21 years between 1983 and 2003.

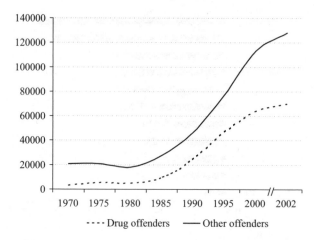

Figure 2.2   Sentenced federal prisoners, US: 1970–2002 (Federal Bureau of Prisons (Fedstat) Website)

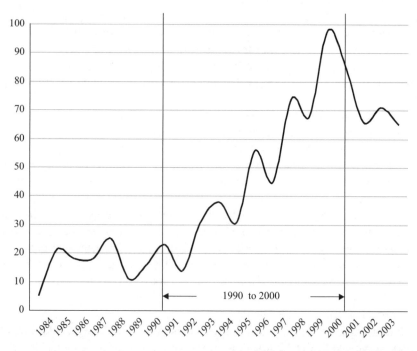

Figure 2.3   Annual executions in America 1983–2003 (Amnesty International US)

We see here a five-fold increase in executions from 1990 to the year 2000, in dramatic contrast to the previous 13 years. The diminishing number of executions subsequent to 2000 is probably accounted for by developments in DNA technology which have resulted in almost one-third of those who might have been executed being 'saved by the bell'. Regrettably, those not saved by the bell included a number of children, the last being Scott Hain in Oklahoma, 13 April 2003, and a number of people with mental disorder such as Larry Robinson (schizophrenia) executed in Texas, 21 January 2000 and Thomas Provenzano (schizophrenia) executed in Florida, 22 June 2000.

It is difficult to avoid the conclusion that these observations have the common thread of reduced tolerance of social deviance, preoccupation with public protection and perhaps a change in perception of offenders, in many parts of the world. We might think of this change of perception of offenders as including a new moral attribution and a new belief in personal responsibility and accountability. It follows from this that those viewing the 'deviants' see themselves differently too. Society has acquired new rights, new authority and new legitimacy over others to punish, castigate, blame, treat and exclude. It appears that there is little political will or ethical drive to reflect on the damage being done by our exercising of this authority. We have been less obliged to understand, have consideration for and mitigate the behaviour of those who transgress. Those who do are themselves castigated for being 'soft', 'wet', 'liberal', 'bleeding hearts'. In this context there has developed a changed perception of what now appears reasonable or legitimate to do with or to offenders. Hallsworth (2005, p. 239) succinctly expresses the trend: 'In the last two decades the tariff of acceptable pain that could be legitimately directed towards deviant populations appears to have increased.' This applies equally to both the punishment and rehabilitation of offenders (Hudson, 2005).

All of this implies a reactionary swing of the pendulum, rather than the liberal one for which the risk–needs orthodoxy seeks credit. Psychologists have been influenced by, contributed to and taken advantage of these trends with contributions to the reduction of offending, child protection, corrections and forensic psychiatry and a preoccupation with the assessment of risk. Some of these contributions have unwittingly institutionalised insensitivity under the guise of empirical purity. For example, some of those applying psychology have exposed offenders to intensive and demanding programmes without individual assessment or preparation to make best use of therapy. Commonly offenders have been considered narrowly, with therapy targeting a 'criminogenic need' rather than the needs of the offenders and often in environments that are not congruent with therapeutic efforts. They are then released into environments that are at high risk of promoting recidivism, without having basic skills to cope with a conventional life.

There is some ground for optimism in changes within the UK penal system. Narey[1] (2005) has described the inadequacies of prisons in the UK in forthright terms and has embarked on a process of management reforms designed to offer value-based leadership and moral direction in prisons and the infrastructure to support risk-reducing interventions. However, this refreshing perspective is a recent and unexpected twist in the evolution of public sector management, which has been dominated by a trend known as new public management (NPM).

The New Public Management

Hood (1991) has described NPM as 'one of the most striking trends in public administration' (p. 3), over the previous 15 years. NPM remains difficult to define precisely but despite the ambiguity NPM has been profound in the effect it has had on public services and professions. Efforts to define NPM hint at how it has influenced psychological practice in the last two decades. Clarke *et al.* (2000) define NPM in five points, adapted here:

1 Focus on outputs and performance rather than inputs.
2 Organisations as chains of low-trust relationships linked by contractual processes.
3 Separation of 'purchaser' and 'provider' and 'client' and 'contractor' rather than integration in service or organisation.
4 Breaking down of organisation and encouraging competition.
5 Decentralisation of budgetary control to 'cost centres'.

Here we see the introduction of commercial ideas into the public sector and the undermining of linkages between every part of the process of service delivery in order to exert financial and management control over them. Indeed it is the process that is lost in this. 'What' is more important than 'how', and 'what' is all that needs to be managed. There is no loyalty to providers, suppliers or supply chains. This means less ownership and control by professionals; accountability is to managers or 'consumers' not professions; there is less commitment to professional training with more commitment to competency-based education which leads to a diluting of the authority of professions. Organisationally it means competitive tendering, fewer links across agency and service boundaries, acceptance of a political agenda and little participation in the construction of values.

Some of this benefits public services. For services involving discrete interventions, such as minor surgery or deciding on social benefit, this kind of focus may be more efficient and equitable. However in any service where protracted involvement is needed, NPM invites error. Opportunities for mistakes are plentiful where there is fragmentation and segmentation, yet the key to success is continuity. Managers in the era of NPM have only to manage their segment. In this environment it should not come as a surprise to see the reaction of managers pressing down costs by narrowing core functions, circumscribing responsibility, defining their service independently of other segments, outsourcing treatment provision when the risk seems too high or when they are temporarily blinded to the real risk. Too rarely are there genuine efforts to build whole treatment pathways and fully fund services. Partition and segmentation is the style of modern public sector management, while integration and integrity are the hallmarks of 'what works'. In practice, this distinction is not quite as clear as this implies.

Gendreau *et al.* (2000) attempt to refocus correctional policy by reference to the value of the 'what works' literature and all that distracts correctional agencies from being guided by it. The commentary reproaches managerial influences and it is easy to be in sympathy with and entertained by it. At the same time its perspective is narrow, missing the larger context. The idea that the introduction of an unnecessary and incompetent managerial class (disdainfully referred to as 'fartcatchers'[2] (Gendreau *et al.*, 2000)) that has accompanied NPM has been a reason why correctional policy has not relied more on empirical psychology and fails to recognise the political context or the revolution in public sector management throughout the 1980s and 1990s that made the influence of psychology in corrections possible. Neither does it acknowledge how psychologists and other correctional programme makers have used the tools of NPM to make this progress.

So many benefits have followed from the risk–needs model that it seems churlish to point out that not every effect has been positive. It can be argued, however, that it is the confluence of 'what works' and NPM that has the seeds of both tremendous advances in correctional interventions and the discrediting of psychology.

In the effort to respond to the pressures of demand and the 'what works' agenda, the advent of 'programmes' has led staff into developing narrow expertise and also the fragmentation of that knowledge. The emphasis on procedure rather than either broad knowledge or process has preoccupied the advocates of the risk–needs model (see McGuire, 2001 and numerous others), so that therapy has commonly been deconstructed into manuals and procedures and passed on to those with hardly any depth of understanding of them to use in therapy.

One effect of this Smithsonian[3] approach to providing therapy on an industrial scale is that it is inclined to acquire staff who are not trained to a high academic or clinical standard. If you need staff to only follow the procedures detailed in the manuals, then you need recruit people capable of doing only that. They need not be psychologists or even have a lengthy training. They do not need a sophisticated understanding of the individuals to whom they apply these procedures; they just need to understand their part in the process.

In this situation there is a risk of developing a cohort of staff who apply psychology without critical awareness or flexibility. Even those who would be 'psychologists' have been known to, for example, employ psychometric instruments without the intention of adapting their intervention according to the results, and they are not expected to adapt in this way. They simply send the psychometric protocols up the chain of programme management as if the data is irrelevant to their own task. They are at risk of never developing the capacity or competence to derive unique psychological solutions for unique psychological problems. They become intellectually dependent 'programme drones', little more than replaceable cogs in the programme machine. Some believe that this is what being a psychologist amounts to. The result is that programmes are applied accordingly and diminish in quality over time and many drop out of therapy or exclude themselves. It might be speculated that this is the mechanism by which there has been a recent spate of disappointing outcomes of programmatic interventions. The concentration on 'What' has encouraged this fragmentation. In this sense, the risk–needs orthodoxy has suited NPM perfectly. Together they have flourished, but there are dangers for psychology in continuing to be associated with management in this way.

Only recently has there been some evidence of this changing. The social exclusion unit (SEU) (2002) has identified nine factors associated with reoffending. They include education, employment, drugs and alcohol misuse, mental and physical health, attitudes and self-control, institutionalisation and life-skill, housing, financial support and debt, and family networks. From within psychology there is a growing realisation that what is done to offenders is not the only range of variables that need consideration. Marshall and Serran (2004), for example, recognise the importance of therapist characteristics in therapy programmes. The authors acknowledge the long history of therapist influence on process and outcome that has hitherto been overlooked in the forensic literature.

There are also recent developments indicating an awareness that offenders have wider needs that are relevant in understanding and reducing offending. Ward and Stewart (2003a) seek to locate our perception of offenders in the wider context of 'human needs', pointing the way to new forms of analysis and intervention. Taking their lead from this general influence Mann et al. (2004) sought to reformulate relapse prevention strategies, which are inclined towards negative avoidant goals that can be demotivating for clients, to more positive goals. In a small sample they found a greater willingness of sexual offenders to make diary entries and participate in therapy. Clearly the manner in which therapists undertake their work with offenders is crucial, and the acknowledgement of this is to be welcomed. In one sense we perhaps need to look more carefully at the basic psychology of our inter-actions with offenders whom we are trying to change. The psychology of such interactions may have a potentially central impact upon outcomes. It does seem that changing our perception of offenders and ourselves does alter what we do, the way that we do it and the response of those we are trying to change.

Treatment programmes in the UK Prison and Probation service that are based on the risk–needs model do now, finally, give some recognition to the need to move away from single interventions and understand offenders as having multiple needs needing multiple interventions. This has been clearly identified in a recent UK Home Office Research Study in which it is argued that the question should not be 'what works?' but 'what works for whom and why?' (Harper and Chitty, 2005). The implication of this recent realisation is that we cannot expect to understand the real value of CBT psychological interventions directed at one problem when the outcome is dependent on neglected variables. Neither should we be surprised that the size and duration of the treatment effects have been small and short-lived respectively.

To be fair to advocates of the risk–needs agenda, none will advocate the reduction of staff to merely cogs in the machine, even if their desire to control content of programmes and their emphasis on procedures rather than process has rather invited it. The offender behaviour programmes unit (OBPU) of the UK prison service would not accept as tolerable the idea of undermining the quality of staff training or stifling therapeutic flexibility by over allegiance to manualised interventions and functional training,[4] even though staff within prisons have complained of being unable to deviate from prescribed activity.[5] Moreover, it would be unfair to criticise the enormous achievement of the OBPU in establishing empirically based interventions on a large scale within England and Wales and of a sophisticated process in which lessons are learnt and research findings are translated into real changes in programmes and research methods (Harper and Chitty, 2005). Despite this we should not remain sightless in respect of hidden dangers to the reputation and identity of psychology.

The New Empirical Orthodoxy

Somewhere during the 1990s the question mark was lost from the expression 'what works?', and with it has gone some tolerance and perspective. There have been assertive representations of opinions that border on ideology rather than science. Some have sought to stifle potentially critical commentary, discourage narrative reviews of the empirical orthodoxy, ironically using the narrative form (Gendreau et al., 2002). Others may have commercial interests in market-ing particular correctional programmes and forensic procedures such as risk assessment. It is possible that this has the capacity to change the perspective of some advocates. In any case, there is an inclination among some forensic psychologists to disparage ideas about intervening with offenders that are not derived from the risk–needs orthodoxy. For example, Ward and Stewart's (2003a) 'good lives' theory has been met with unusual and uncomprehending resistance by some (Bonta and Andrews, 2003) and more gracious resistance by others (McGuire, 2004; Ogloff and Davies, 2004). An argument has been made that the 'good lives' perspective might divert funding from programmes and distract clinicians from attending to 'criminogenic needs' (Ogloff and Davies, 2004), and in any case, all that is good in the 'good lives' approach is already incorporated within the risk, needs or responsivity concepts (McGuire, 2004). It seems unlikely that 'good lives' has contributed nothing as this implies.

Ward and Stewart's (2003b) original contribution and reply to Bonta and Andrews offer a theoretical framework and a values-based perspective of offenders, contrasting with the rather narrow and pragmatic, risk–needs model (Polaschek and Collie, 2004). It is hard to understand why this encouraging development is not more widely welcomed than it has been. In fact Ward and Stewart's second article suggests that the distance between Bonta and Andrews may not be as large as it first seemed. The objectives of these approaches do not appear to the non-protagonist as being mutually exclusive. Even so, the strength of the response to Ward and Stewart reveals something about the partisan nature of this discourse. Some critics might suggest an allegiance to the new orthodoxy of this passion is unhelpful. Others might observe that the implicit values of the risk–needs orthodoxy are being exposed in this exchange. Here it may be useful to distinguish between the implicit values as have emerged in application, and the intended values of what has become a doctrine.

Perhaps it is the crudeness of the distinction between that which is referred to as a 'criminogenic need'[6] and other 'needs' that result in the conflict. Ogloff and Davies (2004, p. 3) remind us of that distinction. McGuire (2004) goes further, arguing that we have no right to trespass on areas outside of what he terms 'criminogenic need' as society 'empowers' (p. 343) us to deal only with these. The narrowness of this perspective is surprising although, like NPM, it has the virtue of apparent clarity and focus. The real difficulty, however, is in the moral/ethical vindication of a particular view of offenders and the implication of that view for the role of psychology. To put this simply, if we believe that individuals can be disaggregated into a series of unconnected problems, we can divide the problems into those we have an intention to change and those we do not. They can be dealt with in a series of disconnected interventions. Each therapist can ignore the big picture because there is no big picture. The only concern is offending behaviour, although responsibility for outcome is with the individual offender, who is responsible for his or her own behaviour

regardless of intervention. In contrast, if we view people as complex intercon-
nected systems, in which changes in dynamic factors in one system influence
those of another, no one can ignore the big picture or the implications of their
actions for the rest of the system. In this construction we must take a more holistic view and accept that problems faced by offenders cannot be partitioned
into convenient segments, and we must accept some shared responsibility for
outcome on behalf of society, from where the offender comes.

A second problem with this distinction is an assumption that the evidence
is conclusive and psychological constructs associated with these 'needs' are
sufficiently clearly demarked that a conceptual boundary may be constructed
between those that are 'in' and those that are 'out' of the 'criminogenic' pad-
dock. Some have been so confident of this distinction that they seek to ridicule
and mock those who are on the 'wrong' side of the boundary fence (Latissa
et al., 2002).

In these commentaries there is much to agree with, and of course there are
eccentricities in forensic work worthy of ridicule, but this is not so in every
example offered and it is here that the new orthodoxy may be losing tolerance, to the detriment of psychology and science. For example, outside the
boundary fence has been placed 'self-esteem'. Although the term has been
generically employed to justify everything from keeping pets to woodworking,
a sophisticated use of the concept recognises its association with shame, anger
and social ranking, for example, among psychopaths (Morrison and Gilbert,
2001). To the extent that social rank is related to self-esteem, there is evidence
that this is important in determining sensitivity and response to antecedent
events to violence such as social 'put-downs' (Gilbert and Miles, 2000). Perception of one's own social rank and that of others is noted to be a determinant
of both expression and suppression of anger (Allan and Gilbert, 2002). Self-
esteem and closely associated variables seem to be important determinants
of angry arousal and violent behaviour. However the connection is complicated, the concepts may need more precise measurement and perhaps they are
unsuited to simplistic generalities necessary for crude algorithms discrimin-
ating between suitable and unsuitable offenders for treatment programmes.
These are not good reasons to dispense with it. In the example of self-esteem, it
seems premature to cast this concept over the boundary fence.

Critics might ask if we are now so certain of what is known and what is
left to be known, then can we cast away all that is outside of our bounded
reality? Does the accumulated knowledge of the meta-analytic reviews of
offender programmes amount to our accumulated wisdom on the subject?
There are numerous issues to challenge and questions to be answered about
that work which has been within the boundary, before we close off access
to alternative conceptualisations. For example, has there ever been a time
when there was evidence that therapist characteristics were unimportant to

the treatment process? It seems that in about 2004 it had been reasonable to ignore such things, although only in the forensic literature (see Horvath and Symonds, 1991; Prochaska, 1999). There is no substantial evidence that supports 'confrontation' as a mechanism of changing people, yet it has been the ubiquitous approach to treating some offenders (Salter, 1988; Calder, 1999). When was a 'one size fits all' approach to psychological treatment defensible on theoretical, empirical or clinical grounds? Has there ever been evidence to support the wholesale inclusion of offenders in groups for therapy when we have known that not everyone is suited to this? The purpose of identifying some questions is not to diminish the many honest efforts there are to reduce offending behaviour. It is to suggest that perhaps not all that is represented as knowledge-based intervention is influenced by all the available knowledge, and some aspects of some interventions are not really supported by evidence at all. In truth, they are driven by expedience, financial and moral imperatives, and sometimes political expectation.

It is also helpful to reflect on the observation that the principles of risk, needs and responsivity do not offer a theory of rehabilitation or psychology. In fact, most studies give little information of underlying theory in respect of interventions. There are often excellent manuals[7] covering theory associated with offending behaviour, but the theory/model of changing[8] individuals is not so apparent. Cognitive therapy is assumed to carry with it a universally accepted and robust theory. However, in the ambiguity of this assumption there is a risk of implicit theory emerging about therapeutic processes, such as 'confrontation', and targets of intervention, such as 'denial' among sex offenders.

Denial has been used to exclude offenders from treatment and obstruct their rehabilitation. In extreme cases this is not unreasonable and, of course, denial can obstruct change, but it must be acknowledged that there is no evidence to implicate denial as adding to risk (Craissati, 2004). Neither is there evidence to support the contention that someone who acknowledges 80% or even 20% of what they are accused or convicted of benefits less from treatment than someone who acknowledges 100%. In all probability 'denial' is normal and those who do not experience obstacles to revealing the full extent of their disturbing behaviour are those we should be most anxious of.

It seems that there is a good argument here for introducing common sense in order to marshal the application of what is known in the context of not knowing everything. Remarkably there have been objections to this. Gendreau *et al.* (2002) may simply be aggregating commonly expressed irritations of psychologists and hence their antagonism towards 'common sense', appears to be without balance. Even so, it is misleading to conclude that 'common sense' is bad by offering examples of where it has come unstuck. This fails to identify, or even search for, illustrations of when 'common sense' did well in ambiguous circumstances. It also assumes that poor decisions that have passed for 'common sense' really were prosecuting sense (knowledge) rather than some political, financial or management agenda. Worse still is the implication that the application of psychology can be conducted without it.

Gendreau *et al.* (2002) have gone much further than a critique of obvious failure. They offer the extraordinary proposition that empirical evidence in psychology should be translated into policy because, unlike 'common sense', 'science' is without 'prejudice', 'judgemental heuristics', 'illusory correlates', 'false consensus', 'self-serving explanations' or poor 'recognition of iatrogenic consequences' (p. 362). This proposition neglects the long history of science being self-serving, mistaken and frankly misleading, such that these comments could well be offered of the scientific method. In the forensic world there is an iconic example of this.

Rice *et al.* (1992) published an evaluation of a state-of-the-art therapeutic community on those assessed as being, or not being, psychopaths. The evidence clearly indicated that 'psychopaths' who were exposed to treatment clearly did worse than non-psychopaths, and worse than psychopaths who were not treated. The conclusion and policy implications were clearly that the means of measuring 'psychopathy' had some credence in determining treatment outcome ('psychopaths' were treatment resistant) and therapeutic communities were unsuccessful as 'psychopaths' did worse in treatment than those without treatment.

Behind the veil of this study is a catalogue of inadequacies, many of which are acknowledged by the authors (see D'Silva *et al.*, 2004, for recent review of this issue). However, the most serious inadequacy has to do with the 'state-of-the-art' intervention. 'Therapy' included 80 hours of therapy per week with little time given over to either vocational training or recreational pursuits. It included two-week, nude marathon encounter sessions in a self-contained chamber where sustenance was provided through tubes through the walls. There was also the use of drugs such as methedrine, LSD, scopolomine and alcohol. The therapy lasted at least two years and the only way out was compliance with the expectations of the programme.[9]

Even by the standards of that time this was extraordinary and to conclude that therapeutic communities do not work or that 'psychopaths' are treatment resistant, or that there is an assessment of personality that may identify those who will not benefit from 'therapy', is a travesty of science. The number of individuals who have been adversely affected by this in institutions around the world cannot be calculated. Rice *et al.* (1992) may well have been trying to bring an end to what they perceived to be eccentric practice and credit should come to them for this. Even so, this example does not inspire blind confidence in psychological science or scientists.

Discussion

This chapter has attempted to consider the socio-political context of correctional programmes, questioning the certainty of belief in the noble cause of liberal rehabilitation and illustrating how social trend and policy has had an impact on the actions of psychologists, programme makers and managers. It has been argued that while psychologists have made an extraordinary contribution to the rehabilitation of offenders, some of their actions have the potential to undermine this good work and damage credibility of psychology and psychologists. It is hoped that by drawing attention to these risks, this can be avoided.

The way forward is not in claiming authority, or polarising opinion, or paralysing commentary with mockery and accusations of destructive intention. Neither does the tremendous value-adding contribution psychology makes emerge in complaining that some psychologists are not influential enough. Psychologists continue to have a very substantial influence on the allocation of resources, and rightly so. Rather, we might ask of psychology and those who apply it why it is not delivering more than recent evidence suggests it is offering. To do this we need to look at the psychology of changing people and not simply at the technology of programmes or the architecture that supports it.

Notes

1. Martin Narey is the Ex-Chief Executive, National Offender Management Services.
2. Gendreau explains that the term 'Fartcatcher' is a legitimate term referring to the role of footman on horse carriages in eighteenth-century North America, presumably because of the proximity of the poor individual to the south end of a horse heading north.
3. See Smith, A. (1776) *An Inquiry into the Nature and Causes of the Wealth of Nations*. This was the first articulation of the industrial process of the division of labour, fragmenting production into specialist areas and generating economic growth.
4. Personal communication from OBPU (2005).
5. The author is also Chief Supervisor for the British Psychological Society, Board of Examiners, Forensic Division. In this capacity he has consulted with very many trainee psychologists and their supervisors on this matter, as it central to the quality of their training.
6. 'Criminogenic needs' is a curious term because it does not usually refer to needs that are experienced as needs by the offender to whom they are attributed. In the 'risk–needs' literature an issue only becomes a 'need' where it is associated with offending. In this sense, 'need' refers to the needs of society rather than the offender. The resulting proposition that 'offenders *need* to change, or be changed, to benefit society' carries many assumptions and raises many questions that psychologists have been slow to address. Recently McGuire (2004) has acknowledged that 'needs' is a term not derived from psychology.

7. For an example see, HM Prison Service, Sex Offender Treatment Programme; Extended Programme Theory Manual. Sex Offender Treatment Team, OBPU. October 2001.

8. Simplistically, with 'what works', a model of change typically refers to the pragmatic association of 'criminogenic needs' with offending behaviour. That is, change the need and the behaviour changes. This is different to psychological models of change, in which the mechanism of moving from one set of beliefs/attitudes/affect/behaviours to another set is determined by a psychological process derived from psychological theory (see Prochaska, 1999). The focus is the process of change, rather than the criminogenic association.

9. These descriptions have been supported by an eye witness account provided by Professor R. Bluglass who visited Penetanguishine, Ontario, Canada (personal communication).

Chapter 3

The Needs of Offenders and the Process of Changing Them

Brian A. Thomas-Peter

Introduction

To understand what it takes to extract the greatest value from psychological interventions in reducing risk, it may be helpful to start by understanding the complexity of people with whom psychologists must work and the circumstances these people are often in. In this chapter the breadth of what has come to be termed 'criminogenic' and psychological needs of offenders are outlined. It is argued that being responsive to the capacities of offenders to change in ways that reduce offending requires a close look and sophisticated understanding of the offender and how they might respond to treatment. It also requires some consideration of how therapists conduct themselves.

To some extent the importance of understanding the breadth of need is illustrated in the conclusions drawn from a review of meta-analytic studies (McGuire, 2002). McGuire describes how the more problems an offender has and the greater their 'criminogenic need', the more likely they are to offend again. The offenders who survive longest in the community will be those who have multiple interventions addressing criminological needs, including practical support in respect of accommodation, education and employment, rather than single problem-focussed interventions.

Harper and Chitty (2005) conclude that the future of offender management must include multimodel intervention targeted at those who will most benefit. Harper and Chitty also report the results of an assessment of 10,000 offenders in 19 areas of England and Wales using the offender assessment system known as OASys (Taylor, 1999). This system identifies 'criminogenic need' on a criterion basis and the results of this unpublished study are presented in Table 3.1.

In their subsequent review, Harper and Chitty note the prevalence of poor basic skills, especially among young offenders, although there is no evidence directly linking a lack of basic skills with offending behaviour. Employment and the quality of that employment, however, are clearly associated with

Table 3.1 Factors associated with offending

Section of OASys		Percentage of offenders assessed as having a problem	
		Community sentences	Custodial sentences
1&2	Offending information[a]	50%	66%
3	Accommodation	31%	43%
4	Education, training and employment	53%	65%
5	Financial management and income	22%	29%
6	Relationships	36%	42%
7	Lifestyle and associates	35%	52%
8	Drug misuse	27%	39%
9	Alcohol misuse	34%	33%
10	Emotional well-being	40%	38%
11	Thinking and behaviour	50%	59%
12	Attitudes[b]	21%	32%
	No. of 'criminogenic needs'	3.99	4.97
	No. of 'criminogenic needs' excluding sections 1&2	3.50	3.21

Notes:
[a] Offending information includes the current offence and criminal history.
[b] The percentage with attitudes needs are likely to rise when an amendment is made to the OASys scoring system, effective from early 2005.

Source: Adapted from Harper and Chitty (2005).

offending and basic skills will influence employability. Unstable accommodation is identified as being significant in reconviction, as is substance abuse, which not only seems to provide motivation to offend, but also diminishes the prospects of an offender re-entering employment. Here we see broad interlinked needs associated with offending, some directly associated and others indirectly associated with crime.

Perhaps as a result of these observations Towl (2005a) describes a policy change in UK Offender Management Services whereby psychological intervention becomes part of the 'mainstream' of prisoner management. In this new strategy, psychology will contribute to interventions directly associated with offending and those that have an impact on offending as well as other needs that may not be directly associated with offending.

All these contributions reveal a convergence of practice, professional development and policy, recognising the importance of seeing offenders in context and resisting two convenient beliefs: first, that offenders can be partitioned into various problems or 'needs' that can be addressed separately; second, that treatment is something we can 'do' or administer to offenders as if psychological therapy can be administered in various dosages, irrespective of the offender's capacity to tolerate the medicine.

The Breadth of Psychological Need

One way of looking at this is to reflect on the evidence about the nature of offenders themselves, looking at what they are and what they have, rather than the criminogenic 'needs' that are attributed to them. In 1997 a survey was commissioned by the Department of Health (DoH) to provide a baseline of the prevalence of psychiatric problems among prisoners in England and Wales (Singleton *et al.*, 1998). Prisoners were randomly selected from a list of all inmates. Selected prisoners were asked to take part in an initial interview (88% complied) and a random subsample of one in five of these was followed up for more detailed examination (75% complied). This resulted in a total of 3,142 full interviews at the initial stage and 505 follow-up interviews. Some key findings from the survey indicated the following:

1   The proportion of respondents with significant neurotic symptoms, such as anxiety, depression and phobias in the week before interview was far higher than found in a similar household survey and ranged from 39% of male sentenced prisoners to 75% of female remand prisoners.
2   Fourteen per cent of women, 10% of men on remand and 7% of sentenced men in a random subsample who took part in a follow-up clinical interview were assessed as having a functional psychosis (such as schizophrenia or manic depression) in the year prior to interview.
3   Among those who had a clinical interview, over three-quarters of men on remand and nearly half of those who were sentenced were considered to have a personality disorder, as were half of the women interviewed.
4   The majority of prisoners (ranging from 69% of female sentenced prisoners to 85% of male remand prisoners) had used illicit drugs at some time in their lives and more than half of the prisoners reported using at least one drug in the year before coming to prison.
5   Women were about twice as likely as men to report having received help for mental or emotional problems in the year before coming to prison: 40% of both remand and sentenced women reported having done so compared with 21% of male remand and 18% of male sentenced respondents.

The message of this survey is that many offenders have significant psychological problems. In fact the Social Exclusion Unit (2002) reported that 70% of prisoners had at least two kinds of psychological disorder. This is the 'raw material' with which psychological interventions must work. Even if psychological well-being is not central to this work it may be associated with offending and the capacity of offenders to engage with intervention. For example, there are offenders whose anxiety, depression or intolerance to stress results in alcohol or substance abuse, which undermines their foothold on a conventional life and creates the circumstances in which an act of violence or theft is more likely. Anxiety or depression may not be sufficient or necessary for violence, but they cannot be said to be unimportant. Equally, there are some disorders that may render some offenders unsuitable for group interventions. An avoidant personality disorder may make public self-disclosure excruciating, resulting in the offender deselecting themselves from treatment. It is clear that engaging offenders in therapy will require an understanding of how disorders might impact on learning capacity and styles, in order to maximise beneficial treatment outcomes.

This is the stuff of 'responsivity', but it might be observed that the 'what works' literature has not generated much guidance in this area. It could be said that responsivity has become the first-forgotten principle of offender rehabilitation. Many authors have simply dropped the term from the 'risk–needs–responsivity' mantra. A most obvious illustration of where responsivity stands in the pecking order is in the work of Latissa *et al.* (2002) in which the term, or equivalents, does not appear in the list of eight programme principles. In the text relating to the fourth principle it is said, 'The assessment also takes into account the responsivity of offenders' (Latissa *et al.*, 2002, p. 45), this comes across as something of an afterthought. While nothing too much should be made of this, we must accept that responsivity remains the lesser of the trio, and this is not an accident. In fact, not only is the low priority of responsivity consistent with implicit values of the risk–needs literature, it is entirely understandable that this is so for practical reasons. There is no time to deal with individual cases and also meet programme targets. However, with 70% of prisoners suffering two or more kinds of problems, there must be many for whom the treatment offered is just unsuitable. It may be that it is this that explains why many fail to take up or take advantage of therapeutic opportunities and risk being castigated for their 'failure'.

Even without formal diagnosis or psychological syndrome, the state of some offenders needs to be accommodated in treatment. For example, sexual offenders typically present themselves having endured public humiliation, sometimes with private shame. Some have lost material and emotional comforts and are hostile towards the institutions associated with this loss. Some are at risk of losing access to opportunities to regain a foothold in the world while others have already lost their liberty. They are all capable of distortion and denial. Typically they have strained relationships with agencies and have an expectation of hostility and negative judgement from others. These identified offenders are generally not successful men who have been caught out with a dark secret, although this is possible. They are commonly inadequate, without coping skills appropriate to their time of life and they are vulnerable to adverse psychological behavioural and emotional reactions to stressful circumstances. Sometimes this means that they repair low mood or status with exploitative or dominant behaviour. They may escape from life's tensions by employing alcohol, substances or disturbing sexual preoccupations. Failing to take these observations into consideration in how we work with offenders may undermine the effectiveness of our own efforts.

If our task is to motivate offenders to accept responsibility for what they have done and will do in the future, to change attitudes and beliefs, to alter behaviour, it would help us if we are informed as to what is most likely to assist or obstruct those changes. We also need to be aware of what we must avoid doing so that we do not make the situation worse either by increasing risk to other potential victims or the offender. In this sense it is insufficient to rely on risk and need assessments in the allocation of offenders to programmes, as has been suggested elsewhere (Hollin, 2002). We must do these assessments, but the real determinant of success or failure will be within the responsivity issue.

Therapeutic Processes with Offending Populations

In this section a number of influences and therapeutic processes are considered. They include the question of making offenders ready for treatment; the assumptions that are commonly made about offenders and how these might help or hinder changing them; questions about a commonly used model of change in treating offenders, which illustrate how a wider view of psychology might inform the process of treating factors associated with the risk of reoffending and add value to the effort to change offenders with psychological therapy.

Readiness for therapy

> There has been a remarkable lack of consideration given to the factors underpinning mentally disordered offenders' motivation for engagement and participation in the treatment process . . . this disregard of motivational matters occurs despite the fact that . . . these factors often bear heavily on clinical decision-making regarding critical issues such as continuing detention and perceived dangerousness . . . examination of motivational issues in this population is long overdue.

> (Hodge and Renwick, 2002, p. 221)

These sentiments expressed by Hodge and Renwick apply equally to prison programmes as it does to forensic hospitals. The associated problems of drop-outs and poor engagement of offenders in treatment programmes is ubiquitous in corrections (Driescher et al., 2004) and the impact on the

effectiveness of Cognitive-Behavioural Therapy (CBT) programmes is substantial. McMurran and Theodosi (2005) reviewed 16 studies comparing
non-completers and untreated offenders and concluded that those who
dropped out of programmes were more likely to reoffend than those not treated.
This was true of programmes in both community and within institutions. However the causal mechanisms involved are unclear. Non-completion and low
engagement have also been reported to be associated with poor staff morale
and inadequate support from institutions.

In response to similar observations in anger management programmes,
Howells and Day (2003) and Ward *et al.* (2004) have introduced the concept of
'readiness' for treatment. This concept of readiness has been recently applied to
those with personality disorder (Howells *et al.*, 2005) and is broadly defined as
the presence of characteristics (states or dispositions) within either the client or
the therapeutic situation that promotes engagement in therapy and enhances
therapeutic change. Described as a more inclusive concept than 'responsivity',
readiness considers cognitive, affective, behavioural, volitional and personal
identity factors within the individual. The concept also accounts for external
readiness conditions in which the conditions of treatment, its timing and
availability of supportive factors is seen as increasing readiness for therapy.

An important aspect of this contribution to psychological therapy in corrections is the implication that the effectiveness of psychological therapy
programmes cannot be evaluated properly unless considered in the context
of external readiness factors. It is also evident that we cannot assume groups
of offenders being subjected to CBT programmes will be homogenous with
respect to internal readiness. Several problems arise from this. It is probable
that therapy will have a more positive outcome on those with relatively high
treatment readiness. A programme designed for high readiness offenders will
be seen as less effective when the group is comprised of both low and high
readiness participants, as the treatment effect is likely to be diluted. The second
problem is the effect on those who would otherwise benefit (high readiness individuals) of having low readiness individuals in the programme. It is probable
that this effect is not likely to be positive and, as a consequence, CBT psychological treatment may be appraised as having had a poor impact on those it
should have done really well with, causing the programme to display poor
general outcome.

There may be a more pernicious effect that makes matters worse. It may
be that the effect of subjecting those with extreme low readiness to psychological therapy programmes will have a paradoxical effect of making them
more resentful, more resistant, more potent in their denial and defiance, more
committed to their oppositional identity and more likely to offend again.

These ideas have several knock-on implications. Perhaps we could postulate
that there is a risk of doing positive harm when internal and external conditions

of low readiness prevail. There may be something about the combination of readiness conditions, rather than just the internal ones that determines bad outcomes.

From this postulate comes a suggestion that our seeking to develop new programmes to accommodate offenders in particular categories, such as 'psychopaths', is misplaced. It may not be their classification or diagnosis, so much as their readiness for treatment that is important (Howells *et al.*, 2005). It becomes apparent that some individuals will require special conditions in order to become ready for and take advantage of therapy. From this perspective, environments and offenders are enabled to extract the most benefit from investment in therapy, in contrast to the current paradigm in which offenders are subjected to therapy without preparation, often in unsuitable circumstances.

A final suggestion has to do with the quality of staff necessary to meet the challenge of making ready and sustaining readiness of both internal and external factors. It may be that many therapeutic processes can be disaggregated into procedures and taught to less educated staff for application, although many have privately expressed doubts about this. However, there is a question about whether all correctional interventions, including the demands of 'readiness', can be reduced in this way and still extract the full potential from the opportunity to change people.

The impact of assumptions about offenders

No greater example is there of the lack of 'responsivity' to a target population than the many assumptions that are proffered about individual sex offenders based on what is known about sex offenders as a group. There has been fair criticism of clinical judgement for being over-reliant on heuristics in predicting risk (Ward *et al.*, 2003), but a comparable criticism can be levelled at some evidence-based interventions for the misplaced assumptions that are commonly made.

The process of developing assumptions is partly an effort to summarise accumulated knowledge, and partly it is an attempt to emphasise the homogeneity of a population, who will be subjected to a fairly homogenous process. Heuristics of this kind have some value in corrections, especially in empowering workers to confront obstacles to intervention with confidence, but there are problems with the approach.

Calder (1999) lists a range of assumptions workers can make about this population which include:

- pre-meditation and choice;
- prior rehearsal in fantasy;
- objectification and targeting of victim;

- grooming of victim and environment;
- multiple victims and offence types;
- unreliable motivation for change;
- high sexual component in offending;
- calculated deception;
- inaccurate and incomplete accounts;
- manipulation of workers.

The value of employing heuristics and presenting them in this forceful way is not simply to reinforce the confidence it offers workers. It contributes to the sense of unquestionable truth of the orthodoxy. There are real economic, programme, political and 'righteous' benefits to relying on assumptions like these. For example, why spend time on complex individual assessments if we already know so much about an individual? Why should we develop costly, bespoke programmes for individuals or subgroups from a homogenous population? If the problems are homogenous we can apply production line methods to dealing with them. Why not simply rely on inexpensive 'competency'-based training of treatment staff rather than invest in high cost 'professional' staff who may be difficult to recruit and manage? What is the merit in making the simple analysis of sex offenders, supported in the popular press and understood by stakeholders, more complicated than it now is? Why divert blame from the sex offender when he fails to be suitable for the treatment we offer or reacts against it?

The problem here is that while these and other assumptions will apply to the population of sex offenders, it is easy to be fooled into thinking that they will apply to each individual sex offender. If, for example, each of these assumptions is accurate for 75% of the population of sex offenders (an unrealistically large proportion in the development of heuristics), applying all of these assumptions to an individual will ensure that we will be significantly wrong in our understanding of that person's behaviour in some important way. Two types of problems may arise from this process.

The first problem arising from failing to be 'case sensitive' is the potential to worsen offence-related factors. For example, exposing a rapist with sadistic interest to empathy training may run the risk of instructing them how much a victim has suffered, and adding to their distorted gratification. Equally, including all of those who are violent on anger management programmes misses the key issue that many violent offenders commit acts of violence without anger and in a social context that expects violence and where physical dominance is rewarded. In either case, treatment outcome will be diminished in the same way that conducting an appendectomy on all of those who report pain in the abdomen will have a limited success rate.

A second problem arises from the damage done to the therapist's credibility as a persuasive authority if he or she persists with an assumption that the offender knows to be wrong. The role of 'source credibility' in changing attitudes has a long history in psychology dating from the work of Hovland and Weiss (1951). From their work we know that a highly credible and trustworthy source will have more persuasive impact than a low credible source. Petty and Wegener (1998) review more recent literature and distinguish expertise and trustworthiness as important contributors to 'credibility'. From this it might be concluded that therapists should do nothing to undermine their own credibility, and perhaps persisting with assumptions that are reasonable for a population but not for an individual would come into this category.

Not everyone is inclined to make such assumptions about the homogeneity of sex offenders, for example, the systematic effort to classify rapist and child molesters (Knight and Prentky, 1990), which clearly indicates a variety of motives among sex offenders and implies a heterogeneity in this group. It follows that their presentations and treatment needs will vary to a similar degree, although this variety is not evident in the treatment literature.

This example of sexual offenders captures a problem for the risk–needs approach, which effectively, and perhaps inadvertently, dismisses the nature of the association between 'need' and offending as being relevant to psychology. All that is required is the pragmatic association. For those providing therapy, understanding the association is not required. In a more case-sensitive approach to allocation and intervention, 'understanding' is the key. In illustration of this, Ward and Hudson (1998) and Ward and Seigert (2003) have reviewed models of sexual offending and proposed a 'pathways' model, which leads to the conclusion that dogmatic assumptions about individuals, their assessment and therapy may be undermining the effectiveness of our efforts. Bickley and Beech (2002) have tested the model and found it helpful in classifying relapse patterns among child molesters. Despite the risks of clinicians' over-reliance on heuristics, it has been argued that this can be overcome through a process of acknowledging base rates, systematic clinical reasoning, hypothesis generation and formulation (Drake and Ward, 2003). It seems that there is sufficient evidence to conclude that making too many assumptions about the similarity of offenders is not necessary and brings error and obstruction along with the empowerment of workers.

Confrontation as an agent of change

Many applied psychologists and other clinicians would agree that pushing too hard in therapy, making demands on patients, and progressing at too fast a pace carries risks for the patient and the success of treatment. This is axiomatic and hardly needs further justification or explanation. With patients who have schizophrenia, it is common to see progress in hospital programmes but relapse when discharged, when the expectations of self-care are made. Among those with personality disorder, reactions to poorly paced and guided therapy may exacerbate psychopathology and result in subjective distress, self-harm, harm to others and suicide. These observations may not have bountiful evidence in support of them. They may have only the ring of 'common sense' about them, but there will be little dissent among those with significant experience of these groups.

Despite this, the use of confrontation as a mechanism for changing people is not uncommon within correctional treatment. There is some support for the use of confrontational methods in the treatment of sexual offenders, although it does not have a strong evidence base. Glasser (1965) has argued that the task of treatment is to confront patients with their behaviour and through the insight derived from confession they may change their self-image and attain self-integrity. Only then are offenders capable of dealing with their lives and taking responsibility for their psychological state.

Davanloo (1978) has developed a brief analytically orientated therapy that employs confrontation. Millon (1999) notes that Davanloo describes his approach as 'relentless', but points out that others use the terms 'remorseless' and 'bullying' (p. 56). While recognising that many patients could not tolerate persistent confrontation, Davanloo argues, without offering evidence, that there are benefits to those who can. The issue is how the group who would benefit might be distinguished from those who might be damaged? At the very least where confrontation is to be used, some effort should be made to make this distinction.

Unfortunately the variation in reaction to confrontation has not resulted in explicit variations in style in dealing with denial and distortions apparent in offenders. On the contrary, we have been extolled to be confrontational in a particular way in order to get to the heart of sex offending (Mark, 1992). Others have argued that confrontation serves a secondary purpose by sustaining 'legitimate authority' by sometimes being persecutory (Sheath, 1990).

Calder (1999, p. 42) summarises this approach rather succinctly. Confrontation

> is characterised by the making of assumptions, by persistence and by structured confrontation. The emphasis is on the breakdown of denial, which is believed to be a manipulative strategy employed by the offender to deceive the worker. Here, the work .... is usually characterised by painstaking dialogue with the offender – where every step, attitude and explanation is challenged unless it is a straightforward acceptance of responsibility.

Three issues are worth noting of this passage. First, it is important to recognise the language. It is relentless, 'remorseless' and 'bullying'. It is unsympathetic to the experience of the person that needs to be different, without any empirical justification. The immediate experience of this process is likely to be challenging at the very least and the consequence of not yielding to this pressure is probably fear for most. Second, an underlying assumption of this approach is that a 'Threat Appeal' of this kind will change attitudes or motivation in individuals for the good. Third, there is a substantial evidence base, which suggests that this is far from certain and may make things worse, especially for vulnerable subjects.

While Boster and Mongeau (1984) conclude that threat and fear can add positively to attitude change, several factors work against this. Considerable evidence supports the conclusion that where an individual believes that they have not the skills to cope with threat or fearful circumstances, a 'threat appeal' to attitudes has an opposite or 'boomerang' effect (Petty and Wegener, 1998). The foundation work supporting this derives from the protective motivation theory offered by Rogers (1983).

Another framework to consider confrontation is within cognitive dissonance theory (Festinger, 1957), which is one of several theories postulating a general motive to maintain cognitive consistency. In brief, where a belief and attitude or an attitude and behaviour are not congruent, they are described as 'dissonant'. The mental state associated with this is argued to be aversive and people will be motivated to redress this by making them congruent. This implies changing an attitude. Within the treatment for sexual offenders, we might consider that confronting someone with the inconsistencies of their beliefs, actions and representation of events amounts to a deliberate creation of dissonance, in the hope that it will be resolved with a constructive change of attitude.

However, it is naive to believe that change will occur in the direction hoped for as resolution can occur equally well with the rejection of the therapist's perspective, as it might well be, for example, where the therapist inadvertently undermines their own 'credibility'. Conventionally, individuals may bolster their pro-offending beliefs and commitment to denial by finding independent means of making apparently disparate beliefs seem congruent. Alternatively they may minimize the significance of one of the dissonant beliefs (Simon *et al.*, 1995).

There is some evidence to suggest that where an attitude and behaviour are dissonant, it is the attitude that is more likely to change in order to become congruent with the behaviour, than vice versa (Festinger and Carlsmith, 1959, reported in Gilbert *et al.*, 1998). This means that among vulnerable offenders where the fragile belief 'I am a good person' is insensitively juxtaposed with their 'bad behaviour', the dissonance may be resolved by the reduction of self-esteem rather than a change of behaviour. If low self-esteem is associated with offending or self-harm, the therapeutic process has put this offender and the public at risk. Alternatively the dissonance might be resolved by embracing the notorious identity associated with the deviant behaviour.

Recently there has been some support for this analysis from work on 'treatment readiness' among offenders (Proeve and Howells, 2005). Apparently, the action tendencies associated with the consequences of confrontation make engagement more difficult. For example, shame, guilt and remorse, resulting in apologizing, undoing and repairing damage, may reduce readiness to engage in treatment.

Convincing evidence is also available to indicate that the aversive experience created by dissonance can be indirectly alleviated, not by a reconfiguration of cognitions or related behaviour, but by any other means that would make someone feel less unpleasant. This would include the use of substances (Steel *et al.*, 1981), watching movies (Cooper *et al.*, 1978) or whatever means of discomfort reduction occurs first (Aronson *et al.*, 1995), which would include, for sex offenders, masturbation to deviant images and perhaps offending behaviour. In other words, we are at risk of generating offence-related behaviour through the process of confrontation.

Regrettably, there is no evidence in support of the use of confrontation for sexual offenders. Belatedly, several authors have started to postulate the value of therapist characteristics and therapeutic climate in particular (Beech and Fordham, 1997) to counteract the damaging impact of confrontation in treating sex offenders.

It appears from this that improvements in the implementation of psychological therapy programmes might be achieved by training designed to assist therapists retain their 'source credibility' by avoiding assumptions and unsophisticated confrontation, and by learning to manage dissonance so that it does not have undesirable consequences.

Group work and the effect of public disclosure

For many years, group therapy has been the treatment of choice for working with offenders. The UK Prison Service Sex Offender Treatment Programme has explicitly acknowledged the importance of treatment style (Theory Manual, 2001) in managing all sex offenders. Group influences can be valuable, however there has been evidence for almost half a century from social psychology that there are risks associated with group work in respect of attitude change.

Forewarning

In general, the process of asking offenders to reveal their stories in front of others has a range of potentially undesirable consequences. The process of exposing a group of people to the intended persuasive message of a therapist emulates a thoroughly researched area known as the effects of 'forewarning' on attitude change. In sum, the evidence suggests that as an audience becomes aware that their individual attitudes will be challenged and as they hear the 'attack arguments' being made, they prepare themselves with counter-arguments, providing they have the time (Friedman and Sears, 1965; Brehm, 1966; Petty and Cacioppo, 1977).

In fact, even before the arguments are heard, simply knowing that someone is going to try and persuade you that they are right and you are wrong about something may be enough for individuals to prepare to resist the persuasive impact of the message (Petty and Cacioppo, 1979). There are methods to counter this effect associated with 'distraction', but they are generally not to be found in conventional offender programmes.

Audience reactions

The group process in treating sex offenders has additional likely effects that may be undesirable. If someone thinks they are accountable to others in respect of an unimportant topic, but is unsure how their opinion will be received, their inclination is to adopt a moderate position to start with. As the group's view becomes known, the attitude of the presenter will move in the direction of the group (Chaikin, 1980). However this is not the situation in treating offenders where the issue for discussion has high importance and where they usually have a good idea of the challenge coming. In these circumstances, individuals are likely to choose the most defensible position in anticipation of the interaction with the audience (Chen et al., 1996). This means that they are encouraged by the process of treatment to minimize, deny and obscure the truth of what they have done, as they have learned that this is the most defendable way to represent themselves.

Other evidence supports the notion that where an individual has already expressed a view on a matter of importance to them, the process of being subsequently accountable to an audience leads them to justify their initial position and polarize their attitudes against the audience (Cialdini and Petty, 1981; Tetlock et al., 1989; Tetlock, 1992; Lambert et al., 1996).

In other words, it may be highly undesirable to ask offenders to tell their story to a group, knowing that it is a distortion and then have them defend themselves against opposing views in a public forum because we know that this may make that story more difficult to change subsequently. It would seem therefore that the common process of treating some offenders has potentially uncertain outcomes. The risks associated with a conventional approach of treating offenders in groups involving the expectation of disclosure and the systematic confronting of issues includes the risks of:

- undermining the credibility of workers;
- hardening offence-supportive attitudes;

- encouraging defensive or helpless reactions;
- creating dissonance with unpredictable resolutions;
- increasing offending potential;
- promoting superficial adaptation to treatment circumstances;
- elongating treatment time.

Discussion

The pragmatic, empirical association between offending behaviour and need tells us something of what must change to reduce offending, but says little about the nature of this association or how to change it. The process of changing this population is made complicated by the observation that psychological problems are more common than not, exceeding that which would be expected in a non-offending population. The challenge is in finding ways of including those with wide-ranging psychological problems into therapy that reduces their risk of reoffending. This means engaging them in a way that they can accommodate. Failing to meet this challenge may result in three kinds of problems. Substantial numbers of offenders may be excluded from treatment as being unsuitable because they have problems that may be associated with, but not pragmatically linked with, offending. Many offenders may exclude themselves as they cannot tolerate the gap between what is provided in treatment and what they can cope with. Finally, there are offenders who will fail to exclude themselves in the hope of obtaining the benefits of complying with expectation and who will fail in treatment or subsequently in the community. In all of these circumstances the credibility and potential contribution of psychological treatments are being underestimated or undermined.

If these observations have some credence, it becomes incumbent on programme providers to develop strategies of engaging the people they hope to change. This requires several kinds of change. First, we must change our belief about what constitutes treatment to include a broader base to what is legitimate to provide. Second, we must become more sophisticated in understanding the role of therapist and therapy processes in dealing with offenders. In this way we might rediscover psychology of what we are trying to achieve. Third, we must no longer attribute to offenders responsibility for their own treatment. While offenders must be held accountable for their own behaviour, it is a *non sequitur* to expect offenders to be accountable for failing to take advantage of, or failing to benefit from, treatment opportunities. Neither are programme providers entirely 'responsible' for offenders failing to participate in treatment or change. However, only programme providers are in a position to change any of this.

Chapter 4

Psychological Research into Reducing Suicides

David A. Crighton

Introduction

Suicide represents a serious problem within prisons with rates of death much higher than in the general community. Historically this has been an isolated and neglected area of research. In recent years though there has been a marked growth in research in this area, with an increasing mainstreaming and methodological sophistication of such work. The key aspects of the current evidence base are considered below in relation to how these might be used to inform efforts to reduce suicides in prisons.

Descriptive Research

There is a lengthy tradition of empirical research into suicides in prisons (Smalley, 1911; Goring, 1913). These early studies were largely an extension of the pioneering work in public health in Victorian Britain. Yet the work of these pioneers was followed by a lengthy absence of further research. The next significant efforts to research this area was in the 1970s (Topp, 1979). This research sought to build on the early empirical and descriptive studies and develop the level of methodological sophistication. Drawing on quite basic available data, overall rates for suicide in prisons between 1880 and 1971 were calculated.

For comparison purposes this data was divided into seven-year periods based on the average daily population (ADP) in prison. Based on the 775 recorded suicides within this time, the rate ranged from 28 to 60 per 100,000 ADP. A more detailed analysis of a subsample of 186 cases was reported, covering the period 1958 to 1971. A basic descriptive analysis was undertaken, and it was reported that 37% were on remand and 63% were sentenced prisoners. Of this sample, 77 took their own lives within the first month of reception into custody. There was, however, no apparent pattern in terms of the time of death or the day of the week when deaths were recorded. High levels of prior contact with mental health services were evident with 70 of the sample of 186 having had such contact and 56 having a history of inpatient treatment. It was also noted that 51% had made 'suicidal threats or attempts'. A number of 'social factors'[1] were also evident at high rates: 79% were single or separated, 54% had been living in lodgings, living alone or were vagrants, and 45% had no contact with family or friends outside prison. High levels of 'parental deprivation' before the age of 16 were also noted.

During this time there were an average of 13.3 deaths per year and an overall rate of 42 per 100,000 ADP. The rate of recorded suicides was also calculated as a proportion of receptions into prisons. This helpfully identified the fact that many more people enter prison than is reflected by the ADP figure. Using the total annual receptions into prisons the overall rate was 14 per 100,000 receptions. A tentative comparison was also made between prisons and a National Health Service (NHS) psychiatric hospital setting in England. Based on data for a single hospital, a rate of 135 per 100,000 receptions was calculated for the hospital.

This study has a number of strengths and weaknesses and it is perhaps helpful to consider some of these in detail, since the study informed much of the research that followed. The study provided an empirical analysis and built on earlier studies in terms of methodological sophistication. A number of themes were also identified which have occurred in later research.

The study also suffered from a number of methodological weaknesses. Most crucially, perhaps, the study was based on a sample of recorded suicides. At first sight this may appear a sensible approach. However, within Common Law systems this approach is likely to result in systematic biases within the data. In England and Wales, where the study took place, suicide was a criminal offence until the Suicide Act 1961. As such, recorded suicides would generally need to be proven using the criminal law's burden of proof; specifically the act would need to be proven beyond reasonable doubt.[2] To date the burden of proof for a suicide verdict remains considerable and it seems highly likely that this will have biased the results from this study, particularly, though not exclusively, in relation to the pre-1961 data. This raises the possibility that some of the reported findings, such as high levels of mental disorder, may have been an artefact of this sampling bias.

A number of conclusions were arrived at based on the data analysis suggesting that a high proportion of those studied were 'attention seeking' or were acting 'on impulse' (Topp, 1979). It has been suggested that such conclusions are not adequately supported by the reported data (Towl, 2000; Crighton, 2000a). However, the study can be seen as having a number of key impacts on the development of policy on suicides in prison settings. First, it acted as a stimulus for others to undertake research in this area, although initial progress was slow. Second, it influenced the approach of future researchers.

And third, it influenced prison service policy and practices for at least a decade.

A similar study was conducted in North America, looking at a number of small-scale studies of correctional facilities in US cities and pooling the data (Hankoff, 1980). There are some clear parallels with the finding reported and those outlined above, with high levels of mental health problems, substance abuse and social exclusion being reported among those completing suicide. Interpretation of the pooled data from this study though is far from straightforward. The US correctional system is one that is split between state and federal systems, with high levels of devolution to local levels. There are wide variations between different parts of these systems that significantly complicate any comparisons with largely centralised systems such as those in England and Wales.

In a reported questionnaire-study of a sample of 155 deaths that happened in Australian prisons between 1980 and 1985, it was noted that 77 of these went on to be officially recorded as suicides (Hatty and Walker, 1986). The other deaths were recorded as misadventure,[3] accidental death or natural causes. The researchers in this study went on to helpfully highlight the limitations inherent in officially recorded suicide data when studying suicides in prisons.

They went on to note higher death rates in women's prisons of 3.3 per 1,000 population per year[4] (333 per 100,000 population). They also noted that the suicide rate for women appeared higher at 1.7 per 1,000 (170 per 100,000) as against 1.2 per 1,000 (120 per 100,000) for men. They did however highlight the fact that these findings were based on very small numbers of women who died, making it inappropriate to draw firm conclusions in relation to gender differences based on these statistical differences.[5]

A pattern in relation to age was identified by the researchers who noted an over-representation of younger and older age groups. The older age groups included an increased number of deaths recorded as being from natural causes. They also reported increased rates of suicide for the 20–24 and 25–29 years age cohorts. The 15–19 years age cohort perhaps surprisingly did not appear at increased risk of suicide. As with the comparisons made between men and women, the researchers noted a need for caution here since small numbers were involved.

The researchers reported an analysis of 'aboriginal' deaths, noting that the rate was 50% higher in the under-35 years age group than for 'non-indigenous' Australians. Unfortunately, particularly given the detailed analysis of the social construction of suicide they did not explore this further. This trend was reported to have continued, with indigenous Australians continuing to show much higher rates of suicide (McCall, 2004).

This study can be seen as part of a trend towards research into suicide in prisons being drawn back into the mainstream of academic research. It began a process of drawing explicitly on sociological and criminological approaches. The researchers also explicitly recognised the social construction of suicide figures. The study suffered from a number of methodological weaknesses. The use of postal questionnaires raises problems with return rates and the quality and accuracy of completion. In this study it was clear that large amounts of relevant data were missing. In turn this makes the interpretation of the data more complex.

Linked studies of suicide in prisons were conducted in England and Wales (Dooley, 1990a, 1990b). These involved retrospective analysis of written prison records from 1972 to 1987, giving a sample of 295 deaths. Suicide rates were calculated on the basis of ADP in prison, using three-year data cohorts. On this basis an increase of 121% was reported between the 1972–5 and 1984–7 cohorts. This compared to a reported increase of 23% in prison receptions and 22% in prison population. It was reported that 98% of the deaths were of men, suggesting that they were slightly over-represented in comparison to the prison population. Contentiously the data for men and women was pooled, based on the researcher's assertion that the two groups did not differ significantly. Similarly questionable was the data that reported absence of differences in suicide rates between ethnic groups. Here ethnicity was assigned on the basis of post-mortem judgements assigned by the researchers. The methodological weakness of this approach makes this conclusion potentially misleading.

In this study, in common with earlier studies, social exclusion was noted as a factor, with high levels of accommodation problems evident prior to reception into prison. Just over a quarter of the sample were recorded as being of no fixed abode. Death rates were highest within the first month of reception with 17% of suicides happening within the first week and 29% within a month. This finding did not appear to be adequately explained by a lack of familiarity with the prison environment since 57% of the sample had previous periods of prison custody recorded.

High levels of mental health difficulties were also noted. Around a third of the sample was reported to have had previous contact with psychiatric services and over a quarter was reported to have had previous inpatient admissions to a psychiatric hospital.

In these studies the period on remand was identified as one of particular vulnerability to suicide. This was based on a calculation of rates of suicide for remand and sentenced prisoners, based on ADP.[6]

Both these studies suffered a number of significant methodological limitations that are worthy of further elaboration. The quality of the data analysed was limited to that contained in general prison service files. Such data was, and indeed remains, problematic. When available in a complete form they are generally, and particularly during the early stages of custody, based on uncorroborated self-report information and often sketchy court records. In common with a number of other studies the sample was drawn from those who received a formal verdict of suicide. As noted above this is narrowly defined and liable to engender systematic biases. In particular the findings on gender and mental health history are open to the alternative view that this was a product of a bias in the legal decision-making process (Snow, 2000).

A study was undertaken in the 1990s looking at a sample of deaths in Scottish prisons between 1976 and 1993 (Bogue and Power, 1995). The researchers reported that during this time 83 deaths had been formally defined as suicide and only these deaths were included. The researchers drew on general Scottish prison files for their data and such records could be located for 79 out of the 83 prisoners. The researchers divided their data into four-year spans, in order to explore trends. Based on this they reported a steady rise in the rate of suicides in Scottish prisons.

This research corrected what had become a dominant, if misguided, view that the period of remand was a time of particular risk. Rates of deaths were calculated on the basis of ADP and receptions into prison. In line with earlier studies it was found that remand prisoners were over-represented when the figures were calculated using ADP. The authors correctly note that this is misleading since remand prisoners will generally represent a small proportion of the ADP. In turn the ADP will only represent a small snapshot of the large numbers of prisoners who are received on remand to prison over a year. They went on to note that the number of receptions provides a better estimate of the rate of suicide for remand prisoners since it more accurately reflects the number of people placed at risk in the prison environment. A similar analysis confirmed this for England and Wales (Dexter and Towl, 1995). When rates were recalculated on the basis of receptions they found no evidence that remand prisoners were at increased risk. They did, though, note that longer sentences tended to be associated with increased rates of suicide, with those serving sentences of over 18 months being at significantly greater risk (Dexter and Towl, 1995).

This study replicated the robust finding that the early stages of custody showed the highest rates of suicide. Two-thirds of suicides took place within the initial three months in custody and four-fifths had taken place within a year. They concurred with earlier research in finding high levels of mental health problems. They reported that 5% had been given a diagnosis of 'psychotic illness' and that 32 individuals had a history of previous intentional self-injury (Bogue and Power, 1995).

Perhaps the most significant contribution of this study was in addressing some of the methodological issues involved in calculating rates of suicide previously leading some researchers to erroneous conclusions. It also provides a useful summary of suicide within Scottish prisons. In many ways the findings parallel those of the studies in England and Wales, although it is important to recognise the fact that the Scottish legal and prison systems are independent from those of England and Wales and have a quite distinct character.

Possibly the most striking thing about the early research in this area is how little interest there was in suicide in prisons. Even when a number of small sample studies are included, the research base remains strikingly limited.

Another striking characteristic of research to this point was a focus on descriptive, empirical and, on the face of it, largely atheoretical research. This provided an important stimulus to a relatively neglected field. The lack of theoretical underpinning however meant that it was more difficult to generate testable hypothesis and develop coherent explanatory models. It could be suggested that what might be termed the 'blind empiricism' of early research acted to limit the further development of the evidence base (Towl *et al.*, 2000).

Methodological Developments

Through the 1990s there was something of a step change in the approach to research into suicide in prisons. This followed on from the development of greater methodological sophistication. These developments came as a result of the increasing mainstreaming of research into suicides in prisons using sociological, criminological and political science models and methods (Tumim, 1990; Liebling, 1992; Liebling and Krarup, 1995). In parallel to this there has been an application of mainstream public health and health behaviour models and methods (Crighton, 1997, 1999, 2000; Crighton and Towl, 1997, 2000).

A study in the late 1980s and early 1990s saw a marked shift from the increasing isolation of this area of research, with a focus on qualitative approaches and an attempt to use current methods and generate theoretical explanations of suicidal behaviour (Liebling, 1991). The study was comprised of two parts: first, a series of semi-structured interviews with offenders and staff in four young offender institutions (YOIs) and, second, a participant observation study of the same institutions. The study drew on criminological and sociological theory in an attempt to explain the behaviours being studied. The most distinctive characteristic of this study was its influence (in combination with a report by HM Chief Inspector of Prisons) on policy and practice (Tumim, 1990).

The research involved an analogue study of 100 young offenders who had a recent history on intentional self-injury and who had also come to the attention of primary health care services. This focus along with the selection of YOIs was described as being pragmatic. The choice of self-injuring offenders as the basis for an analogue study was theory driven and based on the questionable notion that suicide and self-injury form a continuum of self-destructive behaviours. As such the study of self-injurious behaviours has been suggested as a source of valuable insights into suicide. This is a view with a long history and can be traced back to the work of Menninger (1938) and Durkheim (1952) among others.

In contrast to previous studies, Liebling included a matched control group of young offenders from the same institutions, going on to identify a number of statistically significant differences between the groups. Those who self-injured were on average serving longer sentences than the controls. They had also received fewer positive recommendations in reports provided by the Probation Service. Based on interview data a number of differences in social and family background were also reported. Somewhat surprisingly the control group tended to report more unstable family backgrounds. This was potentially at odds with the finding that those who self-injured tended to, for example, show higher levels of placement in local authority care, which might be taken as an indicator of family disruption. Those in the self-injuring group also reported more contacts with mental health services, along with higher rates of suicide and self-injury within their families.

A link between intentional self-injury and drug abuse[7] has been mooted by a number of researchers (Menninger, 1938). Liebling (1991), in her research, found that the young offenders in her experimental group were more likely to have 'major' alcohol-abuse problems[8] than controls. The experimental group also showed higher levels of use of other substances with some evidence that such behaviour was consistent across custodial and community settings. The experimental group was also found to have different experiences of custody. The young offenders who intentionally self-injured tended to be less active and reported disliking activities such as physical education. They tended to show a greater preference for cell sharing. Liebling (1991) also reported that they tended to be more lacking in personal resources that would let them address feelings of boredom and isolation. The research went on to explain such differences in relation to a construct of 'coping' ability devising a profile of those who were described as 'poor copers'.

This work represented part of a move towards a more qualitative approach to research into suicides in custody. It was largely descriptive but did begin theory building and hypothesis testing in a way that had been absent from much of the preceding research (e.g. Dooley, 1990a). The work itself though is not without methodological limitations. As alluded to above the notion that suicide and intentional self-injury are part of a continuum is a hypothesis. It has an intuitive appeal and, if correct, would mean that it is valid and useful to study intentional self-injury as a way to gain insights into suicide. If these behaviours are not part of a continuum then intentional self-injury is less relevant as a means of studying suicide. It is noteworthy that a number of the young people in this study reported engaging in intentional self-injurious behaviours without any apparent intent to complete suicide. This sits uneasily with the notion of a simple continuum and suggests that a more complex explanatory model may be necessary.

The posited theoretical construct of 'coping ability' raises a number of significant issues. In this study it was used in a largely causal way but other explanations may be equally plausible. For example, the profiles of the intentionally self-injuring young offenders suggest that for most observers[9] they were trying to adapt to more difficult circumstances. They tended to be facing longer sentences, with lower levels of family support, with poor contact with friends and poorer levels of contact with professional support. There is a widely recognised bias within human cognition to make internal or dispositional attributions about behaviour rather than situational attributions (Connolly et al., 2000). It might be suggested that this is at least in part an example of such a bias. There is scope for further investigation here for example, by replicating the study using groups more closely matched on this range of variables. There is also a danger that notions of 'poor copers' and 'good copers' are simply tautological (Towl et al., 2000).

The sampling also raises issues about how much the finding may generalise. The study focussed on YOIs with a large proportion of those studied being women. For practical reasons the study also focussed on those in contact with primary health care services. It is unclear to what extent the findings might apply to other groups in custody.

Public Health Approaches

Another approach to the study of suicide in prisons has built on public health models and methods (Charlton, 1995; Crighton and Towl, 1997; Towl and Crighton, 1997, 1998; Crighton, 2000). Public health approaches have generally begun by using operational definitions of suicide most often using international classifications of diseases (ICD) definitions[10] (World Health Organization, 1977). This facilitates the comparison of research internationally across differing legal systems. It also allows for more accurate comparisons of death rates in custody with those in the community (Towl et al., 2000).

The largest and most comprehensive analysis of suicides in UK prisons built substantially on this approach by analysing all the self-inflicted deaths in prisons[11] in England and Wales between 1988 and 1998 using epidemiological methods of analysis (Crighton, 2000). The research involved the retrospective empirical and qualitative analysis of a sample of 525 deaths from a total of 600 deaths over the period. The analysis was based on written records produced as the result of investigation of the deaths undertaken via the Prison Service's suicide awareness support unit.

A clear upward trend in the rate of suicides was noted with a rate of 80 per 100,000 ADP in 1988 and over 120 per 100,000 ADP in 1998. When calculated on the basis of receptions into prisons a similar upward trend was noted with the rate increasing from just over 20 per 100,000 receptions[12] in 1988 to around 40 per 100,000 receptions in 1998.

For the period 1988–98 the rate of suicides for men was 94 per 100,000 ADP compared to a rate for women of 74 per 100,000 ADP. To ensure that this was not largely a facet of the measurement method used, these figures were also calculated for receptions yielding rates of 30 per 100,000 receptions for men and 16 per 100,000 receptions for women. The data did though suggest greater fluctuations in the rates for women and, as a result of this, the rates for women were higher for some years. A trend analysis was conducted which showed higher rates for men. A plausible explanation for the variations in the rates for women prisoner's data is the relatively small numbers involved and the much smaller population of women in prison.

The study also showed rates of suicide for white prisoners of 89 per 100,000 ADP compared to 84 per 100,000 ADP for South Asian prisoners and 13 per 100,000 ADP for black prisoners. This suggested that black prisoners were at lower risk of suicide, a finding that echoes the lower rates found in community studies (Crighton, 2000).

In analysing mental disorder, the levels of prescribed anti-psychotic medication[13] were looked at, with around 6% of the sample receiving such medication at time of death, suggesting the presence of a psychotic disorder. The rates of prescription of anti-depressant medication were surprisingly low at 7%, suggesting low levels of treatment for diagnosed depressive disorders. From this it was concluded that the levels of mental disorder likely to fall within the terms of the Mental Health Acts in the UK were similar or lower than the rates in the prison population as a whole. The levels of such disorders were markedly higher than in the general community. The levels of more broadly defined mental disorders were found to be very high with a rate of more than 30% for abuse of controlled drugs.

The study went on to draw on the very large sample of data to replicate a number of previous research findings. A link between longer sentences and suicide was noted, with the effect being most marked for those serving indeterminate sentences.[14] Those with index offences of violence or drug-related index offences also tended to be at increased risk.

Of those studied, 45% had a recorded history of previous intentional self-injury, a finding that gives some support to the notion of self-injury and suicide in prisons forming a continuum. This finding also casts doubt on the view that those who self-injure are at low risk of killing themselves. Indeed it was a striking finding that 12% of the sample had a recorded history of self-injury during the period in custody when they killed themselves. It was also reported that for 51% of those prisoners who killed themselves an expression of intent to do so had been made. This casts doubt on the notion that those who talk about suicide are unlikely to kill themselves.

Earlier research in prisons had suggested that the early period of custody was a time of increased risk of suicide. The relative level of risk during the first 24 hours after reception was exceptionally high. Extrapolating the rate of suicides over a year the rate of self-inflicted deaths was reported to be around 9,500. From day 2 to day 7 the level of risk remained very high with an annualised rate declining from around 7,000 to 1,500. From day 8 to day 30 there was a steady decrease in the level of risk from an annualised rate of around 1,000 to a baseline level (Crighton, 2000). It is worth noting that just under half of those who killed themselves within 24 hours of reception into a prison had been transferred from another establishment. Interestingly a similar pattern of increased risk has been noted during the first week of psychiatric hospitalisation and the first week post-discharge (Roy, 1982; Geddes and Juszczak, 1995; Geddes et al., 1997; Qin and Nordentoft, 2005). This might suggest that it was not just being new to custody that is relevant but also the change to a different novel environment that is associated with an increased risk of suicide. The mechanisms for this warrant further research although intuitively the breaking of social support networks, both within and outside prison, seems a potential factor. It also seems likely that the initial period after release from prison will be one of increased risk, although the extent of this has been poorly researched.

The study went on to look at the process of care management within prisons. At the time of the research, public sector prisons used a system named the 'F2052SH' system[15] after the standard forms used. This system was designed to provide an administrative framework to support and manage those felt to be at increased risk, as well as providing a structured record of support and monitoring. Around a third of those who killed themselves had been identified as being at increased risk, a finding which replicated earlier small-scale studies (McHugh, 2000). In turn, 18% of prisoners had been subject to such procedures at the time of their death. No level of supervision, including 'continuous watches' appeared to be foolproof in preventing suicide. Routine 15-minute watches, generally carried out at fixed intervals had limited effect, possibly in part related to the predictability of checks. Quantitative and qualitative analyses suggested that the F2052 system was failing for a number of reasons. The system had been explicitly devised on the basis that suicide and self-injury were part of a continuum of behaviour that could be effectively managed using the same system. As noted above this assumption is by no means widely accepted and does not account for the majority of prisoner suicides (Towl et al., 2000). If the general notion of a continuum is accepted it seems likely that behaviour at the extreme ends of the continuum will be quite distinct and that a range of responses will be necessary. Unfortunately such subtleties were largely lost in the F2052 system which imposed a predominantly 'one size fits all' model of managing those at inflated risk of suicide or intentional self-injury.

Another identified weakness was the responsibility placed on prison officers. Previous approaches were criticised, often with good reason, for being unduly focussed on primary care medical practitioners. With the benefit of hindsight there was perhaps an undue focus on prison officers as the key staff involved in trying to manage the risk of suicide and intentional self-injury, often with poor levels of support from health care practitioners. Indeed during the 1990s applied psychologists, for example, increasingly moved away from this area of work. The work of health care teams tended to become increasingly focussed on those with mental disorders that fell within the Mental Health Act (1983). This view was echoed in the response by the Royal College of Psychiatrists (2002) to the earlier thematic review of suicide by the Chief Inspector of Prisons (HM Inspectorate of Prisons, 1999). They argued for increases in primary and secondary health care support. They were also critical of misunderstandings over professional confidentiality issues and the failings of professional staff to give appropriate support to prison officers in a complex and difficult area of work.

Based on his finding a theoretical model of self-inflicted deaths in prisons was proposed (Crighton, 2000). This drew extensively on public health models of multiple causation (O'Carroll, 1993) and also primary research into the development of emotions and emotional regulation (Plutchik, 1980, 1997). This he argued might provide a future framework for future research, as well as a model to direct the work of practitioners trying to significantly reduce the risk of suicides. Causation within this model is brought into line with models used in the community which suggest it is unhelpful to look for 'the cause' of suicide. Each death is the result of a chain of events, and therefore interventions need to be aimed at breaking a link or links within this chain of events. They also need to address a broad range of factors that can be shown to be causally linked to suicide. In turn the strength of such associations and their amenability to intervention, will determine their public health importance. Once this is established researchers will be better placed to identify factors that appear to be 'necessary' components of most suicides.

The structural models of emotion proposed as part of this approach to suicide prevention provide a theoretical basis for generating testable hypotheses. The model sees emotions as having a genetic basis that exists as a means of communication and a survival mechanism. Emotions can be represented as chains of events and feedback loops that are designed to achieve behavioural homeostasis.

Such models suggest that parts of the process are not open to conscious appraisal. As a result individuals may have little insight into their physiological states, or indeed the functions being served by their emotions. Suicidal behaviour here is seen as being based on aggressive impulses, deriving from the emotion of anger. Clearly anger and aggression have an evolutionary survival value. The way such impulses are dealt with by an individual varies significantly and these impulses might be amplified and attenuated. These effects are likely to be central to both risk assessment and risk management with those at risk of suicide. The Cambridge risk assessment model (CAMRA) (see Figure 4.1) provides a logical framework for the assessment of management of risk (Towl and Crighton, 1996).

Within this model the emotional states, the interaction of individual and environmental factors and the way that individuals manage these are likely to be central to stage 3, the identification of factors that might increase or

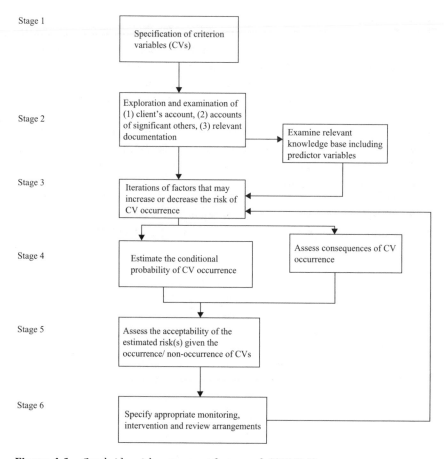

Figure 4.1   Cambridge risk assessment framework (CAMRA)

decrease risk. Such factors are also likely to be key aspects of the later stages of seeking to intervene and the monitoring and feedback processes outlined.

One clear and testable hypothesis generated from this model is that those who show high levels of violence towards others will, when prevented from doing so, be more likely to be violent towards themselves. This is consistent with the finding that those convicted of violent offences tended to be at greater risk of suicide than those who were not (Towl and Crighton, 1998; Crighton, 2000, 2002).

There are a number of practical implications from this proposed theoretical model. It moves away from the largely atheoretical empirical approaches that have tended to characterise this area of research and which, it can be convincingly argued, have run their course. In doing this the model provides a source of testable hypotheses which, in turn, will allow the theoretical model to be tested and refined, or replaced with a more powerful explanatory model. In doing this it allows the research base to move away from the use of essentially circular explanations such as 'attention seeking' and replaces these with concepts derived from fundamental research into emotions as illustrated in Figure 4.2. In linking suicide to anger and aggression, it also moves away from an unduly exclusive emphasis on depression (Plutchik, 1997).

The model also suggests that there are a number of points at which intervention might be effective within what may be termed a 'biopsychosocial' approach. These could include efforts to reduce initial anger and aggression by working to improve self-regulation. Equally interventions might be made earlier in the process to reduce levels of perceived threat and loss of control experienced in the environment.

For illustrative purposes, for example, prisoner A might be received into custody with a lengthy history of violent offending, a diagnosis of personality disorder and a history of substance abuse. Drawing on the CAMRA framework

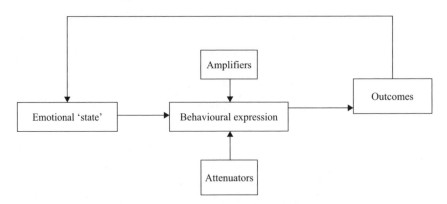

Figure 4.2   A model of emotion in suicide (modified from Plutchik, 1997)

it is important to identify factors that increase and decrease risk. Screening for depression might show that A is not depressed. Given their previous history though it is likely that feelings of anger and aggression will be amplified rather than attenuated by a change of environment. The prison environment also places stronger controls on the expression of aggression towards others, so increasing the likelihood that such feelings will be turned inward. Possible withdrawal is also likely to make the identification and regulation of emotions more difficult. From this brief outline, a number of avenues for intervention can be identified. Reducing the level of threat within the environment is likely to be helpful. This would include professional reception processes that make clear what is happening, how it will happen and that the environment is a safe and secure one. Effective interventions to reduce the negative effects of withdrawal are likely to be useful in reducing risk. In the longer term, efforts to improve A's ability to identify emotions and regulate these more successfully are likely to be helpful in addressing A's patterns of responding to events.

Of course this is by necessity a simplified example for illustrative purposes and each person will be different but, as outlined above, there are common underlying emotions associated with suicide and broad-based interventions might be used to address these. Specific interventions may then be used to address particular problems. It seems from the evidence base that approaches which assume a single cause for suicide, or that adopt a 'one size fits all' approach to intervention, do not work effectively.

Conclusions

Overall it seems likely that public health models will be most effective in terms of identifying approaches to reduce levels of suicide. Such models suggest multiple points at which risk of suicide in prisons might be reduced.

The evidence relating to the early period after reception into a prison is striking and gives rise to a number of practical implications. Perhaps most striking of these is the fact that increases in the movement of prisoners between establishments is likely to increase risk.

The first day of reception into an establishment is clearly a critical period where the risk of suicide is at its highest. There is a clear case for redesigning reception processes to take account of these findings. Similarly the early period following this remains one of high risk and again there is a case for minimising the levels of change during this time.

The notion of a link between intentional self-injury and suicide needs to be considered carefully. The lack of linking between assaults and intentional self-injury also needs to be questioned. For most prisoners most of the time the notion that suicide and self-injury are part of a simple continuum does not stand up to scrutiny.

In the longer term, links to fundamental research into the nature of emotions provides a promising avenue for investigation. Such research holds out the promise of facilitating the development of more effective ways of intervening.

Notes

1. In his paper Topp (1979) uses descriptive terms such as 'social factors' and 'parental deprivation' to describe what might now be seen as aspects of social exclusion. Unfortunately these are not operationally defined in the paper, making comparisons across time more difficult.
2. In England and Wales suicide verdicts are returned by the coroners courts. While suicide is no longer a criminal offence the burden of proof required remains high and it has repeatedly been made clear to coroners that in law suicide needs to be proven rather than presumed.
3. The legal distinction between misadventure and accidental death is a complex one which goes beyond the scope of this chapter. In general terms a misadventure verdict tends to be returned where the individual's actions are thought to have played some significant role in their subsequent death.
4. Hatty and Walker reported rates per 1,000 population. It is not fully detailed in their paper whether this is per 1,000 ADP. The use of figures per 1,000 is different from normal practice in epidemiological studies where figures are generally quoted per 100,000 of average population over a given time interval. In this chapter figures have been quoted per 100,000 of average population wherever possible.
5. This is a recurrent challenge in making gender comparisons with prison populations that are predominantly male. For example in 2002 it was reported that 40% of deaths in custody in the Australian state of Victoria were women: two women and three men died. For the whole of Australia the figures were 5 women and 63 men (McCall, 2004). This highlights the need for caution when calculating rates on the basis of such small numbers.
6. This method of calculating rates is potentially very misleading as noted by Bogue and Power (1995) and Towl and Crighton (1997). Despite this it led to a long-standing and incorrect view that remand prisoners were at inflated risk of suicide.
7. The term drug abuse is used here to refer to the abuse of drugs, both licit and illicit. The term therefore includes the abuse of alcohol and prescribed medication, as well as the illegal use of controlled drugs such as heroin.
8. A major alcohol-abuse problem was operationally defined as an average consumption of more than eight units of alcohol per day.
9. The data here might more accurately be described as having high levels of inter-subjective agreement rather than objectivity.
10. ICD provides a system of coding all deaths and a number of these codes are for self-inflicted deaths. This is a much broader category than many legal definitions of suicide but more accurately reflects the rates at which people kill themselves than do officially recorded suicide statistics.

11. The term self-inflicted death is used because the sample included cases in which prisoners had killed themselves but a formal verdict of suicide had not been returned. The selection of cases for inclusion was based on ICD classification of deaths.
12. The receptions data was corrected for double counting of rereceptions of prisoners released on bail and for other reasons.
13. Classification of prescribed medication was based on British National Formulary (BNF) categories.
14. This group included those sentenced to life, detention for life and detention at Her Majesty's Pleasure.
15. Contracted prisons did not generally use the F2052SH system but all had developed similar systems for care management of prisoners identified as being at increased risk of suicide. Due to the relatively small number of deaths in contracted prisons no reference is made to the specific care management processes used.

Chapter 5

Psychological Understanding of Self-Injury and Attempted Suicide in Prisons

Louisa Snow

Introduction

There has been increasing governmental, political, academic and media interest in what may be termed 'suicidal behaviours' in prisons in recent years. In spite of ongoing political and academic interest, and in the context of the introduction of revised management strategies for suicidal and self-injuring prisoners, the overall number of 'self-inflicted deaths' (SIDs)[1] and incidents of attempted suicide/self-injury have continued to increase. There were 95 SIDs in prisons in England and Wales during 2004[2] (calendar year), matching the previous record number of deaths in previous calendar years. The provisional rate of SIDs (i.e. the number of SIDs expressed as a proportion of the total prison population) for 2004 is 127 per 100,000 prisoners, slightly lower than the highest recorded rate of deaths, which was 141 per 100,000 in 1999.

Earlier academic interest in 'suicidal behaviours' in prisons focussed almost exclusively on retrospective analyses aimed at identifying the individual characteristics of those who died or otherwise injured themselves (e.g. Wool and Dooley, 1987) such that the factors associated with heightened risk are now relatively well understood. Recent years have seen a shift from the almost-exclusive focus on individual factors, towards an understanding of the social, situational and environmental context of these behaviours conceptualising suicidal behaviour from self-injury to suicide as being best understood as a continuum (e.g. Liebling, 1992) as well as towards individuals' interpretations of these contexts (Snow, 2002). Despite this broadened research focus, little attempt has been made to develop a comprehensive understanding of the similarities and differences between suicide and self-injury within prison populations. The research reported in this chapter attempts to address this shortcoming by describing the key differences between attempted suicide and self-injury as experienced by a group of prisoners in England.

Various factors relating to attempted suicide and self-injury are examined, namely: (1) prisoners' background characteristics, (2) the extent to which they have experienced negative life events, (3) their different mood states, (4) their motivations for attempting suicide or otherwise injuring themselves and (5) their own interpretations of the functions of these behaviours. Based on in-depth interviews with prisoners, the research focuses on individuals' own accounts of their actions and experiences. The results of these interviews provide empirical evidence for there being different psychological 'routes' to attempted suicide and self-injury, a finding that has clear practical consequences. Before we start, it is important to define the behaviours being studied.

Definitional Issues

There are problems inherent in the various terms used to describe what may be loosely termed 'suicidal behaviours'; indeed, it is argued that one of the most common methodological problems relating to research in the area surrounds the question of definition (Neuringer, 1962). The term 'suicidal behaviours' is currently used to incorporate a variety of actions that involve the intention of or actual infliction of harm, ranging from suicidal thoughts, self-harm/injury, attempted suicide and completed suicide[3] (O'Connor and Sheehy, 2000). Before outlining the terms currently adopted, the inherent definitional difficulties associated with the terms 'suicide', 'attempted suicide', 'self-harm' and 'self-injury' are briefly described in turn.

1. The term 'suicide' is, conceptually, straightforward in that, expressed simply, it is a wilful, self-inflicted, life-threatening act which results in death (Beck *et al.*, 1974). According to this interpretation, all situations in which the circumstances surrounding an individual's death led to the conclusions that they undertook the act with the primary purpose of ending their life would be defined as suicide. However, assessments of an individual's intent are somewhat arduous given the (inevitable) retrospective nature of investigations into suicides. Further, in England and Wales, a person's death can be classified as suicide only by a coroner who adopts a level of evidence comparable to a criminal court. Consequently, a suicide verdict must be supported by evidence of both *actus rheas* (the 'guilty' act) and *mens rheas* (the 'guilty' intent) (Dorries, 1999). Therefore, to return a verdict of suicide, a coroner must establish that a person killed themselves and that they intended to. If there is doubt about an individual's intent (e.g. there is no suicide note) an alternative verdict is recorded. Consequently, published statistics are believed to underestimate the true suicide rate in the population (Jobes *et al.*, 1986).

2. Although seemingly straightforward, the term 'attempted suicide' is also complex and can be misleading. Taken literally, the term relates to the intentional infliction of injury aimed ultimately, albeit unsuccessfully, at death. However, in practice the term is applied to a broad range of different behaviours (Fairbairn, 1995) ranging from the very safe (e.g. superficial cutting) to the highly lethal (e.g. attempted hanging or self-strangulation). It is only since the 1970s that researchers and practitioners have begun to distinguish between 'failed' acts of suicide and the infliction of injures for reasons other than cessation of life. Prior to this, different behaviours on the suicidal behaviour 'spectrum' tended to be grouped together on the assumption that they were similar, by virtue of the fact that they were self-directed and because they were thought by some to be determined by the same (or at least similar) motivations (e.g. Menninger, 1935, 1938). Later writers questioned the perceived similarities between the behaviours, emphasising the inappropriateness of such all-inclusive interpretations. However, while some authors argued that the very basis on which a distinction should be made rests on the key concept of an individual's intended outcome (e.g. Walsh and Rosen, 1988) others contested this on the basis of problems associated with interpretation of an individual's intent retrospectively, particularly if death has taken place (e.g. Kreitman, 1977; Morgan, 1979). Despite the validity of these debates, the position currently adopted is that there are clear differences between attempted suicide and injures inflicted for reasons other than cessation of life. Differences exist, for example, in individuals' motivations for engaging in the behaviours, as well as in the functions they may serve.

3. As with the attempted and completed suicide there are no universally agreed definitions as to what constitutes 'self-harm' or 'self-injury', although the terms are generally used to describe a very wide range of self-inflicted, self-destructive, culturally acceptable and/or 'unhealthy' behaviours. For the current purposes, self-harm is perceived to be distinct from self-injury on a number of levels, including the cultural acceptability (or otherwise) of the behaviours and whether or not the injury (or harm) is directly inflicted. Others' attempts at classifying the behaviours within these subgroups are summarised in order to give clarity to this distinction. Ross and McKay (1979) make the distinction between 'direct' and 'indirect' self-injurious behaviours. In 'direct' behaviours (such as cutting) the link between the action and the consequences is unequivocal and immediate. In 'indirect' behaviours (such as alcohol misuse or eating disorders) the link is remote and unequivocal. Similarly, Favazza (1996) distinguishes between three subtypes of behaviours: 'suicidality', 'self-mutilation' and 'unhealthy behaviour'. Favazza's (1996) description of 'unhealthy behaviour' is broadly equivalent to Ross and McKay's (1979) definition of indirect self-harm, while 'self-mutilation' is broadly akin to 'direct' self-injury.

While acknowledging that differences between them exist, Babiker and Arnold (1997) emphasise an important parallel between self-injury and other 'unhealthy', 'self-harming' behaviours (such as sexual promiscuity and substance misuse) namely the *functions* that they serve. For example, both substance misuse and self-cutting may be used as distraction from negative emotions or distress or as means of self-punishment. The authors argue that these behaviours differ simply in the extent to which they are socially acceptable (or not). For example, it may be more acceptable to get drunk following an argument with one's partner than slash one's face with a razor blade. Both alcohol and drug use constitute acceptable social behaviour (unless taken to extremes) whereas self-injury does not. Perhaps as a function of its social unacceptability, self-injury is explicitly 'psychiatrised'. While excessive alcohol intake may be regarded as a *social* (rather than an *individual* psychiatric) problem, the reverse is true with regards to self-injury. Perhaps because of the fact that it is outside of the ordinary range of managing feelings and emotions it is considered indicative of 'madness', at least when compared with other forms of 'unhealthy' behaviour (Babiker and Arnold, 1997).

Definitions currently adopted

Having outlined some of the definitional difficulties associated with the behaviours currently explored, the adopted definitions are as follows:

1 'Self-injury' is interpreted as an act in which an individual purposefully and directly injures themselves, irrespective of the method employed, where the motivation for the behaviour is something other than cessation of life. According to this definition, self-injury does not involve an intention to die but, in some case, quite the reverse. Many of those who injure themselves intentionally regard it as an attempt not to end life, but to preserve it, in the sense that inflicting and feeling pain reinforces the fact that one is alive (Arnold, 1995; Babiker and Arnold, 1997).
2 For the current purposes the term 'attempted suicide' is used to describe all incidents that involved self-inflicted injury engaged in by a single individual, with the sole intent of ending their life.

Where appropriate, the different behaviours are differentiated by use of the applicable term (i.e. attempted suicide or self-injury). The generic term 'suicidal behaviour' is used if no distinction is intended. For further discussion on definitional issues relating to suicidal and self-injurious behaviours, see Crighton and Towl (2000).

Method

The series of studies currently reported is based on research conducted with 124 prisoners in prisons in England who had either attempted suicide or injured themselves for other reasons (i.e. without suicidal intent).[4] In order to gain the fullest appreciation of participants' *interpretations* of what motivated them to attempt suicide or injure themselves, a series of in-depth interviews was conducted (Minichiello *et al.*, 1990).

Prisoners who had attempted but survived a potentially lethal incident of self-injury or attempted suicide were approached by a representative within the prison and asked whether they would consent to participating in the research. Participants were given an information sheet, which outlined the purposes of the research as well as other important ethical information (e.g. participants could withdraw from the research at any time without adverse consequences). Once agreement in principle had been gained the researcher visited the prisoner in question, resought their consent and outlined the limits of confidentiality, namely that any information indicating a risk of harm to self or others would be communicated to staff, and undertook the interviews. The interview schedule, which was based on factors identified within previously published prison and community-based research into 'suicidal behaviours', was designed to elicit information relating to a broad range of general and background characteristics of the sample, including individual, social, situational, offence-specific and demographic factors, as well as detailed and in-depth information about recent incidents of attempted suicide and self-injury. The elicited data were subject to various statistical techniques, as explained in more depth presently.

The sample, who were interviewed over approximately a 12-month period, included 36 adult men (of whom 20 had attempted suicide and 16 had self-injured), 49 young male offenders (of whom 24 had attempted suicide and 25 had self-injured), 28 adult women (of whom 9 had attempted suicide and 19 had self-injured) and 11 young female offenders women (of whom 5 had attempted suicide and 6 had self-injured). Each participant was located in 1 of 10 prisons in England. The participants were aged from 16 to 56 years (mean = 23 years and 10 months, SD = 7.47). Slightly fewer than half the participants (44%, $n = 54$) were unsentenced, with the remainder (57%, $n = 70$) being sentenced. The most common offences of those in the sample were as follows: violence against the person (27%, $n = 33$); burglary (22%, $n = 27$); and theft/handling stolen goods (11%, $n = 14$). Of the 70 prisoners who were sentenced, 29% ($n = 20$) were serving up to 12 months; 31% ($n = 22$) were serving between 1 and 3 years; 31% ($n = 22$) were serving in excess of 3 years; and 9% ($n = 6$) were serving life sentences.

Key Findings

Socio-demographic, personal and criminological factors

Previous researchers have considered the relevance of a wide range of socio-demographic, criminological and personal factors on suicidal behaviours in prisons. For example, it has been consistently reported that a disproportionate number of prisoners who both attempt and die by suicide are white (Meltzer *et al.*, 1999). Similarly a disproportionate number of prisoners who kill themselves are charged with or convicted of violent offences (Crighton and Towl, 1997) or are drug dependent (Meltzer *et al.*, 1999). The findings of previous research have been practically applied to the identification and management of suicidal/self-injuring prisoners, such that the risk factors associated with these behaviours are relatively well understood. However, few previous studies have considered whether differences exist between those who injure themselves and those who attempt suicide, a shortcoming the current research aims to address.

In order to further explore the relationship between 'suicidal behaviours' and the various background characteristics commonly explored in studies of this type, a series of univariate (namely χ^2 analyses and t-tests) and multivariate analyses (namely logistic regression) was undertaken, comparing those who had attempted suicide with those who had injured themselves on the factors shown in Table 5.1. The inclusion of variables in the analysis was based

Table 5.1   Record based results

Variable	Result
Marital status	
Single	$\chi^2(1, N = 124) = 0.046, p = 0.831^*$
Married/cohabiting	$\chi^2(1, N = 124) = 2.452, p = 0.484$
Divorced/separated	$\chi^2(1, N = 124) = 2.350, p = 0.125$
Widowed	$\chi^2(1, N = 124) = 0.008, p = 0.927$
Ethnicity	$\chi^2(2, N = 124) = 2.690, p = 0.261$
Age	$t(120) = -1.187, p = 0.238^{**}$
Previous domestic situation	
NFA	$\chi^2(1, N = 114) = 1.303, p = 0.254$
Hostel	$\chi^2(1, N = 114) = 0.391, p = 0.532$
Parent/s	$\chi^2(1, N = 114) = 0.959, p = 0.327$
Partner	$\chi^2(1, N = 114) = 0.132, p = 0.716$
Friends	$\chi^2(1, N = 114) = 2.995, p = 0.084$
Alone	$\chi^2(1, N = 114) = 0.008, p = 0.930$

(Continued)

Table 5.1 Continued

Variable	Result
Qualifications	
None	$\chi^2(1, N = 115) = 0.004, p = 0.947$
GSCE/O level	$\chi^2(1, N = 115) = 0.935, p = 0.334$
A level and higher	$\chi^2(1, N = 115) = 0.013, p = 0.911$
Legal status	$\chi^2(1, N = 124) = 0.991, p = 0.320$
Offence type	
Violence	$\chi^2(1, N = 123) = 0.014, p = 0.905$
Sexual	$\chi^2(1, N = 123) = 0.036, p = 0.849$
Burglary	$\chi^2(1, N = 123) = 1.204, p = 0.272$
Robbery	$\chi^2(1, N = 123) = 0.769, p = 0.381$
Theft	$\chi^2(1, N = 123) = 2.046, p = 0.153$
Fraud	$\chi^2(1, N = 123) = 1.756, p = 0.185$
Drugs	$\chi^2(1, N = 123) = 1.366, p = 0.243$
Other	$\chi^2(1, N = 123) = 0.262, p = 0.609$
Sentence length	
<12 months	$\chi^2(1, N = 124) = 0.366, p = 0.545$
>12 months <3 years	$\chi^2(1, N = 124) = 2.403, p = 0.121$
>3 years	$\chi^2(1, N = 124) = 0.019, p = 0.891$
Life	$\chi^2(1, N = 124) = 0.458, p = 0.499$
Previous imprisonment	$\chi^2(1, N = 124) = 1.571, p = 0.210$
Psychiatric illness	$\chi^2(1, N = 123) = 0.118, p = 0.731$
Substance use	
None	$\chi^2(1, N = 122) = 0.095, p = 0.758$
Opiates only	$\chi^2(1, N = 122) = 0.417, p = 0.518$
Stimulants only	$\chi^2(1, N = 122) = 1.409, p = 0.235$
Cannabis only	$\chi^2(1, N = 122) = 0.849, p = 0.358$
Multiple (inc. opiates)	$\chi^2(1, N = 122) = 0.853, p = 0.356$
Multiple (ex. opiates)	$\chi^2(1, N = 122) = 0.034, p = 0.853$
Opiate-dependent on imprisonment	$\chi^2(1, N = 117) = 1.393, p = 0.238$
Physical health problem/s	$\chi^2(1, N = 115) = 0.319, p = 0.572$
Previous attempted suicide/self-injury	$\chi^2(2, N = 115) = 1.007, p = 0.604$
Age at first incident	$z = -2.036, p = 0.042***$
Method of injury	
Hanging/self-strangulation	$\chi^2(1, N = 124) = 27.397, p = 0.000$
Cutting – wrist/throat/artery	$\chi^2(1, N = 124) = 0.699, p = 0.403$
Cutting – other	$\chi^2(1, N = 115) = 35.162, p = 0.000$

on a replication of previous research (e.g. Toch *et al.*, 1989; Liebling, 1992; Bogue and Power, 1995; Power *et al.*, 1997; Towl and Crighton, 1998) and incorporated those shown in Table 5.1.

Groups of variables included in initial analysis

The results of the initial univariate analysis revealed almost no differences between participants who had attempted suicide and those who had injured themselves. In fact the only variables that distinguished between the groups were age of first incident and method of injury. Prisoners who had attempted suicide were slightly older than at the age of first injury when compared with those who injured themselves without suicidal intent. Prisoners who had attempted suicide were significantly more likely to have hung themselves or self-strangulated. Conversely, prisoners who injured themselves (without suicidal intent) were significantly more likely to have cut themselves in locations which were less likely to be fatal (e.g. forearms or legs).

That none of the other variables distinguished between the two groups of participants could possibly be explained by the fact that single variables are simply not capable of distinguishing between the groups. In order to test this possibility, the data were subjected to logistic regression, a technique that can enable one to predict a discrete outcome (such as group membership) from a group of variables. In the present case the discrete (dichotomous) outcome was 'attempted suicide' or 'not attempted suicide' (i.e. self-injury). In order to achieve this, a model containing both the dependent variable ('DV') and a set of 'predictor' variables (e.g. the 'socio-demographic factors' illustrated in Table 5.1) is compared with a model including only the DV (i.e. without any of the predictor variables). The difference between the two models (based in the difference in log-likelihood values) is then compared. The χ^2 test is used to evaluate the difference of any change (Tabachnick and Fidell, 1996). As with the univariate analyses described above, none of the multivariate analyses successfully distinguished between participants who had attempted suicide and those who had injured themselves for other reasons. There are a number of possible explanations for this. First, the current sample size ($n = 124$) is relatively small for quantitative analyses. A large sample size is much more likely to yield significant results (Tabachnick and Fidell, 1996). Second, it could be argued that prisoners who attempt suicide are more similar than different from those who self-injure, at least in terms of the variables currently examined: socio-demographic, criminological and psychiatric/health-related factors.

Prisoners' mood states and key emotions

Having established that prisoners who attempt suicide are broadly similar to those who injure themselves on the range of socio-demographic, criminological and psychiatric/health-related factors, the next stage in the analysis involved an attempt to explore the differences between the groups on factors which have been found (in non-prison-based research) to be related to *either* attempted suicide or self-injury beginning with participants' mood and general emotional states. The reason for this focus is two-fold. First, there is little research examining how cognitive mechanisms related to suicidal behaviours change with fluctuations in mood (Hawton and Van Heeringen, 2000). Second, although there is convincing evidence of a relationship between emotional experience and suicidal behaviours *generally*, the specific emotions typical of those who complete suicide and those who injured themselves without suicidal intent are different (Williams, 1997). The mood types currently examined are variously associated with attempted or completed suicide or self-injury, as follows: boredom (Liebling, 1992); anger (Williams, 1997); anxiety (Beautrais *et al.*, 1998); stress (Van Heeringen *et al.*, 2000); depression (Michel, 2000); and loneliness (O'Connor and Sheehey, 2000).

Working on the basis that mood is not static, the relationship between mood type and 'suicidal behaviour' (not hitherto assessed within the prison context) was examined in the current research by examining prisoners' perceptions of mood at three different stages: (1) *generally within the prison setting*; (2) preceding incidents of attempted suicide/self-injury; and (3) following such incidents.

Participants' generalised mood states and emotions

In order to measure participants' *generalised* mood states, a six item, five-point scale was devised, which included the following items: boredom, anger, stress, anxiety, depression and loneliness. Participants were asked to report how frequently they experienced each of the mood states (never, rarely, sometimes, most of the time or always) and were given a score based on their response. Those who reported that they never felt bored scored one, those who rarely felt bored scored two and so on, to a maximum of five. Table 5.2 shows the mean scores and standard deviations across all participants on each of the six measures. As shown, the highest mean score relates to participants' reported boredom levels (4.31) and the lowest are for reported anxiety levels (3.43). That the scores across all variables are relatively high (indicating high levels of measured negative mood states) is notable.

As the majority of participants reported experiencing each of the negative mood states 'most of the time' or 'always' the two categories were combined. In keeping with the main research focus on the *differences* between attempted suicide and self-injury, each participant was coded according to whether or not they had attempted suicide or injured themselves, in order to examine (via univariate analysis) whether there was an over-representation of either group

Table 5.2 Mean scores and standard deviations on self-reported mood states

Variable	No.	Mean	Std. deviation
How often do you feel bored?	105	4.31	0.87
How often do you feel depressed?	105	3.69	1.16
How often do you feel stressed?	105	3.58	1.14
How often do you feel lonely?	105	3.54	1.27
How often do you feel angry?	105	3.53	1.12
How often do you feel anxious?	105	3.43	1.20

within each mood category. This analysis revealed that those who reported feeling depressed 'most of the time' or 'always' had a greater chance of attempting suicide than those who reported feeling depressed infrequently (Pearson $\chi^2(1, N = 105) = 10.333, p = 0.001$).

The next stage in the analysis involved an exploration of the *structure* of participants' experiences of the mood states examined and, more specifically, an examination of the extent to which the variables co-occurred. In order to meet this end the data were analysed using one in a series of multidimensional scaling (MDS) techniques. All MDS techniques have essentially the same purpose: to represent empirical relationships in a dataset as points in space, with the aim of making more apparent aspects of the data that may be obscured in the original data matrix (Donald and Cooper, 2001). The current data were analysed using smallest space analysis (SSA-1; Lingoes, 1973), a technique increasingly used to examine psychological concepts such as emotion that have traditionally been examined using factor analysis (e.g. Plutchick and Conte, 1977). SSA-1 is preferable in that there is no assumption that the dimensions or structures are linear. This is important in view of the growing evidence that individuals' experiences cannot be adequately displayed using linear dimensions (Donald and Cooper, 2001). The SSA-1 programme computes association coefficients between all variables and rank orders them. The SSA output then represents the items in the analysis as points in an n-dimensional Euclidian space, such that the rank of the distances between the points is the inverse of the rank of the inter-item correlation coefficient. Thus, the closer together two points in the space are, the higher their positive association is. The researcher then identifies regions in the resulting plot that include items representing similar substantive issues or underlying domains. The SSA programme provides a coefficient of alienation (Guttman, 1968), which is a measure of the goodness of fit between the rank order of the association coefficients and the rank order of their spatial representations. The smaller the value of the coefficient, the better the fit of the plot to the original

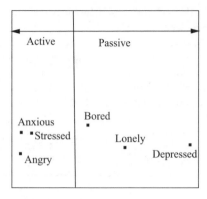

Figure 5.1   The two-dimensional SSA solution

correlation matrix (Shye *et al.*, 1994). The coefficient ranges from 0 to 1, with 0 representing a perfect fit of the geometrical representation to the input similarity data.

The two-dimensional SSA solution[5] is shown in Figure 5.1. Each point of the plot shown in Figure 5.1 represents one of the negative mood states as outlined above, and the empirical relationship between each mood type is represented by the distances between the items on the plot. These regions, which have been termed 'active' and 'passive', include the following two sets of three items: anger, anxiety and stress; and depression, loneliness and boredom. The term 'passive' was chosen to represent the variables bored, lonely and depressed, because of their general association with apathy which, in itself, is related to suicide (Williams, 1997). Self-injury, on the other hand, is more commonly related to external verbalisations of anger and stress (Babiker and Arnold, 1997) hence, for the current purposes, the region is termed 'active'. That the plot can be partitioned into two distinctive regions suggests that these two sets of items represent conceptually different elements of the overall domain of negative mood states.

The two regions that resulted from the SSA analysis can be interpreted as representing two separate scales, each measuring different elements of the overall domain of negative mood states – that is, 'active' and 'passive'. Participants' overall mean scores on each of these scales were examined to ascertain whether differences existed between those who attempted suicide and those who self-injured. First, participants' overall scores on each of the two scales were calculated and then submitted to reliability analysis using Cronbach's alpha values (Cronbach, 1951). Having established acceptable reliability coefficients for each of the two scales, participants' scores on each of the three items within the two scales were summed and a mean calculated for each mood domain. Each participant was then classified according to whether they had attempted suicide or injured themselves, the sum of scores for all participants within each of these groupings was calculated and independent samples t-tests were conducted to ascertain whether there were any statistically significant differences between the attempted suicide and self-injury groups.

Given that self-injury is commonly associated with externalised or verbalised anger or distress (Babiker and Arnold, 1997) it was hypothesised that those who self-injured would have higher mean scores on the 'active' domain and that those who attempted suicide would have higher mean scores on the 'passive' domain, given its association with depression (Williams, 1997) and social isolation (Durkheim, 1887/1952). The mean scores for those who attempted suicide and those who injured themselves were 3.42 and 3.60 respectively. Although this difference was not statistically significant, the difference was in the predicted direction. The mean score for attempted suicide participants on the 'passive' domain was 4.02 and 3.70 for self-injuring participants. The independent samples t-test was statistically significant ($t(N = 103) = 2.053; p = 0.43$) indicating that participants who had attempted suicide felt *more* depressed, lonely and bored than participants who had injured themselves for reasons other than death.

Mood states prior to attempted suicide/self-injury

Continuing with the focus on participants' mood states and emotions, self-report data were collected on prisoners' feelings *immediately prior* to the incident of self-injury or suicide attempt. The qualitative data arising from this item were examined using content analysis and each participant coded for the presence or absence of each emotion-descriptor. A total of 99 participants were included in the analysis. Only five different emotions were elicited from participants' responses, as follows: 'depressed', 'angry/frustrated', 'anxious/stressed', 'bored' and 'in emotional pain'. The emotions 'anger'/'frustration' and 'anxiety'/'stress' were combined as participants tended to use the terms interchangeably. Each of these mood states was examined independently to ascertain whether any was more or less prevalent among those who had attempted suicide rather than injured themselves and vice versa. Interestingly, the vast majority of participants who had attempted suicide (89%) reported feeling depressed prior to the incident. This compares to slightly more than half (55%) of self-injury participants, a difference that was statistically significant (Pearson $\chi^2(1, N = 99) = 13.451, p = 0.001$). Further, a significantly higher proportion of participants who experienced anger prior to the incident had injured themselves rather than attempted suicide (Pearson $\chi^2(1, N = 99) = 23.188, p = 0.001$).

Mood states post attempted suicide/self-injury

A number of theorists have remarked on the *functional* aspects of self-injury. For example, it is deemed to be effective in regulating distress (Babiker and Arnold, 1997), reducing anxiety (Cullen, 1985; Coid *et al.*, 1992), attracting sympathy or comfort (Cullen, 1985) or for instrumental purposes, such as securing a change in location (Cullen, 1985). Others suggest that self-injury occurs in the context of generalised prison-specific frustration and helplessness and that it can provide temporary relief from frustration, anxiety or depression by enabling prisoners the ability to exert control over their environment (Cookson, 1977).

In order to test the assumption that self-injury may have some functional element, participants were asked to describe how they felt *immediately after* the incident. It was hypothesised that those for whom self-injury served some function or purpose, for example, a reduction in tension, would report feeling better afterwards. When asked if they felt better afterwards, 41% responded in the positive and 59% in the negative. Each participant was coded according to his or her response and the totals in each category compared to ascertain whether either category contained an over-representation of either group of participants. The binomial test was used to evaluate whether the proportions that fell into each category were equal to hypothesised values. In this case, the two categories were as follows: felt no better (coded 1); or felt better (coded 2). The hypothesised proportion in each category is 0.50 (i.e. half of each category felt either no better or worse). A two-tailed binomial (z-approximation) test was conducted to assess whether population proportions for participants who felt better following the incident was greater than 0.50 (the proportion that would be expected if there was no difference between the groups). The majority of participants who felt better (81%) had injured themselves, rather than attempted suicide (two-tailed $p \leq 0.001$). Conversely, the majority of those who felt no better or worse after the incident (83%) had attempted suicide (two-tailed $p \leq 0.001$). These findings give further support to the view that self-injury is functional in providing relief from negative feelings or emotions.

Previous life experiences

A recent influential study considered significant life events and experiences of a group of prisoners who had attempted suicide and compared them with a group of prisoners who had not (Meltzer *et al.*, 1999). This approach has been applied to the current sample although, as with other studies reported here, has been extended to include a comparison between prisoners who attempt suicide and those who self-injure for reasons other than cessation of life.

Meltzer *et al.*'s study included the use of 15 key life events, which were categorised according to three broad groups, as follows: 'personal', 'relationship' and 'educational/economic'. The authors reported a number of key differences between the groups. For example, those who had attempted suicide were more likely to report having experienced a greater number of such events. A higher number of those who reported having experienced seven or more negative life experiences (indicating a very high level of negative life events) had attempted suicide; 46% of prisoners who had attempted suicide had reported seven or more such events, compared with only 15% of those who had not attempted suicide.

An adaptation of Meltzer *et al.*'s key life events categorisation was used in the current study, with participants being asked (during the course of an interview) whether they had experienced each of the included key life events. Working on the assumption that both qualitative and quantitative differences exist in participants' experience of negative life events, the *structure* of participants' negative life experiences was analysed using SSA-1 analysis, which revealed three distinct categories of events: 'negative home life', 'rejection events' and 'personal violence and loss'. This finding represents an important departure from Meltzer *et al.*'s work (1999) in which the events were categorised on the basis of assumed similarity. These empirically defined negative life event categories were then examined to determine whether there were any differences between those who had attempted suicide and those who had self-injured in their experiences of the events within the different categories, as well as in their overall experience of negative life events. A series of between-subjects analysis of variance tests revealed no differences between the groups, thereby demonstrating that suicidal and self-injuring prisoners' (quantitative) experience of the various life events was comparable, both overall and at the level of negative life event category.

Further analysis of the data was undertaken using POSA (partially ordered scalogram analysis) which, like other MDS techniques, represents empirical relationships in a data set as points in geometric space and makes visually clear apparent aspects of the data that might be obscured in an original data matrix. POSA differs from SSA-1 in that the former allows a simultaneous examination of quantitative and qualitative differences in a data set. Separate analyses were conducted on each of the empirically defined categories of negative life events, the main results of which are summarised thus:

- An analysis of the variables in the 'rejection' events and 'personal violence and loss' categories revealed that the combination of participants' experiences of these events was similar. Follow-up univariate analyses revealed no differences between the groups, confirming that participants who had attempted suicide and those who self-injured did not have different experiences (either qualitatively or quantitatively) of 'rejection' events.

- An analysis of the variables in the 'negative home life' category revealed that participants who had self-injured were more likely to have run away from home, been homeless and experienced violence at home or had financial problems. Further, a significantly higher proportion of participants who had experienced all of the events in this category had attempted suicide.

The aim of this analysis was to ascertain whether differences (qualitative or quantitative) exist between prisoners who attempt suicide and those who injure themselves in terms of their experiences of previously identified negative life experiences. The structure of participants' experiences was analysed using SSA-1, which revealed three distinct categories of events ('negative home life', 'rejection events' and 'personal violence and loss'). These empirically defined negative life event groupings were examined in detail to reveal that there were statistically no differences between prisoners who attempted suicide and those who self-injured in terms of their experience of events within the different categories, as well as in their overall experience of negative life events. Verification of the possible dual (i.e. qualitative and quantitative) effect of negative life events was undertaken using POSA analysis which highlighted some differences between prisoners who attempt suicide, when compared with those who injure themselves. This analysis revealed that those who experience three events in the 'negative home life' category were more likely to have self-injured, while those who experienced all four events were more likely to have attempted suicide suggesting, perhaps, that there exists a process whereby medium levels of negative home life events may be, to some extent, tolerable (perhaps with the amelioration effect of self-injury) while the combination of all experiences may conspire to create a process whereby people may look for an escape from life.

Motivations for attempted suicide/self-injury

As outlined above, a number of theories exist as to individuals' motivations for engaging in 'suicidal behaviours'. A recurrent theme of this chapter has been the implicit observation that there is a dearth of research into the *differences* between self-inflicted injuries depending on whether or not the individual intended to kill him/herself. Two of the few papers available on the differences in motivation between individuals who attempt suicide and those who self-injure are now overviewed.

A cluster analysis conducted on data arising from interviews with women prisoners who injured themselves revealed two distinct groups (Coid *et al.*, 1992). The first (and largest) group of women had injured themselves in order to relieve negative feelings (e.g. anxiety, depression, etc.), which were clearly linked to negative childhood experiences. These prisoners were more likely (than the second group) to be experiencing impulse or personality disorders. The second group injured themselves in response to more recent, significant life events or psychotic episodes.

A more recent study found a number of significant differences between prisoners' stated motivations for attempting suicide or otherwise injuring themselves (Snow, 2002). Qualitative data from in-depth interviews were subjected to content analysis before being analysed using MDS techniques, in order to fully understand the structure of participants' expressed reasons for attempting suicide/self-injuring, as well as the inter-relationships within the structure. The resultant MDS (SSA-1) plot was partitioned according to five separate regions, each containing items that relate to a separate theme or element of motivation, thereby suggesting that (for the dataset in question) there are five major motivational dimensions to self-injury and attempted suicide, which were classified as follows: offence-related; interpersonal; symptom-relief; instrumental and situational. In order to ascertain whether either group of prisoners (i.e. those who had attempted suicide compared with those who had injured themselves) had a tendency to adopt a particular motivational typology, prisoners' explanations for their behaviour were examined and each participant assigned a 'predominant motivational style' based on the explanations they gave. The results of this analysis are summarised as follows:

- all of those who were motivated by 'relationship' related issues had attempted suicide;
- the majority of those who were motivated by a desire to relieve negative experiences or feelings (83%) had self-injured;
- the majority of those who gave explanations categorised as being 'instrumental' (60%) had self-injured; and
- the majority of those who gave explanations categorised as being 'situational' (74%) had attempted suicide.

The results of this analysis highlight the complex and multifactorial nature of attempted suicide and self-injury in prisons, in that prisoners give multifaceted explanations for their behaviours, which are rarely related to one incident, event, feeling or emotion.

In summary, Snow (2002) reported very clear distinctions in prisoners' motivations, depending on whether or not they *intended* to kill themselves. Attempted suicide was precipitated by *concrete* events, such as relationship problems, drug withdrawal or a court appearance, while self-injury was motivated by negative feelings or emotions. For example, a substantial proportion of prisoners who self-injured reported that they injured themselves in order to relieve feelings of anger, stress or frustration.

Research summary

Socio-demographic, personal and criminological factors

The current study drew on previous research findings, which had associated various socio-demographic, criminological and psychiatric/health-related factors with 'suicidal behaviours', in order to assess differences and similarities between attempted suicide and self-injury. A range of univariate and multivariate analyses demonstrated that the prisoners who attempted suicide were more similar than different from those who injured themselves for other reasons, at least on the variables examined.

Prisoners' mood states and key emotions

The focus on prisoners' emotions and mood states at key periods during the phase in question was undertaken in order to ascertain whether there existed any clear differences in this regard between those who attempted suicide and those who self-injured. The results of the presented research demonstrated that, indeed, differences do exist. The results of multidimensional analysis were used to develop two separate scales, each of which measured different elements of the overall domain of generalised mood states, as follows:

- the 'active' mood domain included the items 'anger', 'anxiety' and 'stress';
- the 'passive' domain included 'depression', 'loneliness' and 'boredom'.

Follow-up t-tests demonstrated that participants who had attempted suicide had higher mean scores on the 'passive' domain, indicating that they felt *more* depressed, lonely and bored when compared with participants who had self-injured.

The second stage of the analysis focussed on participants' self-reported emotions *immediately prior to* attempted suicide or self-injuring. The data arising from an open-ended question in the interview schedule were content-analysed and the following five broad emotion types were reported: 'boredom', 'depression', 'anger', 'in-pain' and 'anxious'/'stressed'. It was demonstrated that those who self-injured (rather than attempting suicide) were significantly more likely to report feelings of anger prior to the incident.

The final stage of the analysis examined the possible functional aspect of 'suicidal behaviours', by assessing whether either group was more or less likely to report feeling better after the incident. That participants who injured themselves were significantly more likely than those who attempted suicide to feel better after the event gives further support to the well-established finding that self-injury can provide relief from negative emotions or feelings (e.g. Cookson, 1977).

Negative life events

A replication of parts of the analysis undertaken previously by Meltzer *et al.* (1999) was undertaken in order to assess whether there existed differential experiences among prisoners who attempted suicide, compared with those who self-injured. The authors reported that the proportion of prisoners who experienced such events was nearly always greater among those who had attempted suicide (when compared with a sample of prisoners who had neither attempted suicide nor self-injured).

The current research examined the relative difference in experience of negative life events between prisoners who attempted suicide and those who self-injured. Rather than simply grouping the variables according to assumed similarity, the data were analysed using SSA-1. This enabled the development of an empirical model, which facilitated detailed examination of the underlying psychological structure of prisoners' negative life experiences. The model, which makes clear the pattern of co-occurrence of these events, revealed three *discrete* negative life event types, which were termed 'negative home life', 'rejection experience' and 'personal violence and loss'. Each of these experience-types contained clusters of variables that shared some psychological commonality.

'Rejection experience' included the following variables: the experience of being bullied at school, expulsion from school, and having been dismissed or made redundant from employment. 'Negative home life' included the following: homelessness, the experience of running away from home, violence at home, and severe financial problems. Finally, the 'personal violence and loss' category included the death of a child or partner, the death of a parent or sibling, the death of a close friend, and sexual abuse. The model provides a theoretically and empirically based typology from which a richer and more valid understanding of prisoners' life experiences may be drawn.

More detailed analysis revealed subtle differences in the various categories. For example, in the 'negative home life' category, prisoners' experiences varied qualitatively *and* quantitatively. Some had low levels of negative home life experience, others medium levels and still others experienced the highest level (i.e. they had experienced all events in this category). Interestingly it was found that while those with low levels of negative life events were neither more likely to attempt suicide nor self-injure, those who experienced medium levels were more likely to self-injure, whereas those experiencing high levels were more likely to attempt suicide. This suggests a process in which medium levels of negative home life events may be, to some extent, tolerable (perhaps with the amelioration effect of self-injury), while the combination of all experiences may conspire to create a process whereby people may look for an escape from life itself. Together these models contribute a far richer picture of prisoners' negative home life events and their relation to suicidal behaviours than was previously available.

Motivations for attempting suicide/self-injuring

The reported model of prisoners' motivations was based on participants' own explanations for the incidents, rather than them being provided with predefined constructs by the researcher. This approach, as well as being rich and detailed in nature, enables a full examination of suicidal behaviours from participants' own perspectives. The model was based on participants' varied and complex accounts of the events or emotions that precipitated their attempts at suicide or incidents of self-injury. These data were content analysed and classified according to broad explanation types, which were then submitted to SSA. The resultant model revealed five dimensions to prisoners' motivations for engaging in these behaviours namely 'situational', 'offence-related', 'interpersonal', 'instrumental', and 'symptom-relief'. The main associations between attempted suicide/self-injury and each of these motivational categories are summarised thus:

- those who attempted suicide were more likely than those who self-injured to be motivated by events in the 'interpersonal relationships' category;
- those who self-injured were more likely to be motivated by events in the 'symptom-relief' category;
- 'instrumental' motivations are most common among those who self-injured; and
- 'situational' factors are most common among those who attempted suicide.

Participants who attempted suicide were far more likely than those who self-injured to report being motivated by the factors that include:

- homesickness;
- grief;
- hopelessness;
- relationship problems;
- the award or expectation of a lengthy prison sentence.

Participants who injured themselves without suicidal intent were more likely to be motivated by:

- anger, stress or tension;
- the absence of alternative ways of dealing with negative feelings (e.g. drugs and/or alcohol).

These results highlight the complex and multifactorial nature of suicidal and self-injurious behaviours. In very few cases were there single reported causes. Rather, the majority of participants described a number of precipitating or motivational factors related to concrete events or feelings/emotions or both. For further discussion on prisoners' motivations for attempting suicide or otherwise injuring themselves, see Snow (2002).

Dual Path Model

The findings presented above in relation to the similarities and differences between prisoners who attempt suicide and those who injure themselves are drawn together and presented in Figure 5.2, which indicates different psychological routes to attempted suicide and self-injury. As illustrated:

- socio-demographic, criminological and psychiatric/health-related factors do not discriminate between prisoners who attempt suicide or otherwise injure themselves;
- prisoners with medium levels of negative home life events were more likely to have self-injured;
- prisoners with high levels of negative home life events were more likely to have attempted suicide;
- those who self-injured were more likely to be 'passive' in terms of generalised mood states;
- those who attempted suicide were more likely to be 'active' in their generalised mood states;
- the motivations of prisoners who attempted suicide differ from those who self-injured;
- self-injury is *functional* in that prisoners felt better afterwards.

Implications for Policy and Practice

The research has highlighted a number of issues that have implications for Prison Service policy and practice with regards to the management of suicidal and self-injurious behaviours, which are covered sequentially below.

First, the very clear distinctions that have been established between prisoners who attempt suicide and those who injure themselves (in terms of

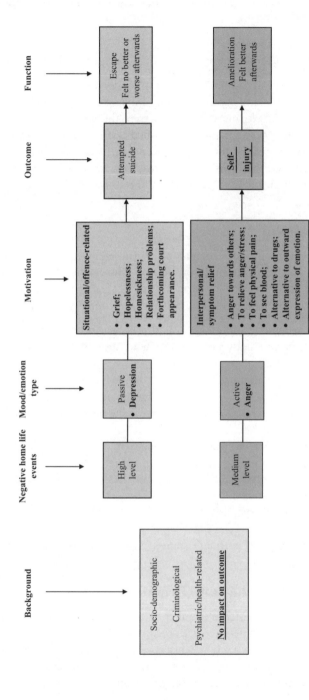

Figure 5.2   Dual path model

motivations, preceding emotions and perceived functions of the behaviours) support the recent move away from the 'generic' management approach (under the F2052SH system) towards a more behavioural-specific approach (under the ACCT (assessment care in custody and teamwork)[6] system). Given that people who attempt suicide or injure themselves do so for very different reasons, it follows that they require different management approaches and interventions.

Despite the theoretical and empirical distinction between prisoners who attempt suicide and those who injure themselves for other reasons, it is acknowledged that the latter are substantially more likely than those who do not injure themselves to die by suicide (Gunnell and Frankel, 1994). Consequently, all prisoners who injure themselves should be perceived as being at *some* risk of suicide. The ACCT approach, which is based on three levels of risk (low, medium and high), may be preferable in this regard, in that it is more sophisticated in terms of risk assessment and management.

The research demonstrates how prisoners' interpretations of events play a key role in their suicidal behaviours. As mentioned, almost none of the prisoners who injured themselves in order to manage negative feelings or experiences had received any help or therapeutic support since being in prison. The psychological impact of self-injury – on the individuals concerned, on their families, on other prisoners and on prison staff – is substantial. It follows, therefore, that enabling such prisoners to express themselves or manage their feelings in more positive ways would be hugely beneficial. Structured interventions (such as cognitive-behavioural therapy, cognitive analytical therapy and problem-solving therapy) have been shown to be effective in other settings (e.g. Linehan *et al.*, 1991). A range of services, such as individual counselling, group therapy, psychotherapy and peer support (Snow, 2000), as well as the cognitive-behavioural approaches outlined above, should be offered to suicidal and self-injuring prisoners. Any such intervention should be individually tailored and based on the factors that precipitate these behaviours. In addition to formalised interventions mentioned above, evidence suggests that creating a productive, full and active regime for prisoners may protect them against suicidal behaviours (Borrill *et al.*, 2005). It is, of course, vital that all prison staff positively support any intervention or regime improvement and encourage prisoners to participate if appropriate.

Conclusions

It has been argued that, despite the substantial body of prison-based research into completed and attempted suicide, as well as self-injury (without suicidal intent), these behaviours remain poorly understood. The current research aims to improve this understanding by drawing on wider theoretical models of these behaviours (e.g. Shneidman, 1985; Walsh and Rosen, 1988) as well as broader social and behavioural psychological theories.

The conclusions drawn from the current research have implications for academic psychology as well as policy and practical implications for the Prison Service. In summary, these are as follows:

- Background factors do not clearly discriminate between those who attempt suicide and those who injure themselves for other reasons.
- The majority of the participants in the sample had experienced similarly negative life events and experiences. The analysis identified different typologies of such events, of which few discriminated between those who tried to kill themselves and those who did not. Theoretically, it would be interesting to explore further what leads some of these people to attempt suicide, but others to intentionally injure themselves without wishing to die.
- It is possible to distinguish between the generalised mood states and emotions of those who attempt suicide and those who injure themselves for other reasons.

  A model of moods and emotions preceding their suicidal behaviours was developed which indicates two broad dimensions: 'active' and 'passive'. Very clear differences were found between prisoners who attempted suicide and those who injured themselves in their generalised mood states, providing further support for previous work that has drawn the distinction between these two groups (e.g. Williams, 1997). For example, feelings of depression ('passive' mood types) characterised those who attempted suicide. Those who injured themselves were far more likely to report feelings of anger, anxiety or stress. This has important practical implications in the sense that any therapeutic interventions should be based on the specific group's needs, rather than being generalised to all of those who engage in the broad spectrum of 'suicidal behaviours'.

- Reasons for attempted suicide and self-injury differ.

  A model of prisoners' motivations for their suicidal behaviours was developed. It shows how motivations operate within five different dimensions: offence, interpersonal, symptom-relief, instrumental and situational. A number of different motivational factors were found to be more prevalent among participants who attempted suicide. These included, for example, relationship problems, concerns about forthcoming court appearances and factors relating to drug withdrawal. Those who attempted suicide were more likely to report that *concrete events* or experiences had affected their decision to act in the way they did. On the other hand, those who injured themselves without suicidal intent were much more likely to describe precipitating factors related to *negative feelings* or *emotions*. For example, a substantial proportion reported that they injured themselves in order to relieve feelings of anger, stress or frustration, or that they would prefer to hurt themselves than direct their anger towards others. There was a small, but important, minority who injured themselves with the sole intention of affecting a change in their circumstances.

- There are clear distinctions between attempted suicide and self-injury in the functions they serve.

  Prisoners who injured themselves felt significantly better after doing so. This was not the case for those who attempted suicide, who invariably felt no better or worse. This finding provides further support for theories regarding the functional aspects of self-injurious behaviours. This is not to suggest, however, that the Prison Service should accept as inevitable that some prisoners will injure themselves. Rather, it should explore ways of channelling prisoners' negative experiences and resultant emotions in more positive and less destructive ways.

- These findings are drawn together in a dual path model, indicating the different psychological routes to attempted suicide and self-injury.

In conclusion, the current research has made a significant contribution to the understanding of suicidal and self-injurious behaviours in prisons. It has provided empirical support to some of the earlier work on suicide and self-injury in prisons. Further, it has developed a richer picture of prisoners' lives in relation to their suicidal behaviours. Combined, the research provides a more accurate and sophisticated view of attempted suicide and self-injury from which the Prison Service can develop future policy.

Notes

1. The Prison Service uses the term 'self-inflicted death' to refer to all apparent suicides in custody. This is broader than the strict definition of 'suicide' as defined by a coroner and includes all deaths where it is apparent that the individual's actions led to their death, irrespective of intent. It is, therefore, broader than community-based definitions.

2. Safer Custody News, January/February 2005, HM Prison Service.

3. The term 'completed suicide' is far preferable to the more commonly used term 'committed suicide', which implies that a 'crime' has been 'committed', as Barrington writes: 'in itself the tendentious expression "to commit suicide" is calculated to poison the unsuspecting mind with its false semantic overtones, for apart from the dangerous practice of committing oneself to an opinion, most other things committed are, as suicide once was, criminal offences' (1969, 231).

4. For further information on inclusion criteria, see Snow (2002).

5. The SSA-1 on self-assessment mood data was carried out using the Phi coefficient of association, which is appropriate for the ordinal scale used in the analysis. As only six items were included in the analysis, a two-dimension plot was deemed sufficient for interpretative purposes. The resultant two-dimensional SSA-1 solution had a

Guttman-Lingoes coefficient of alienation of 0.32 in 15 iterations. According to Borg and Lingoes (1987), ideally, the coefficient should be around 0.20 although there is no universally agreed upper limit. Given that published papers present SSA-1 with similar coefficients (e.g. Canter and Heritage, 1990) it was deemed acceptable for the current purposes.

6. During the next two years it is intended to replace the F2052SH (Self-Harm At-Risk Form) with a new system to support the identification and care of prisoners at risk of suicide or self-harm.

Chapter 6

The Effective Management of Bullying in Prisons: Working Towards an Evidence-Based Approach

Jane L. Ireland

Introduction

Interest in researching the bullying that occurs among prisoners has increased in the last few years. A review of peer-reviewed studies appearing between 1999 and 2004 indicates 18 published studies, most appearing between 2002 and 2004 (e.g. Ireland, 2002a, 2002b; Ireland and Power, 2004), with seven appearing prior to 1999 (e.g. Power *et al.*, 1997). There is some research available published in professional journals or briefings (e.g. Livingston and Chapman, 1997), or unpublished as in-house surveys (e.g. Livingston *et al.*, 1994), but the quality of this research is limited, partly because they have not been subject to independent peer review and also by the fact most are based on small samples. There are other papers and texts available exploring aggression among prisoners but these have focussed on general violence and the precautions taken by victims (e.g. McCorkle, 1992; O'Donnell and Edgar, 1996), on sexual victimisation (e.g. Dumond, 1992), or on 'predatory' behaviour (Shields and Simourd, 1991).

The focus of most prison research has been on bullying between male prisoners, with few studies exploring women. The first study exploring women appeared in 1996 (Ireland and Archer, 1996), with eight peer-reviewed papers discussing bullying among women available up until 2004 (i.e. Ireland, 1999a, 1999b, 2001a, 2001b, 2002a, 2002c; Ireland and Archer, 2002; Leddy and O'Connell, 2002), and one currently in preparation (Ireland *et al.*, 2005). Little is also known of the bullying that occurs among juveniles in comparison to young and adult offenders (Ireland and Ireland, 2003; Hafiz and Ireland, 2005).

Despite gaps in knowledge regarding specific prison populations, the field of research in bullying is advancing, not only with regards to the number of studies being produced but also with regard to the content of these studies. Researchers are now beginning to move away from focussing solely on the nature and extent of bullying towards a more detailed exploration and explication of the predictors and characteristics of those involved. To date, the characteristics explored by researchers include prison behavioural characteristics such as negative behaviour towards staff and prison rules (Ireland, 2001b); empathy and pro-victim attitudes (Ireland, 1999b; Ireland and Ireland, 2000); beliefs about aggression (Ireland, 2001a; Ireland and Archer, 2002); anger, aggression and hostility (Ireland and Archer, 2004); assertiveness (Ireland, 2002c); attachment styles and emotional loneliness (Ireland and Power, 2004); social self-esteem (Ireland, 2002a) and health (Leddy and O'Connell, 2002; Ireland, 2005b).

Providing a comprehensive review of the findings of these studies is outside the scope of the chapter. Their findings will be reflected on, however, to provide evidence, where possible, for the opinions outlined in this chapter regarding the effective management of bullying. It is important to be clear that although there have been recent advances in prison bullying research, as a field of academic study it remains in its infancy. Social-criminological and social psychology theories exploring intergroup dynamics exist (e.g. Turner, 1987), but few have been developed that attempt to provide an understanding with regards to prison bullying. The focus on developing a theoretical understanding of prison bullying began only in 2002 (Ireland, 2002d), and has more recently been a focus of academic interest, with the first book exploring the theory published in 2005 (Ireland, 2005c). To date there are four theoretical models: first, outlining an interaction model of prison bullying (Ireland, 2002d); second, outlining a model of applied social information processing (Ireland and Murray, 2005); third, an applied-fear response model (Ireland, 2005d); and, finally, a biopsychosocial and ecological interaction model (Gilbert, 2005a). A summary of the core themes of these models will be described later.

An appropriate place to start is the provision of an outline of how bullying is defined in prisons and the different groups of prisoners involved. Following this will be a summary of the core theories underpinning prison bullying followed by a focus on implications for effective evidence-based intervention. The aim of this chapter is not to provide an all-inclusive outline of evidence-based intervention, however, rather to delineate some examples of core issues that should be accounted for.

Defining Bullying

Definitions of bullying first used by prison researchers were influenced largely by the school-based literature. Such definitions generally indicated that in order for a behaviour to be classed as bullying it must contain physical, psychological or verbal attack, involve an imbalance of power, that the victim must not have provoked the bully, that the aggression had to have occurred more than once and that the bully must intend to cause fear or distress (Farrington, 1993). Problems with this definition have been noted, not just by prison researchers but also by school-based researchers. Consequently, the only criteria most commonly accepted by school researchers are those of the behaviour having to be repeated and an imbalance of power having to be evident (Smith and Brain, 2000).

These two criteria, however, have been criticised by prison researchers who argue that the transient nature of prison populations prevent the development of stable social networks required that allow repeated acts of aggression to occur. Rather it is argued that it is the *fear* of repeated aggression that should drive definitions, not the actual incidence (Randall, 1997; Ireland, 2002d). Prison researchers also argue that some examples of prison bullying are not clearly based on an imbalance of power, providing 'baroning' as one such example (Ireland, 2002d). Such behaviour refers to where goods (e.g. tobacco, drugs) are provided to another prisoner by a prisoner acting as a baron. The rates of exchange are high, with the victim expected to pay extortionate levels of repayment. Since the victim enters this relationship 'voluntarily', it is not based on an imbalance of power, at least initially.

Due to difficulties in defining bullying in prisons, broader prison-based definitions have consequently been suggested, for example:

> An individual is being bullied when they are the victim of direct and/or indirect aggression happening on a weekly basis, by the same perpetrator or different perpetrators. Single incidences of aggression can be viewed as bullying, particularly where they are severe and when the individual either believes or fears that they are at risk of future victimisation by the same perpetrator or others. An incident can be considered bullying if the victim believes that they have been aggressed towards, regardless of the actual intention of the bully. It can also be bullying when the imbalance of power between the bully and his/her victim is implied and not immediately evident.

> (Ireland, 2002d, p. 26)

Defining prison bullying is, however, fraught with difficulty. It is unlikely a fixed measurable definition of bullying will be settled on and at best 'bullying' should be considered a working term that encapsulates a range of aggressive behaviours between individuals. Recognising the problems in defining bullying is important, however, since this has connotations for how bullying is managed. This issue will be reflected on later.

The Groups Involved

Early research focussed on two core groups – bullies and victims. This was consistent with the early school-based research and symptomatic of the wider aggression literature whose focus, at least initially, was on the perpetrators of aggression and victims as independent groups. More attention is given now, however, to the 'bully/victim' group and the 'not-involved' group. The former group represent those reporting the perpetration of aggression who also experience victimisation, whereas the latter represent those not involved in bullying either as a bully and/or a victim. Bully/victims are a sizeable group among prisoners, in general making up one-third of the population (Ireland *et al.*, 2005). The not-involved group are a particularly important inclusion since they are symptomatic of recognition that bullying is a product of the peer group and not a behaviour occurring in isolation between the 'bully' and the 'victim' (Ireland, 2005c).

Thus, among prison research there are four groups of prisoners who have been researched: 'pure victims' – those reporting behaviours solely indicative of being bullied; 'pure bullies' – those reporting behaviours solely indicative of bullying others; 'bully/victims' – those reporting behaviours indicative of being bullied and of bullying others; and, 'not-involved' – those not identified as belonging to any of the other groups. It has been suggested, however, that future research should focus on separating these groups further, perhaps following the lead of school researchers (e.g. Sutton *et al.*, 1999) who separate groups into:

1   'Ringleader' bullies: those initiating bullying, serving as active leaders of the aggression.
2   'Assistant bullies': active bullies but more followers than leaders of the aggression.
3   'Reinforcers': those acting as part of an inciting audience to the bully.
4   'Defenders': those actively defending the victim.
5   'Victim': those reporting victimisation.
6   'Outsiders': those demonstrating no evidence of membership to the previous groups.

The identification of these groupings is achieved via a 'peer nomination' approach in which the peer group places each member into one of the categories. Such an approach works well in schools where classes are small and peers have known each other for a sufficient period of time. In a prison where the population is large and transient, such an approach becomes difficult to implement. It is also unlikely prisoners will engage in an approach that essentially ensures they are informing on their peers to staff, a behaviour in violation of the inmate code that may be considered sufficient for the informer to be subjected to 'justified bullying'. It is important to remain mindful of these further groups, however, particularly in the development of intervention programmes. Being able to identify if the prisoner you are working with is a 'ringleader', a 'reinforcer' or 'assistant', for example, will determine the specifics of an intervention programme. These issues will be reflected on later.

Thus prison researchers have been left with what are arguably four crude groups (i.e. pure bullies, pure victims, bully/victims and those not-involved) as a basis with which to explore the characteristics associated with bullying. There are changes planned to these groupings currently in development. These are changes reflecting recent amendments to the measures developed to assess bullying that will allow for a more complete assessment of the frequency of the behaviour and the different groups involved (see Ireland, 2005c, for a fuller explanation of these changes).

Theoretical Models to Aid Understanding

It can be seen from the previous sections that a number of advances are being made in the prison bullying field. The need to develop theoretical models is the next step in the evolution of such research, with increasing focus on this already identified (Ireland, 2002d). Provided here is a summary of the theoretical models proposed that provide a grounding for many of the suggestions for intervention outlined later. Four models have been put forward to date as follows:

1 *Interaction model* (Ireland, 2002d): The model reflects on the wider aggression literature by including attention to theories such as material deprivation, indigenous origins, direct importation, social categorization and evolutionary approaches. These are combined with a review of the prison literature to outline an eclectic model that explains bullying as an expected behaviour in prison. The core basis of this model is its reflection on how the social and physical aspects of prison environments serve to encourage and maintain bullying. Within this setting are placed individuals who have a predisposition to engage in interpersonal aggression and/or individuals who deal with situations poorly. This model places emphasis on the role of the environment in promoting bullying and places de-emphasis on the role of the individual, arguing strongly against over-attention to individual psychopathology models.

2 *Applied social information processing model* (Ireland and Murray, 2005): This model draws heavily on the original social information processing model of Dodge (1986) and the reformulated model of Crick and Dodge (1994) in terms of structure and content. It also incorporates the unified model of Huesmann (1998) by attending to both emotions and normative beliefs.

In this applied model there is explicit emphasis on displays of aggression as an adaptive (although not acceptable) solution to the threat of or actual experience of being bullied. The applied model was not intended to replace social information processing models. The focus instead was on how such models could be applied and reformulated in parts to explain prison bullying. It incorporated the specific role of the prison environment, emotions such as anger and fear, the promotion of aggressive scripts (i.e. internalised 'guides' that determine a behavioural response) over non-aggressive scripts, the influence of normative beliefs on the evaluation and subsequent activation of a behavioural response and the reinforcement of scripts. It argued that prisons encourage a learning of aggressive scripts to deal with social problems such as bullying. The process by which this learning happens is expected via 'socialisation' into prison culture and an acceptance of the inmate code and belief system.

3 *Applied fear response model* (Ireland, 2005d): This model specifically explores the responses of victims following exposure to bullying and the precautionary behaviours prisoners engage in to avoid exposure. It focuses on fear as a motivating factor in explaining victim responses. Emphasised in particular is the concept of 'flight vs. fight' responses to threat, with reference to cognitive neoassociation theories of aggression (Berkowitz, 1998). The fear response model outlines how responding aggressively to victimisation represents both a fight and a flight response, with the target of this aggression unimportant (i.e. it can be the perpetrator, other prisoners or staff). It describes how fear can represent a motivating drive in prison that serves to protect prisoners against bullying.

This model also proposes the concept of a 'delayed-flight' response, suggesting that responding aggressively following an incident of bullying, either by aggressing towards others or towards themselves in the form of self-injurious behaviour, represents a *delayed*-flight response since both can, eventually, lead to removal from the prison unit. The application of the concept of a delayed-flight response is considered essential to prisons where the options to demonstrate an *immediate*-flight response is limited by the constraints of the physical environment.

4 *Biopsychosocial and ecological interaction model* (Gilbert, 2005a): This model outlines the biopsychosocial interactions in bullying, focussing on evolutionary functions and cultural regulators. It has a number of similarities with the interaction model outlined by Ireland (2002d) in that it also attends to the complex interactions between the prison environment and those housed within it. Like Ireland's (2002d) and Ireland and Murray's (2005), this model emphasises the potentially 'adaptive' nature of aggression, reflecting on its role as a strategic solution to the challenges of social competition. Gilbert's (2005a) model, however, accounts much more clearly for the value of evolutionary theory, with the author outlining the influence of group living on social interactions and the influence of ecology in the recruitment and success of aggressive or affiliative strategies.

The mention of biological factors in this model (e.g. genes, hormones, neurochemistry and immunity) is also a novel aspect. In the same vein as the models put forward by Ireland (2002d) and Ireland and Murray (2005), the biopsychosocial and ecological interaction model places emphasis on 'depsychopathologising' bullying.

All of these models, although recent, provide some basis for a more detailed understanding as to why prison bullying occurs and how it is maintained. All have implications for evidence-based approaches to managing bullying.

Evidence-Based Intervention into Prison Bullying: Setting the Scene

The aim of this section is to explore key issues that should be accounted for in the design of any intervention into prison bullying. As outlined at the start of the chapter, it is not intended to provide here an exhaustive list but rather to outline some useful considerations. It does, however, commence with a caveat. Currently there are no evaluations exploring the effectiveness of interventions into prison bullying, whether these represent interventions conducted at the organisational or individual level. Organisational interventions primarily represent anti-bullying policies and procedures whereas individual interventions refer here to individualised approaches to the management of bullies and/or victims such as engaging them in treatment and/or management programmes. In view of the resources placed into the management of interpersonal aggression within prisons, this lack of evaluation is surprising but perhaps symptomatic of a fairly new area of empirical research.

It can be argued that theory-driven approaches represent those with the highest potential for positive impact. There is an absence of theory-driven approaches at present, with a tendency for attention to be placed on the school-based literature, individual psychopathology models, punishment-orientated approaches and intuition models (i.e. the 'it feels right and so should work' approach). Such criticisms have been mentioned previously in the literature (Ireland, 2002d). This section aims to provide suggestions grounded in theory that should provide guidance to those involved in managing bullying. This section commences with an outline of the aims of intervention and provides a broad framework within which theory-driven approaches should operate.

Setting the scene: Aims

The starting point for any effective approach is an acceptance that bullying should be expected to occur among prisoners. There are physical and social aspects to the prison environment that promote bullying and reinforce it once it continues. All the models outlined in the previous section emphasise the role of the prison environment. Some elements of the prison environment, known to contribute to the promotion of intergroup aggression, represent static elements of prisons unlikely to change. These include evidence of social hierarchies based on dominance, the existence of a regime, a transient prisoner population, limited spatial density, limitations on opportunities to avoid actual or potential aggressors, limitations on available stimulation, low genetic and attachment relationships between prisoners, a high prisoner-to-staff ratio restricting supervision, low levels of material goods and a prisoner subculture that encourages prisoners not to inform to staff (interaction model: Ireland, 2002d). Prisons indicating they have no or 'very little' bullying are arguably not measuring the nature and extent of bullying appropriately. I have long held the view that prisons making such statements are the most ineffective in managing bullying and commonly fail to acknowledge the more subtle forms of bullying known to occur among adolescents and adults, leading to artificially low estimates of bullying.

With regards to this latter point, I am referring here specifically to indirect forms of bullying such as gossiping, spreading rumours and ostracising (Björkqvist, 1994). In a prison, indirect aggression has been found to occur to at least the same extent, if not more frequently, than direct aggression (e.g. Ireland, 1999a, 2002d; Ireland and Monaghan, 2005). Indirect aggression is an effective way of victimising in prisons since it combines a high cost for victims in terms of harm with a low cost for the bully in terms of identification by staff (Ireland and Monaghan, 2005). Such an explanation is based on the 'effect-danger' ratio theory proposed by Björkqvist (1994), according to which aggressors will choose an aggressive strategy based on an evaluation of the effect of their aggression and the associated personal danger. Prisons reporting little or no bullying, therefore, are likely to be failing to measure bullying correctly and to be focussing on the more direct types of aggression that are easily observable or detectable by staff, that is, physical and theft related.

The starting point therefore is that bullying should be expected to occur in prisons and approaches to managing bullying should be focussing on reducing bullying and not eradicating it. The latter is an unachievable goal and will serve only to discourage staff.

Setting the scene: Framework

First, there needs to be an acknowledgement that bullying is not an individual phenomenon: prisoners do not bully and/or are victimised solely because of the intrinsic characteristics they possess. Individual characteristics may be important in adding to an explanation of bullying but they are insufficient on their own to explain bullying and to provide guidance on an effective approach to management. It is not possible to manage the individual who is bullying and/or being victimised without also managing the environment in which they are placed. This certainly fits with all of the models outlined earlier, particularly the interaction model (Ireland, 2002d) and the biopsychosocial and ecological interaction model (Gilbert, 2005a).

There does remain a tendency for a focus on individual psychopathology approaches to managing bullying. Examples of these include 'anti-bullying' units or wings where alleged perpetrators are placed in order to have their behaviour 'corrected' before returning to a standard wing or unit. What is not attended to by these interventions, however, is the environment in which the bullying is taking place. Not only do you have bullying within such 'anti-bullying' units (highlighting again the role of the environment), but also when the perpetrator is returned to their original unit they are essentially returned to the same environment in which the bullying first occurred. Thus, it should not be surprising that they continue to bully or become subtler in the selection of their aggressive strategy. Also it cannot be guaranteed with such approaches that the 'bully' placed within these anti-bullying units are not in fact victims who have chosen to display aggression towards others in order to obtain respite from their aggressor(s). Such victims learn that displays of aggression may lead to placement on another unit where they will be watched more closely by staff (and hence the opportunities to be bullied by others are consequently reduced). This adaptive victim response to bullying is certainly consistent with the applied-fear response model (Ireland, 2005d).

Other individual management approaches have included the use of 'stage systems' described as 'a series of procedures that are put in place each time a bullying incident occurs' (Ireland, 2002d, p. 179). Essentially such systems are designed to provide specific graded targets for the bullies on each occasion that they bully others, with the severity of the intervention applied increasing as the number of bullying incidents increases (Ireland, 2002d).

The term 'intervention' is used here cautiously. Although approaches like anti-bullying units/wings and stage systems are described and marketed more as rehabilitation style approaches, they are much more similar in nature to punishment-orientated approaches. Such approaches also risk the potential punishment of victims via their incorrect assignment to a 'bully' group.

Furthermore, in order for punishment to be '*effective*', it must be inevit-able, immediate, severe, include alternative options to the negative behaviour, with the link between the negative behaviour and the punishment understood by the perpetrator (McGuire and Priestly, 2000). In order to be effective in managing bullying, any approach influenced by punishment-orientated con-siderations therefore needs to respond to each and every occasion of bullying; to occur immediately after the bullying; to match the severity of the bullying; and to provide bullies with an attractive alternative to using aggression. Such conditions, most notably the first three, cannot be met (Ireland, 2002d).

It remains the case that punishment-orientated approaches, despite their title and how they are marketed by those involved in their design, underlie the majority of approaches to managing the behaviour of bullies. Interestingly, the questions posed when management strategies are designed remain reflective of this with the most common question that of 'How do we stop bullying' or 'How do we stop this prisoner from becoming involved in bullying'. Any focus on 'stopping' a behaviour remains the core tenet of punishment (Huesmann and Podolski, 2003). Even use of the term 'anti-bullying' is reflective of a punishment-orientated approach.

A more effective and theory-driven approach would be one that promotes the notion of a positive and healthy community since this encourages a focus on true rehabilitation and treatment. Such an approach is also more motivational and focussed on *changing* behaviour as opposed to simply 'stopping' it. Thus, when a prisoner becomes involved in bullying either as a bully and/or a victim the question that should be posed as a starting point should be 'How can we encourage them to interact more positively with their peers?'.

Equally, when prisoners enter a prison they should not, in my view, be faced with 'anti-bullying' posters and associated literature. Rather, literature should focus on the promotion of the positive and healthy aspects of the prisoner culture. Posters and literature would benefit from being retitled 'prison communities' or 'wing communities', focussing on the promotion of the existence of a positive community. Anti-bullying strategies would also benefit from being retitled accordingly. Terms such as 'Safer Prisons' are in existence but again this carries with it the connotation of potential danger and risk and a focus on stopping negative behaviour. A more useful term would instead be 'Healthy Prison Communities'.[1] It is unlikely that changes to the title of anti-bullying strategies will occur in the immediate future, however, since the terminology has been used for a number of years and is embedded in wider policy and documentation. There is no reason, however, as to why the associated paraphernalia (i.e. posters, leaflets, etc.) cannot be redesigned to represent a more positive, 'community spirit' approach.

Evidence-Based Intervention into Prison Bullying: Specific Approaches

Now that the aims and the broad framework of effective management have been outlined, a number of specific approaches that should be expected to aid the management of bullying can be suggested. Approaches will be separated into 'environmental' and 'individual' for ease of interpretation. As indicated previously, particular attention should be placed on environmental intervention and how environmental characteristics interact with individual characteristics to promote bullying.

Environmental approaches

The importance of the environment in managing bullying is crucial. It should never be the case that individuals, whether they are bullies, victims or both, should be managed in isolation from the environment in which they are placed. It is, for example, recommended that all 'action plans' developed following an incident of bullying should account for the changes that can be made to the environment (Ireland, 2005e). Environmental changes should be construed in broad terms to reflect both social and physical aspects known to promote bullying in accordance with the principles highlighted by the interaction model (Ireland, 2002d) and biosocial and ecological interaction model (Gilbert, 2005a) in particular. A focus on the elements of culture change, currency management and supervision style is likely to be among the most effective. To some extent these different elements are interlinked but they are separated here for ease of interpretation.

Culture change

Attempting to change a social ecology that is accepting of bullying is a useful focus for management approaches (Gilbert, 2005a). The focus here should be on the implementation of methods likely to influence the views and opinions of those influential in the management of bullying. As highlighted previously, bullying is a product of the peer group and not a behaviour that occurs in isolation from this group (Ireland, 2002d). Culture change therefore needs to account for the entire peer group, including those not involved in bullying, and attend to the involvement of both prisoners and staff. The starting point of any approach should be the acknowledgement, therefore, that all prisoners and staff form part of a peer group. Although culture change is likely to be slow with resistance to change with regards to some elements, positive long-term impact on culture should be considered possible. Elements that an effective evidence-based approach can consider to address include the following:

1 *The inclusion of a policy designed to promote pro-social community-focussed behaviours*: Environments where there is a proactive approach towards the development of community strategies focussed on the management of interpersonal aggression and conflict should be expected to reduce bullying. Attitudes are described as elements of the social environment that promote bullying and specifically encourage its use within some situations. 'Informing' on another prisoner or 'fraternising' with staff are elements of the inmate code (Tittle, 1969) likely to lead to 'justified' bullying (Ireland, 2002d). Although justifying attitudes are likely to provide a motivation for bullying, attitudes of indifference are likely to promote bullying over and above those supporting the behaviour of bullies and the stigmatisation of victims

(Rigby and Slee, 1991). The absence of a policy focussed on the value of positive community-based behaviours and the unacceptability of interpersonal aggression is likely only to communicate an attitude of indifference (Ireland, 2002d). This is likely to promote bullying by communicating to prisoners that it is not a behaviour placed firmly within the agenda of change for a prison. The development of such policies should ideally be developed as a collaborative strategy between prisoners and staff, an issue that will be emphasised later.

2 *Raising awareness of bullying*: Ensuring that all members of the peer group, both prisoners and staff, have a complete and up-to-date understanding of the range of behaviours known to represent bullying is important. This can be communicated via structured group work sessions and via literature such as posters and leaflets. Subtler forms of bullying, namely indirect aggression, are particularly likely to be either ignored or minimised. The latter is commonly a result of lack of understanding of the negative impact of such behaviours on victims coupled with a desensitisation to the unacceptability of such behaviour as a result of its increased occurrence in comparison to direct aggression. The prevalence of such aggression in prisons coupled with a rationale for its increased occurrence has already been outlined. It remains the case, however, that indirect bullying is less likely to be considered aggression than its direct counterpart (Ireland and Ireland, 2003).

Similarly, discouraging the use of terms such as 'horseplay', 'playfighting' and 'skylarking' is also important. Such terms can be used to describe interactions between prisoners, with less focus on the discrete behaviours actually being displayed (i.e. punching, hitting, name-calling, etc.). The use of such labels serves only to minimise such behaviours and fails to recognise the role that such behaviours play in the formation of social hierarchies based on dominance, particularly among all-male groups.

Awareness strategies designed to explore all types of interpersonal aggression should be considered an important element therefore of changing a culture of acceptance, particularly with regards to indirect bullying. Importantly, such awareness strategies would benefit from opting for a collaborative approach between staff and prisoners. Structured awareness sessions co-facilitated by staff and prisoners, for example, would be valuable to consider as a method of moderating the 'them' and 'us' culture in existence (Ireland, 2002d), by helping to communicate that bullying is not a 'prisoner's problem' alone and that the strategies adopted to manage it are joint ventures between staff and prisoners. If the identification of appropriate prisoner facilitators is not possible, consideration needs to be given to at least having joint awareness sessions for both prisoners and staff. At the least prisons should be giving consideration to the development of literature that has more than a superficial input from prisoners.

3. *Enhancing community behaviours*: As indicated in the interaction model (Ireland, 2002d), bullying can be a product of a transient population, with the moving of prisoners between and within prisons likely to lead to a destabilisation of the social hierarchies already in place. Social hierarchies are always going to be in existence in prisons and the suggestion here is not to try and remove their existence. Rather the suggestion here is to try and moderate the other factors likely to increase the negative aspects of social hierarchies based primarily on dominance, namely the existence of low-attachment relationships between prisoners (Ireland, 2002d). Focussing on the development of initiatives likely to develop a sense of community should be expected to begin to offset the influences of low-attachment relationships coupled with evidence of a transient population.

Community activities can include the development of general discussion groups, community meetings and wing-based activities. With regards to the latter, increasing opportunities to engage prisoners in meaningful activity is likely to reduce displays of bullying for two reasons. First, it should reduce feelings of boredom known to precipitate some acts of violence as a solution to the 'monotony' of prison living (Ireland, 2002d). Second, by encouraging investment in a wing community it should be expected that prisoners have more to lose if they engage in behaviours that go against such a community (i.e. bullying), with an increased chance of social retribution. Indeed, as stated by Gilbert (2005a), 'Leaders only get their power because. . .subordinates are too weak to oppose them'. In a prison setting the power of bullies would be reduced if the social group as a whole opposed their behaviour.

In prison settings where there is evidence of a competitive subculture (Ireland, 2002d) and little sense of a community, this leads to a restricted range of social roles available to prisoners. The development of a prisoner community should, however, increase the potential for a wider range of social roles to become available, roles not focussed solely on aggression versus subordination. This is summarised eloquently by Gilbert (2005b) who describes how the more threatening and competitive a social environment is, the less pro-social and warm affiliations are likely to develop and the more bullying and intimidation become a strategic way to 'get on and survive' in that environment. Focussing social ecologies on welfare issues, therefore, should be expected to reduce the existence of negative behaviour (Arrindell *et al.*, 2003). Gilbert (2005a) also makes the important point that pro-social behavior and concern for the welfare of others is created in similar ways to bullying and violence, 'that is, they need to be co-created by mutual stimulation through interaction in appropriate ecologies'. He further outlines how pro-social behaviour emerges when people feel safe, have pro-social role models, when pro-social behaviour is rewarded and therefore pro-social behaviour is associated with positive effect.

Although it should be acknowledged that this would be both ambitious and difficult to develop with a prison (Gilbert, 2005a), a focus on community-based interventions designed to encourage pro-social and affiliation behaviours should be expected to assist with the discouragement of bullying.

Currency management

Currency in prisons includes any type of material goods that carry some degree of value. The range of material goods attractive as currency includes tobacco, food, toiletries and drugs (illegal and prescribed). Material deprivation is identified as an important factor in the motivation of bullying, with resource acquisition an identified motivation for aggression both within animal and human groups (Gilbert, 2005a). Being able to acquire additional material goods via aggression in an environment where goods are controlled and minimal in comparison to the community is indicative of an 'adaptive' solution to such deprivation (Ireland, 2002d; Ireland and Murray, 2005). The theft and/or extortionate trading of material goods does form a sizable proportion of the amount of direct bullying that occurs between prisoners (Ireland et al., 2005).

Although strategies are in place to monitor material goods in prisons there is a need to continually revise strategies in accordance with the types of goods featuring as significant currency. Revising and updating systems designed to increase the monitoring of such goods becomes a valuable method of reducing bullying. If the cost of detection is increased, the 'effect–danger' ratio for the aggressor (Björkqvist, 1994) becomes weighted more towards a risk of personal danger for them and less towards a positive effect of sustained currency acquisition.

Supervision style

The role of staff supervision is outlined both in the applied-fear response model (Ireland, 2005d) and the interaction model (Ireland, 2002d) as important factors both in promoting bullying and in determining victim responses. The interaction model focuses in particular on the amount and predictability of supervision: bullying will occur in situations where the amount of supervision is low. In a prison setting where the prisoner-to-staff ratio is unavoidably high, it is unrealistic to expect all prisoners to be watched continuously 24 hours a day, seven days a week. Aggressors will always find opportunities to engage in bullying. The predictability of supervision, however, is perhaps a more important factor.

In a prison setting where there is a clear regime in place, supervision patterns will be to some extent explicit and predictable, for example, staff-handover times and food-provision times may represent occasions where staff supervision is momentarily reduced. The subtler elements of predictable supervision patterns are perhaps just as important. This includes the patterns of behaviour that staff adopt that might not be immediately evident to staff as an informal pattern but will be to prisoners monitoring them. These include occasions when staff have regular conversations, when they go to obtain a drink and/or when making telephone calls.

Inmate aggressors have been likened to residential burglars who will watch the vacation patterns of householders before going into the property to commit the offence (Toch, 1992). Inmate aggressors will behave in a similar way by observing the explicit and subtle staff-supervision patterns. An obvious and potentially effective intervention would be the encouragement of variability both in explicit *and* subtle supervision patterns adopted by staff, and raising their awareness of the subtle patterns they may have developed. Raising the potential for the aggressor to be detected will, in accordance again with the 'effect–danger' ratio theory, reduce the potential for occurrence as the chance for detection is increased. Aggressors will undoubtedly find other opportunities to bully but the focus here is on making these opportunities more difficult to detect.

Individual approaches

The term 'individual strategies' will be used broadly here to encompass strategies designed to 'treat' or manage individual psychopathology aspects perceived to be associated with bullying. The management of these aspects has, historically, been through the provision of individual or group treatment programmes to bullies and/or victims designed to ameliorate the aspects of their psychopathology felt to relate to bullying. Although emphasis has been placed within the current chapter on the environment, there are occasions where individual approaches are important to consider. They can be useful to employ in conjunction with environmental intervention and should be construed broadly to consider a range of individual approaches, and not just those focussed on treatment *per se*. Individual approaches therefore should include aspects associated with investigation/assessment and treatment. Each of these will be considered in turn.

Investigation and assessment

Prior to the implementation of any individual-focussed intervention strategy is the importance of completing a full investigation into the incident(s) of reported bullying. Such investigations operate on the principle that all incidents are alleged until there is supportive evidence. There has been a tendency in the past to focus on the self-report of those involved in the bullying either as victims and/or as bullies, and to use this as the focus of decision making.

Evidence that bullying has occurred does not have to be focussed on the self-report of those involved but can attend to other sources of evidence. This includes the behavioural characteristics associated with being bullied or the fear of being bullied. These are outlined in the applied-fear response model (Ireland, 2005d) in which fight responses, immediate- and delayed-flight responses, and precautionary behaviours are outlined. Fight responses include displaying aggression towards staff and other prisoners (and not necessarily towards the perpetrator of the bullying); immediate-flight responses include avoidance strategies; delayed-flight responses include self-injurious behaviour and aggression; and precautionary behaviours include avoidance, aggression and role-playing, namely occasions where prisoners adopt a certain 'image' that will help them to avoid victimisation. All these behaviours are valuable to attend to since they provide some evidence for the existence of bullying.

Suggestions for the specific approaches towards investigation and assessment are outlined in detail elsewhere (Ireland, 2002d) and readers are referred to this literature for a more complete outline of the specific approaches. In essence, however, the focus should be on attempting to determine the specific roles of those involved in bullying (i.e. pure bully, bully/victim, pure victim or not-involved). Once the general roles have been identified it would be valuable, if possible, to determine the subgroup roles associated with the bully groups (i.e. leader, assistant or reinforcer bully), and those 'not-involved' (i.e. defenders and outsiders). Determining these roles assists with the refinement of treatment approaches, an issue that will be outlined later. Equally, it is important to recognise that prisoners can alternate between these groups: for example, although at one point a prisoner may be classified as a bully/victim, at another they could fall into the pure victim group.

In keeping with the view bullying is an expected behaviour that cannot be eradicated, coupled with the view that much bullying occurs when opportunities to do so arise, any investigation should follow the core principles associated with risk assessment. The focus should therefore be on the prevention and management of future incidences of bullying by determining, via a complete investigation:

- the probability of the bullying reoccurring;
- the frequency and the nature of the bullying;
- an estimate of the consequences of the bullying;
- the conditions under which the bullying is most likely to occur;
- the conditions under which the bullying is not likely to occur (i.e. protective factors).

In addition, the focus should also be on determining the motivations and function of the behaviour. Determining the function of the behaviour, using the principles of functional assessment, allow for the development of an individualised treatment approach. Such approaches can utilise the SORC approach (Lee-Evans, 1994) detailed below to include the following:

- **S**etting conditions, that is internal and external triggers for the bullying.
- **O**rganism variables, that is conditions underlying individual responses to triggers such as learning history, individual beliefs and so on.
- **R**esponse variables, namely the frequency, duration and severity of the bullying.
- **C**onsequences, namely the consequences of the bullying serving to reinforce it and encourage its reoccurrence and/or consolidation as an appropriate behavioural strategy.

If the function of the bullying can be described then it can either be replaced with a pro-social behaviour and/or what is preventing the occurrence of the pro-social behaviour can be determined, for example, is it a skills deficit?

Treatment

Ideally any treatment approach should be informed by a functional assessment. It also needs to account for the adaptive nature of bullying in a prison (Ireland and Murray, 2005), and in doing so recognise that replacing the adaptive nature of bullying will be difficult. There is a need for recognition of the limits within which a treatment programme operates with an acceptance that 'treatment' approaches might be better outlined as a 'management' approach designed to contain bullying as opposed to amending or altering it. Should treatment approaches be designed, however, there are some core principles that should be adhered to. These are as follows:

1 *Specialised group programmes*: Group interventions designed specifically for 'bullies' and/or 'victims' should be avoided for a number of reasons. For example, being identified as a victim in a prison carries with it a stigma, with pure victims in particular at the bottom of the prisoner dominance hierarchy (Ireland, 2002d). 'Victim groups' quickly become labelled as such, contributing to the further stigmatisation of this group. Groups designed for bullies are also fraught with difficulty for two core reasons. First, bullying carries with it a certain degree of status among prisoners, particularly among younger prisoners (Ireland and Ireland, 2003). Thus the formation of any 'bully' treatment group should be expected to lead to an encouragement for prisoners to secure a place on such a group to benefit from the status connected to this. Second, there are problems in identifying 'true' bullies, with the majority of prisoners being classified as 'bully/victims' with few classified as 'pure bullies' by comparison (Ireland *et al.*, 2005). Thus the risk here is that such programmes may be inadvertently mixing bullies and victims together. Rather, if group programmes are

to be employed then they should represent those already available within prisons for a wider range of prisoners, and not those designed 'specially' for bullies and/or victims.

2 *Individual programmes*: Any decision to implement treatment programmes on an individual basis should take advantage of the increasing literature exploring the intrinsic characteristics associated with pure bullies, bully/victims and pure victims. Examples of specific interventions that could be considered for each group on the basis of this literature are as follows.

Pure bullies. Although identification of the intrinsic characteristics associated with this group remain difficult to determine, there is evidence this group presents with deficits in cognitive and emotional empathy (Ireland, 1999b). Victim empathy work, therefore, may be of limited value with pure bullies. Instead, they may benefit from a structured management approach outlining what is acceptable and unacceptable behaviour, with a focus on the costs of bullying. Indeed, there is evidence that pure bullies favour aggression as an appropriate response to being bullied (Ireland, 2001a) and evaluate the consequences of using aggression as a positive and preferred solution in some bullying situations (Ireland and Archer, 2002). Exploring the costs to them of engaging in bullying may therefore be of greater value than exploring the actual or potential harm to their victim(s).

It is important to remain mindful, however, of the potentially different subgroups within 'pure bullies', that is ringleader bullies, reinforcers and assistants. This has not been explored within the research to date although it should be expected that different intervention approaches might be of assistance. Ringleader bullies may be best targeted using a 'costs–benefits' approach, whereas reinforcers might benefit from an approach that also includes exploration of the consequences of reinforcing the bullying of others. Assistant bullies, on the other hand, may be more similar to bully/victims and, as will be outlined, may benefit from approaches designed to raise their potential to widen their social network beyond a primary association with aggressors, with possible attention given to training them in specific assertiveness skills.

Bully/victims. This group do not appear to present with the same difficulties in empathy as pure bullies (Ireland, 1999b), suggesting that engaging them in victim empathy work might be valuable. This group also presents with difficulties in displaying assertiveness, with specific difficulties noted with regards to the assertiveness displayed during conflict situations (Ireland, 2002d). This suggests that intervention focussed on developing specific assertiveness skills might be of value. Assertiveness training should, however, be used with caution. There is a danger that teaching such skills could expose victims to an increased risk for potential injury if they attempt to use them *during* an incident, and have not refined their skills enough to ensure they are being assertive and not aggressive. Getting assertiveness 'wrong' during a potential conflict situation may serve to escalate the situation. Rather the focus should be on the use of assertiveness *following* an incident and the use of immediate avoidance strategies as a preventative approach to being exposed to bullying. As noted in the applied-fear response model, however, immediate avoidance strategies are difficult to implement in a prison setting and thus those designing interventions should remain mindful of this.

Unlike pure bullies, however, bully/victims are not inclined towards favouring aggression as a response to being bullied (Ireland, 2001a), although they do report positive consequences related to using aggression following being bullied (Ireland and Archer, 2002). This could suggest that their use of aggression in response to bullying represents more of a response to victimisation than a chosen strategy to aggress towards others in the absence of being victimised. This would fit with the applied-fear response model and suggests bully/victims would benefit from learning some further non-aggressive approaches to managing bullying.

Bully/victims do, however, present with higher levels of hostility and anger than pure bullies (Ireland and Archer, 2004). This could suggest they may be more sensitive to the identification of potential aggression in comparison to other aggressors, particularly in ambiguous situations. This increased sensitivity to threat may serve an adaptive function in prisons (Ireland and Murray, 2004), although it may be of value to teach them skills focussed on distinguishing between actual and ambiguous threat. Finally, research also suggests bully/victims are characterised by higher levels of emotional loneliness than the other groups, with an increased tendency towards avoidant attachment (Ireland and Power, 2004). Although there has been no research to date exploring the actual quality of the social network accessible to bully/victims, this research suggests they are emotionally isolated from a peer group from whom they are more likely than other prisoners to perceive hostility. Assisting them to engage successfully with a social network might therefore serve as a protective factor for them with regards to victimisation.

Pure victims. The focus of intervention for this group should primarily be on supportive approaches designed to limit the opportunities others have to victimise them. Attending to the environmental suggestions for managing bullying are therefore of particular importance since all are designed to reduce bullying at an organisational level. Pure victims do, however, present with general difficulties in assertiveness across domains of functioning (Ireland, 2002c), suggesting they would benefit from general training in assertiveness skills and not on assertiveness skills specific to conflict. Pure victims in particular would benefit from assertiveness training focussed on the assertiveness communication of their difficulties. Pure victims also present with lower levels of self-esteem in comparison to the other groups that could point to a need for intervention focussed on raising their self-esteem and their perception of self-efficacy (Hafiz and Ireland, 2005).

Conclusion

The current chapter aimed to provide a brief overview of the advances in the prison research field to date and to outline how these advances might inform an evidence-based approach to managing bullying. It highlighted how researchers have begun to move away from exploring the nature and extent of bullying to examining in more detail the intrinsic characteristics of those involved, with a more recent focus on the development of theoretical models designed to aid a further understanding of prison bullying. It remains the case, however, that prison bullying research remains in its infancy when compared to the bullying explored in other settings such as schools. Despite its infancy, the increasing attention given to the development of theoretical models is one of the most notable recent advancements in the field to date. Such models should provide a basis for the development of potentially effective approaches to managing bullying. All of the models outlined in the current chapter place emphasis on the role of the prison environment in promoting and maintaining bullying, providing evidence against a focus on approaches attending solely to individual psychopathology.

A theme running through this chapter has been the need to focus on the inclusion of the whole prison peer group in the management of bullying, with attention in particular given to the value of community-based approaches as opposed to those influenced by punishment models. The chapter also placed emphasis on the complexities of prison bullying and the difficulties in managing this behaviour effectively. Any approach adopted should recognise the limits within which it operates, with an acknowledgement that bullying, although not acceptable, is arguably an adaptive behaviour in a prison that can be reduced but not eradicated. In this way a focus on managing bullying as opposed to eradicating it is perhaps a more realistic approach to take. Connected to this, evaluating the effectiveness of both organisational and individual management approaches aimed to reduce bullying would appear to be an area that future research could focus on if further developments in this area of study are to be made.

Note

1. Such changes have been considered within high secure forensic hospitals, notably at Ashworth High Secure Hospital (Mersey Care NHS Trust), with proposals to

have policies focussed on 'Healthy Ward Communities' as opposed to 'Patient-to-Patient Anti-Bullying' made (Ireland, 2005e). However, such terminology within health settings is likely to be confused with physical and mental health needs more readily. Terms such as 'community' are also already in existence in relation to other initiatives. Thus the acceptance of such a revised title, although promoted, is not likely to occur within secure forensic health settings in the near future, with the chosen working title for such policies remaining 'anti-bullying' for the time being.

Chapter 7

Drug-Misuse Intervention Work

Graham J. Towl

Introduction

Drug misuse is a major problem in two key ways. First, and foremost, drug abuse represents a major public health problem; the misuse of drugs can result in a range of health problems both in terms of physical and mental health. Second, there is evidence of some clear links between drug-misusage and crime. In this chapter the policy context of arrangements for drug-misuse interventions is captured with an emphasis on health and offending, rather than simply one or the other. It is important to remember that many of those who misuse drugs do not commit offences to, for example, fund their drug habits (Gossop, 2005). Similarly not all offenders misuse drugs. That said there are some strong correlational links between much drug-misusing behaviours and offending (Martin and Player, 2000). Indeed about one-third of 'problematic drug users' (PDUs) in England and Wales are in the care of correctional services at any one time (NOMS, 2005). Links between drugs and crime can be complex and either activity can serve to amplify, if not necessarily 'cause' the other (Lee and George, 2005).

Interventions to address drug misuse in prisons will be considered in this chapter particularly in terms of their efficacy. The relative lack of involvement among applied psychological staff in prisons in this important area of work will then be touched upon. The Home Office (HO) strategic framework for the delivery of psychological services (HM Prison Service and the National Probation Service, 2003) will be drawn upon to examine possible future developments in improvements in service delivery and intervention effectiveness.

Health and Offender Partnerships are a division of the Care Services Directorate of the Department of Health (DoH). The partnership consists of units working within both the DoH and HO or more specifically within Offender Management Services. The Applied Psychology Group (APG) is organisationally located within Health and Offender Partnerships working with policy colleagues from both the DoH and HO. Colleagues from the HO include the

Drug Strategy Unit which retains some key responsibilities in relation to drug-misuse-based interventions in prisons. This is important in terms of the potential linkages between drug-misuse intervention work and the role or potential roles of psychological staff from whatever applied psychological specialism.

Previously, applied psychological services had been located within HM Prison Service's personnel directorate with a remit to work across Probation Services and prisons. The comparatively recent repositioning of APG sits well with recent developments regarding the professional regulation of applied psychologists through the Health Professions Council (HPC).[1] This development has also, in part, served to arguably define the work of forensic psychologists within the broader health context.

The Policy Context

Tackling drug misuse is a key UK government priority. This is reflected in the strategy for the management and treatment of PDUs within correctional services, where the wider context of the work is acknowledged: the NOMS Drug Strategy is an integral part of the Government's National Drug Strategy. Its aim is: 'To address the needs of PDUs during their engagement with the correctional services, irrespective of age, gender or ethnic background, with a view to reducing their reoffending and the harm they cause to themselves and others' (NOMS, 2005).

This aim resonates coherently with the theme of not viewing the activities of offenders solely in terms of their potential impact upon reoffending, but rather reflecting the importance of considering health needs too. This helps to develop a very healthy relationship in terms of the potential for effective partnership working across both the DoH and HO. Shared aims are important in much partnership working for it to be truly effective. Interestingly research into the effectiveness of drug-misuse interventions have tended increasingly to look at effectiveness in both domains, that is, reoffending and improved health outcomes.

The government strategy for addressing the needs of PDUs is based on the assumption that there are around 250,000 PDUs (Home Office, 2005). This is drawn from some of the work looking at prevalence rates (e.g. Frisher *et al.*, 2004; Miller *et al.*, 2004). Prisons are where the greatest concentration of PDUs may be found with around 140,000 offenders a year passing through them. It has been conservatively estimated that there will be around 40,000 PDUs in prison at any given time (Lee and George, 2005).

A great deal of public money is being spent on drug-misuse interventions in prison and probation, estimated to be in something of the order of £152.7 million in 2004/5. The work in prisons started before the formal advent of the launch of National Offender Management Services (NOMS). However the strategy has developed with three key themes: (1) reducing demand through structured interventions, (2) reducing supply through intelligence-led interventions and (3) developing and augmenting community drug service linkages (Lee and George, 2005). One key milestone was the introduction of CARATS workers into prisons in the late 1990s. CARATS stands for counselling, assessment, referral, and advice through care services (HM Prison Service, 2002). The CARATS system of support is widely available within prisons and forms the foundation of the drug-misuse interventions in place. There are some clear potential linkages between the work of the CARATS teams and the care programme approach (CPA) as used in mental health services. The CPA provides an administrative tool as part of the case-management process, to structure the arrangement of health services for an individual patient. These may be deemed as needing to be either 'enhanced' or 'standard'. This is an important potential linkage partly because of the National Health Service taking responsibility for the delivery of health services in prisons (Cinamon and Bradshaw, 2005). It is also important because the effective management, organisation and delivery of drug-misuse services is needed if the related and unrelated health needs of offenders are to be effectively addressed and interventions to reduce reoffending are to have their potential fully realised. These policy and practice developments reflect a government-driven desire to ensure that health services are of an equivalent standard for prisoners, to what is provided outside prisons (Lane-Morton, 2005). Underpinning the CARATS service is the 10-year national strategy 'Tackling Drugs – To Build a Better Britain' (HM Prison Service, 2002). In turn this built on, as indicated above, the national strategy for Offender Management Services (Home Office, 2005).

Within the criminal justice system it is also important to mention the national initiative of the Drug Interventions Programme (DIP). This is aimed at reducing offending among drug misusers through treatment. DIP was established in 2003 and is characterised by a case-management-based approach. This fits well with developments within both health in the use of the CPA and also in offender management with the advent of the introduction of both offender managers and offender supervisors driving the tiered, needs-based, approach to offender assessment.

Do Drug-Misuse-Based Interventions Reduce Reoffending and Drug Misuse?

It is difficult to try to estimate the full potential impact of drug-misuse-based interventions in contributing to reducing crime. This is because of a number

of factors, two of which are highlighted below chiefly because of their pertin-
ence, although not exclusivity, within the criminal justice context. First, we
do not know how effective the interventions would be for those who do not
consent to participating in them. Evaluation studies have tended to be based
upon 'volunteers'. The nature of 'voluntariness' within the coercive environment of criminal justice settings is a moot but necessary caveat (Towl, 1994).
Second, because there are a number of well-documented difficulties in establishing whether or not any changes in behaviour are as a direct result of a
specific intervention or other factors (see, e.g. the discussion by Martin and
Player, 2000). Drug-misuse interventions in a criminal justice context as with
elsewhere also have the explicit aim of reducing the chance of drug misuse and
thereby improving health outcomes.

The broader research context of the work on drug-misuse interventions is
important, particularly as this affects the evaluation of such interventions in
prisons. As a starting point it is important to consider what success would look
like. Looking at two broad areas, first, the likely impact of drug-misuse interventions to increase the chances of desistence from drug taking and second,
the likely impact of drug-misuse interventions in decreasing the chances of
reoffending. It is probably worth drawing attention to a point which applies
across these two distinct behavioural categories, namely that there can be
degrees of success. We are by no means simply considering two categorical
variables.

One potentially positive outcome of drug-misuse interventions is abstinence
from drug taking. Another could be a reduction in the frequency or quantity
of drugs taken. Moving from a previously preferred drug to a lower category
of drug, or a drug that causes less physical or psychological harm to the individual, may also potentially be deemed a success. The temporal propinquity of
any drug use after intervention can also be an important aspect of attempts to
measure success. Arguably a more controlled use (or misuse) of drugs, whereby
the drug-taking activity is no longer linked to crime, could also be deemed at
least a partial success in some cases.

The second area of interest in measuring the efficacy of drug-misuse interventions is in the area of reducing reoffending. Just as with drug taking this
could be complete desistence from offending or a reduction in the seriousness
or frequency of offending. Similarly considerations of temporal propinquity
also may play a part. So, for example, if previously an offender has reoffended
after three months of release from prison it may be viewed as a limited success
if after intervention the prisoner reoffends after one year of release instead. In
terms of offence severity if a prisoner is released and commits an offence of
burglary, rather than an offence of robbery, this may also be deemed a limited
success. However questionable and limited, the time-honoured tradition within

much criminological research is to focus, sometimes exclusively, on reconviction levels at two- and five-year points after release and compare them usually with predicted reconviction levels, to test the efficacy of interventions aimed at reducing the risk of reoffending. Needless to say, then, such temporal categories are somewhat arbitrary conceptually, although it is true that there can be problems with an over-reliance on reconviction data for comparatively short periods after release from prison. This is, in part, because of the potential problem of 'pseudo-convictions'. Here convictions may be recorded for offences that occurred some time before existing convictions. Thus it would not necessarily be that the individual had committed a further offence, indeed they may have desisted from offending but the criminal justice process would result in such past offences being subsequently recorded as convictions (Martin *et al.*, 2003).

With the above in mind some key research studies addressing the issue of the efficacy of drug-misuse interventions are considered below.

Three Key Research Studies

This section is intended to be illustrative rather than comprehensive, hence the focus on three research studies.

The first study outlined is the National Treatment Outcome Research Study (NTORS). Drug misusers in this study reported very high levels of pre-treatment crime. Much of this was acquisitive but a substantial proportion also related to the selling and distribution of illicit drugs. There were substantial reductions in reported crime levels after treatment. Acquisitive and drug distribution related crimes reduced at the five-year follow-up point to about 25% of the pre-treatment levels.

Clinical services tend to be more focussed on health outcomes in a fairly narrow sense, thus findings concerning the reduction in the risk of criminal behaviour may not always have been given the prominence that perhaps it could have, especially if such behaviours are seen as an important part of the broader public health domain. In the study, just over 1,000 drug misusers reported more than 27,000 acquisitive offences during the three months prior to the drug-misuse treatment. Seventy-one individuals (7% of respondents) reported a staggering 35,000 drug-distribution offences in the three months prior to treatment (Gossop, 2005). In terms of a potential impact on crime levels, these figures illustrate that even a relatively modest treatment effect would potentially result in substantial reductions in the levels of such crimes.

At a one-year follow-up point, acquisitive crime was down to one-third of intake levels; at five-year follow-up this had further reduced to less than a quarter of intake levels. This finding is particularly encouraging because often the expectation might be that treatment effects would attenuate over time rather than be consolidated and even enhanced. An additional explanation here might be that maturation is having an effect in reducing levels of crime. For many drugs, the historical pattern has been that levels of use attenuate with age, except for a small core of heavy lifetime users. These two effects might be interacting. This area would probably benefit from more focussed research. Drug-distribution crimes were down to less than 20% of intake levels at the one year after treatment point. There were also some gender differences in treatment outcomes, broadly women faired worse. This is important because much research in the criminal justice arena tends to focus upon young white men from lower socio-economic groups. The applicability of the research base which may underpin evidence-based practice needs to be considered perhaps rather more carefully than it sometimes is.

To put the NTORS findings into their international context, they broadly mirror some of the results from North American research. For example, patients undertaking treatment in one study were reported as having committed property crimes at a rate of about one-third of pre-treatment levels (Hubbard et al., 1997). However, direct comparisons are notoriously difficult to make with confidence because of a range of cultural and research design differences.

One increasingly prominent change in research evaluation studies testing the efficacy of defined interventions in criminal justice and also in health has been the introduction of economic measures of success. On the whole, health economics is comparatively well developed within the UK, but less so are economic considerations within correctional services. The economic costs of drug misuse are significantly linked to the amount of crime committed. Thus the savings from drug-misuse interventions tend to be within the criminal justice system rather than simply with the health sector. Although it is important to recognise that drug misuse has significant health costs including A&E treatment, treatment for Hepatitis B, HIV infections in users and transmission to the broader community. It has been estimated that for every extra £1 spent on drug-misuse treatment there are savings of £3 to be made (Gossop, et al., 1998; Gossop, 2005). Of course, such financial assessments are only one fairly crude measure of the broader societal benefits, which are far more difficult to measure. Other measures may be linked to the quality of life for the patient and also the avoidance of distressing experiences for those who would otherwise have been the victims of patient crimes. Patients themselves can be, as with other offenders, likely to experience higher levels of crime as victims too. The world is not simply populated by two categorical groups; offenders and victims, we all may benefit from a reduction in drug misuse.

Before moving on from this study it is probably worth making explicit some cautionary points raised by the author of the study. The NTORS results were from a group of volunteer patients who were not necessarily involved with the criminal justice system, although some appear to have potentially narrowly avoided such contact. Perhaps legal processes can be used productively to improve the motivation for change even if this is initially of a fundamentally instrumental nature (e.g. to avoid imprisonment).

Some drug misusers (those who used heroin in particular) had worse outcomes when followed up in terms of their drug use; however there were still reductions in crime for this group (Gossop, 2005). This serves to illustrate the potential complexities of the relationships between crime and drug misuse. Both are multifaceted terms. The term 'crime' can include a wide range of sometimes very different sets of behaviour. Similarly drug misuse may involve a range of drugs and lifestyles. As with much evaluation research it is probably worth mentioning the likely historical bias of under-reporting negative results. This can result in an unduly positive appearance of treatment outcome studies; this is of course by no means exclusive to the drug-misuse field, far from it.

Another influential study which has informed the development of much drug-misuse work in prisons is the evaluation work on the Rehabilitation of Addicted Prisoners Trust (RAPt)12-step interventions (Martin and Player, 2000; Martin et al., 2003). RAPt, previously called the Addicted Disease Trust (ADT), set up its first structured intervention work at HMP Downview in Surrey, England, in 1992. Formal funding from HM Prison Service began in 1995 and in 1997/8 the first 12-step-based interventions were made available for young offenders (YOs) at HMP Norwich. At the time of writing there are nine full treatment interventions in nine prisons, these include seven prisons accommodating adult male prisoners, one young offender institute (HM YOI Aylesbury) and one prison which accommodates women prisoners (at HMP Send). The notion of 12 steps is based upon breaking down into stages the processes or steps that an individual needs to take or make in order to change their drug-misuse behaviour to abstinence. The model is basically one that is predicated on viewing drug misusage as an addiction where the treatment outcome of choice is abstinence. The 12 stages themselves are clearly underpinned by a spiritual dimension. Arguably the approach also involves a mix of principles based on restorative justice approaches. For example the notion of acknowledging the hurt of victims and seeking to make amends could just as well be part of a restorative justice-based approach to reducing reoffending.

Two evaluations of the RAPt interventions are considered below. The first study which involved 200 prisoners over four prisons was conducted in the late 1990s. The sample was broken down into three groups: 'graduates', 'dropouts' and 'non-starters'. All participants were voluntary and at the time of the research there was no specific selection criteria used. Participants in the treatment process who were graduates completed all three broad stages of the 12-step process. The 12-step process included three main stages of therapeutic activity. The first was a preparative stage, the second an action-based phase and finally a consolidation period. These stages reflect the reciprocally iterative nature of assessment and interventions, with both informing each other (Towl, 2005b).

Over half the sample had served four or more custodial sentences often for crimes such as robbery, burglary or drug offences. Less than a third of participants were serving a sentence for violence, however 59% had a previous conviction for an offence involving violence. There was virtually no disagreement with the proposition that their drug use was a problem. Most of the participants reported that their drug misuse had played a major role in their offending. Half reported having previously tried to give up drugs. Participants' accounts of why they had not previously succeeded in giving up drugs fell broadly into two explanatory categories; those who blamed themselves for their lack of commitment at the time and those who attributed their lack of success to challenging circumstances (Martin and Player, 2000). A potentially fruitful avenue for future research might be to follow up these reported attributions and their impact on outcomes.

The study involved an interesting and more sophisticated measurement of behavioural change than is often the case in evaluation studies of this type. A tiered approach was taken to measuring 'successes'. Tier one involved abstinence from drug use. Tier two involved abstaining from the participants' drug of choice. Whereas the primary purpose of the RAPt intervention is to enable participants to abstain from drugs and alcohol, including a second tier of potential success adds to the sensitivity of the measurement of change which might otherwise be missed.

The researcher's analysis of the data went further than just these two tiers though. For example, they also looked at the persistence of participants' drug misuse as well as whether it was of the same degree as prior to treatment. They also looked at whether those relapsing were able to re-establish recovery subsequently.

Of the three groups included in the analysis of outcomes ('graduates', 'drop-outs' and 'non-starters') the graduates did best with much lower levels of substance misuse than either drop-outs or non-starters. The attitudes of the participants to different types of drug misuse appeared discerning in that they clearly distinguished between substances that they thought not universally harmful and those that they thought were. Those who had alcohol as their drug of choice had much higher levels of returning to previous levels of misuse. Eight out of ten alcohol abusers in the subsample that were followed up on release had relapsed compared with less than half of the other drug users.

One potentially very important finding was the evidence in support of the hypothesis that contact with RAPt staff and former RAPt prisoner participants and related self-help groups such as Alcoholics Anonymous (AA) was linked to improved outcomes. This may be associated with more general links to a richer network of social support. Graduates were more likely to have received formal support from drug workers and had been more successful in gaining employment. There was also very strong evidence from the study of marked reductions among participants in drug usage while still in prison both during and after participation in the treatment. The researchers appear to have cross-checked some of their results by linking self-report measures with drug-testing procedures.

Although the primary outcome focus, understandably, with such interventions is to help participants to live drug-free lives those participating are also given the opportunity to reflect on the need to reduce their risk of reoffending. There has been some evidence that high rates of criminal behaviour tend to be associated with periods of more active drug misuse for some offenders. Conversely, lower rates of criminal behaviour may be linked with periods of abstention (Ball *et al.*, 1983).

Overall the chances of reconviction of graduates of the treatment were significantly related to drug misuse. Offenders who relapsed in terms of usage of their drug of choice were twice as likely to have been convicted as those who had not. Following release from prison, graduates were more likely to have abstained from drug misusage and also had much lower levels of reconvictions than others. This is despite graduates having the most entrenched pre-treatment profiles (Martin and Player, 2000). Where they did report having committed crimes they tended to be less serious than previously.

The authors of the study plausibly claim that their findings broadly accord with some international research in this area. Arguably, nowhere is this more so than with the findings highlighting the importance of the levels of social support received after release from incarceration as being very much linked to outcomes. Indeed the likelihood of criminal behaviour including drug misuse can be seen to be amplified in materially deprived environments (Martin and Player, 2000).

The next study of interest is one which built upon some of the work by Martin and Player albeit in a restricted way because of a narrow, and some would say seriously limited evaluation method. The research was based upon a larger sample than the previous study outlined above. The measure of treatment efficacy here though failed to build on the impressive breadth of the Martin and Player (2000) study and simply assessed the one-year and two-year post-release reconviction data.

The study looked at 274 RAPt graduates who had been released for a year or more. As with the sample from the previous study, graduates tended to have a large number of reconvictions. About a quarter of graduates were serving sentences for drug offences and a slightly smaller percentage were serving sentences for burglary when they undertook the treatment.

About 25% of RAPt graduates had been reconvicted within one year of release. In the study this is compared with a broadly matched sample in which 38% were reconvicted within the same timeframe. This is a highly statistically significant and positive difference. Drug of choice proved an interesting variable in terms of linkages with rates of reconviction. For example, only 18% of those who favoured alcohol misuse were reconvicted after a year (Martin *et al.*, 2003).

Expected reconviction rates can be statistically predicted by using criminal history and a number of demographic variables. In this study the offender group reconviction scale (OGRS) was used. The variables used in the calculation of risk are age (at time of sentence), gender, number of youth custodial sentences, current offence, age at current conviction, age at first conviction, rate at which convicted, history of burglary and breach. One hundred and thirty seven RAPt graduates had been released for at least two years at the time of the fieldwork for the study.

Two-year reconviction data revealed that 40% of graduates had been reconvicted compared with an expected rate of 51% using OGRS scores. This is a statistically significant positive result. Graduates also compared favourably with a matched comparison group, again at a statistically significant level.

Data on offence type of graduates served to add evidence in support of the efficacy of the treatment intervention. For example, only 8% of released graduates were convicted of drug offences up to two years after release. This would seem to indicate that the intervention potentially had a marked impact on reducing the absolute potential number of crimes which would have occurred had participants not undergone treatment.

Another key finding from this study was that the amount of time spent with RAPt was negatively correlated with the percentage of graduates reconvicted. Thus, for those who had contact with the treatment process for 18 to 24 months there was only a 20% reconviction rate at the two-year, post-release point.

So, it seems that in terms of the evidence there are findings to suggest that such drug-misuse interventions can at least be effective for potentially significant numbers of prisoners. Although there are a number of approaches to working with drug misusers, the focus of this chapter has tended to be primarily but not exclusively upon the RAPt treatment interventions and their effectiveness.

Reflections and Conclusions

On the whole the evidence in support of effectively working with drug misusers seems to support continued development and delivery of such interventions, as part of broader offender management and care planning with offenders. As outlined above the evidence base for the effectiveness of these interventions can be judged both in terms of improved health outcomes (by reduced risk of continued drug misusage and the associated direct and indirect improvements to health) and by reduced risk of reoffending. Particularly given what can be very high frequency crimes such as drug offences, reducing reoffending in such cases can have a disproportionately high impact on reducing criminal behaviour.

As with cognitive-behaviourally based manualised interventions, routinely and widely undertaken by psychologists in prisons, drug-misuse interventions can be and are run by staff other than psychologists (Towl, 2004b). It is though perhaps disappointing that psychologists as a professional group have not become more actively involved in the development and delivery of drug-treatment intervention work in prisons. This is particularly so with the many psychologists and trainee psychologists directly employed in prisons. In terms of evidence-based practice it would seem that there is a strong case for more involvement in this area, particularly so given concerns over the need to increase the chances of reducing reoffending and improving public health outcomes.

The likely formalisation of the statutory registration of applied psychologists by the HPC has the potential to help to broaden the scope of the work of many applied psychologists by moving their work away from the narrow area of practice, or indeed 'practice silos' in which they have found themselves.[2] With health services in prisons now being entirely provided via the National Health Services (NHS) rather than through the previous in-house system[3] there are likely to be growing numbers of a fuller range of applied psychologists working in prisons. These applied psychologists will include those traditionally referred to as, for example, 'clinical', 'health' or 'counselling' psychologists, all of whom would be potentially well placed to provide services for drug misusers too. This is all entirely in keeping with the strategic framework for improvements in the delivery of psychological services in prisons (Home Office, 2003).

With the introduction of NOMS bringing together services working with offenders in both custody and the community, a helpful organisational backdrop has been established from which to contextualise potential service improvements in the drug-misuse field. For graduates of drug-misuse-treatment interventions in prisons it appears crucial that there is a continued support and follow-up during the period after release. The evidence shows the importance of such follow-up in maximising the benefits of treatment effects.

Psychologists work across both custodial and community-based settings. In the criminal justice field there remains, albeit for historical reasons, a marked skew in the numbers of psychologists working in custodial rather than community setting with offenders. This is not a distribution of psychological staff which reflects the psychological needs of offenders or the need for psychologists to contribute most effectively to the protection of the public. To a large

degree such organisational and professional arrangements reflect the historically based specialist silos referred to early. However, fortunately the majority of
psychological therapies may be delivered by many groups of workers other than
psychologists. And as we have seen this is generally what happens in the area of
drug misuse. Psychologists, alongside other social researchers, potentially have
much more to contribute in this important area, especially in taking forward a
number of future research directions some of which have been touched upon
in this chapter. In conclusion, in terms of future research there is a clear need
for a broad range of outcome measures and also a case for looking afresh at
challenging methodological issues linked to the levels and types of motivation
for change.

Notes

1. The HPC is responsible for the statutory regulation of a range of health professions
   for the protection of the public.
2. Largely for historical reasons training in different branches of applied psychology
   in the UK developed largely on the basis of place of employment rather than function, this despite a very high degree of overlap across all specialisms. There have
   been a number of recent developments that have sought to break down these
   'silos' and improve the delivery and use of applied psychology across a full range of
   government-supported settings (e.g. Home Office, 2003).
3. Historically HM Prison Service provided an in-house service essentially delivering
   primary care. Secondary and tertiary services were often provided by the NHS but
   on an ad-hoc basis. This resulted in primary care services that were professionally
   isolated and out of step with developments in NHS practice. Secondary and tertiary
   service tended to be patchy and poorly integrated with mainstream service delivery.

Chapter 8

Research into High-Intensity Training (HIT) with Young People

Derval Ambrose

Introduction

This chapter explores the history and development of the high-intensity training (HIT) regimes in England and examines the available evaluation data on effectiveness Farrington *et al.* (2000, 2002, 2002b). This chapter draws heavily upon the work of David Farrington. In addition, some available evidence from North America is reviewed to provide context and comparison.

Young adults aged between 18 and 20 make up 42% of first-time offenders, and account for one-fifth of all reconvictions. Statistics show that of this group of offenders 63% are unemployed at the time of arrest and 34% have problems with basic literacy and numeracy (Crime Reduction Website, Young Offenders targeted with New Community Penalty – ICCP, 2003). Interventions to reduce reconvictions among young adults have grown over the last decade.

The Australian Institute of Criminology (AIC) produced a review of current literature on youth crime prevention in 2002, taking an international perspective. The review looked at 155 references, 24% of which were described as evaluations, and it provides an overview of current thinking on what is effective in preventing and reducing offending in young people aged 12–25 years of age. The review focuses on interventions described by 'program type', the setting in which it was delivered and effectiveness in terms of achieving the aims of the approach.

The authors conclude that interventions which focus on individual needs are most effective (AIC, 2002) and suggest that a more holistic case-management approach to intervention with young people who offend is likely to yield the best results. In general the following principles are proposed:

- interventions addressing many risk factors have a greater effect than those addressing only one per intervention;
- interventions that work across social settings – within the family, school, peers and the community – can impact on the whole of the young person's

life. These are more effective in reducing offending than concentrating on one area of influence;

- interventions containing skills-based components to increase educational attainment, improve employment prospects and increase positive reintegration into the community can have positive impact;
- school-based interventions striving to keep young people in formal education, focussing on the way school and classes are run and emphasising behavioural skills appear to be effective;
- interventions which focus on altering the way a young person thinks and acts are particularly effective. Offending behaviour is linked to poor problem-solving and decision-making skills and therefore social-skills-based interventions can also be beneficial (modified from AIC, 2002, p. 8).

Furthermore, the authors refer to the intensive 'strict' regimes such as 'boot camps' as being generally ineffective unless they also contain more therapeutic elements that are generalisable to the young person's usual environment.

In addition, a recent literature review commissioned by the Scottish Executives' Social Work Services Inspectorate explores the relevant evidence base in terms of the desistance from offending literature and psychotherapy literature (McNeill *et al.*, 2005). The authors focus on the diversity and variation among offenders versus a homogenous theory of change. The more recent criminal justice system's focus on individual need and responsivity is well supported in research evidence from the field of psychotherapy, which suggests that it is not the specific type of intervention that determines change but more the existence of 'common factors'. Common factors involve:

- accurate empathy, respect, or warmth, and therapeutic genuineness (sometimes referred to as therapist factors and at other times described as relationship factors);
- establishing a 'therapeutic relationship' or 'working alliance' (mutual understanding and agreement about the nature and purpose of treatment);
- an approach that is person centred, or collaborative and client driven (taking the client's perspective and using the client's concepts) (McNeill *et al.*, 2005).

It would seem, unsurprisingly, that the relationship between practitioner/worker and client/offender is critical to effective interventions. The authors also refer to broad findings in the desistance from offending literature. Notably research findings suggest that desistance requires social capital (opportunities) in addition to human capital (capacities) (McNeill *et al.*, 2005). The authors go on to suggest that this implies the need for an 'advocacy role' for practitioners that targets societal systems as well as the individual offender.

Definitional Issues

Within the context of England and Wales a young offender (YO) is described as being 17 years of age or younger and over the age of 10. Offenders who are in the age group 18–21 are referred to as young adult offenders.

Within this chapter the term young offender or young person will generally be used to refer to those involved in the research. Farrington *et al.* refer to 'experimental' groups and 'control' groups. These terms will be retained in their original context, but not outside of that as the terminology can imply a dehumanising of participants and a de-emphasis on the individuality of young people involved.

American 'Boot Camps'

Spiralling rates of incarceration of young people in the US led to experiments with alternative approaches to custody for this population. So-called boot camps were one of these developments starting in the early 1980s and gaining a high political and public profile. The years that followed saw a proliferation of boot camps across the north of America. There is no agreed definition but such approaches tend to have four common features that distinguish them from other types of imprisonment. Namely they adopt a military atmosphere, require offenders to participate in military drills, individuals are kept separate from other YOs and they are considered an alternative to lengthier custodial sanctions (MacKenzie, 1990 in John Howard Society of Alberta, 1997). In addition, it could be argued that they are seen to provide a dual function of cost-effective intervention and punishment, being seen as 'alternative sanctions with teeth' (MacKenzie *et al.*, 1995). The UK experience of cost effectiveness in terms of this approach will be returned to later. It has been suggested that the goals of boot camps can be divided into three levels: (1) system level goals, (2) individual level goals and (3) public relation goals (MacKenzie, 1990). System level goals are concerned with reduction in the numbers of incarcerated YOs. Individual level goals involve changes in those who participate. Public relation goals include improving the public image of the penal system and the belief that such approaches are a politically popular form of sanction.

The early research in the US on the impact of such approaches on future recidivism focussed on the first camps to be established in the US. For example, Georgia state in 1983, Florida in 1987 and New York in 1987. These early approaches focussed on the creation of a 'military atmosphere, with drilling, physical training, strict discipline and hard labour. Staff and inmates wore military uniforms and inmates entered in groups as squads or platoons' (Farrington *et al.*, 2002, p. 1). Later such approaches were modified to be broader in approach, adding rehabilitative aspects such as counselling, education, cognitive-behavioural skills training and substance-use interventions. Such approaches gained considerable popularity in the US with 36 states running such programmes by 1994 (Farrington *et al.*, 2002). The addition of more rehabilitative aspects to the regimes represented a shift away from the primary 'punishment' focussed approach.

The approach used in the US state of Georgia was originally named the special alternative incarceration (SAI). Evaluation of the SAI (Flowers *et al.*, 1991) looked at 'graduates' of SAI and compared two other groups of offenders: those who were sentenced to prison and those who were sentenced to probation. The prison group was categorised into four subgroups determined by length of time served (less than six months versus more than six months) and prior periods in custody (none versus one or more). The probation group was categorised in terms of the type of community sentence served, for example, intensive supervision versus diversion centre (Flowers *et al.*, 1991 in Kempinen and Kurlychek, 2000). The analysis also controlled for a number of other potentially contributory factors such as risk level and race. There was a follow-up period of at least three years (majority were followed up for four years and a significant number for up to five years) and recidivism was measured in terms of participants in each group being returned to or sentenced to custody (Flowers *et al.*, 1991; Kempinen and Kurlychek, 2000).

Flowers *et al.* (1991) reported that at the three-year follow-up point the recidivism levels of SAI offenders was significantly lower (41%) than those who went to prison (ranging from 50% to 60% depending upon the subgroup) and those on intensive probation (50%), but significantly higher than those on regular probation (33%). After five years the recidivism rates increased for all groups, though the rate was still lower for the SAI group (50%) than the prison groups (ranging from 57 to 70%) and the intensive probation group (54%). Offenders on regular probation continued to have the lowest recidivism rate (37%) (reported in Kempinen and Kurlychek, 2000).

The New York approach was interestingly named 'shock incarceration'. Evaluation was conducted by the New York Department of Corrections and the Division of Parole. Again the evaluation covered a three-year follow-up period. After a period of two years it was reported that 'graduates' were less likely than the comparable prison group to be returned to custody for the commission of a further offence (15% versus 19%) or a technical violation (failure to comply with conditions of pre-trial release, probation or parole, excluding alleged new criminal activity) (14% versus 17%). After three years 'shock' graduates were still less likely to be returned to custody for the commission of a new offence (21% versus 26%), yet both groups were returned to prison for technical violations with equal regularity (19%). In terms of offence type it was concluded that the shock incarceration programme was most effective for young people convicted of drug offences (Kempinen and Kurlychek, 2000).

As mentioned earlier 'boot camp'-based approaches quickly gained popularity and proliferated across North America. However, differences between the various approaches make it difficult to generalise outcomes (Kempinen and Kurlychek, 2000). MacKenzie and colleagues have conducted the most extensive research on the effectiveness of these types of interventions in the US and have attempted to address such differences in their evaluation approach.

MacKenzie *et al.* (1995) conducted an evaluation covering eight US states: Florida, Georgia, Illinois, Louisiana, New York, Oklahoma, South Carolina and Texas. They noted a number of similarities and differences across all eight states. All programmes selected in the eight states shared military aspects to their regime, such as physical training, strict adherence to rules and engagement in work. However, other aspects differed such as engagement in education, vocational training and interventions to reduce substance misuse. Furthermore, programmes differed on other aspects such as differing lengths of confinement, rates of completion, differing lengths of time devoted to rehabilitative interventions and differing types of community supervision post release (e.g. intensive supervision versus regular probation supervision) (MacKenzie *et al.*, 1995).

Recidivism measures were broadened to incorporate arrest rates as well as a return to prison for either a new crime or a technical violation. MacKenzie *et al.* recognised that there were several different ways of approaching the measurement of recidivism and therefore adopted a multiple indicator approach. The follow-up period was one year in four states and two years in the other four states. Overall the findings of the study were mixed, reporting that recidivism rates were lower than control groups in three states, higher in one state and no different in four states (MacKenzie *et al.*, 1995). The state which was reported as having higher rates of recidivism between graduates and control group was the Georgia boot camp, where graduates were reported to be significantly more likely than probationers to have a conviction for a new crime (17% versus 5%), while there was no significant difference when compared to prison releases (16%). The authors propose that this is partially a result of specific aspects of the Georgia regime: less treatment intervention, offenders sentenced to the programme by the court, low rates of drop-out, significantly less activity in the daily schedule and graduates released on traditional probation (MacKenzie *et al.*, 1995).

Conversely, three states (Illinois, Louisiana, New York) were reported as demonstrating lower rates of recidivism, though not all of the findings were significant. In Louisiana, graduates were reported as having 'fewer arrests then any of the comparison groups, fewer revocations than the parolees and drop-outs, fewer new crimes than parolees and fewer technical revocations than drop-outs' (MacKenzie *et al.*, 1995). In all three states, boot camp graduates were less likely than the prison release group to be returned to custody for a new crime. This finding was not significant for the graduates of the New York camp. Illinois boot camp completers were less likely to be returned to prison for a new crime, but more likely than prison releases to be returned for a technical violation. It is proposed by the authors that this may have been affected by the intensive supervision element of the Illinois programme, in that graduates were released on intensive supervision and therefore may have been returned for a technical violation before they became involved in new criminal activity (MacKenzie et al., 1995).

The authors conclude that the lowest levels of recidivism were associated with extra emphasis on rehabilitation and resettlement issues, such as providing rehabilitative activities and intensive supervision after release. The three programmes that were reported as showing lower rates of recidivism had a number of similarities such as over three hours of therapeutic activity per day, intensive supervision on release, voluntary participation and all were of similar longer periods (120–180 days) (MacKenzie et al., 1995). Overall, MacKenzie et al. concluded that the military aspects of boot camps were not effective in reducing criminal recidivism.

The important question of whether programmes which incorporate the characteristics of the New York, Illinois and Louisiana programmes, but remove the militaristic elements, would produce equal or more positive effects on recidivism, is raised. They refer to past research on the effectiveness of prison drug-treatment approaches suggesting that that it is the intensive treatment and good-quality aftercare which are the most effective components in reducing recidivism (Andrews et al., 1990; Anglin and Hser, 1990 in MacKenzie et al., 1995; Andrews and Bonta, 1994).

Furthermore, MacKenzie et al. (2001) identified 29 studies resulting in 44 samples examining the effects of 'correctional boot camps' on offending. A meta-analytic approach was applied. The scope of the review was experimental, and quasi-experimental evaluations examined 'boot camp-like programs' for juveniles and adult offenders (MacKenzie et al., 2001, p. 128). Overall 27 studies reported no effect, nine found that 'boot camp' approaches reduced recidivism and eight reported an increase in recidivism. The overall mean odds ratio was 1.02 (95% confidence interval of 0.90 to 1.17), indicating 'an almost equal odds of recidivating between the boot camp and comparison groups, on average' (MacKenzie et al., 2001, p. 130). The authors concluded that the military elements of boot camps do not effectively reduce recidivism.

History and Context of the HIT Regime in England

The mid-1990s in the UK was characterised by public debate about the treatment of children and young adults who offend. A number of highly publicised events intensified this debate such as public reaction to the murder of

Jamie Bulger (a young boy murdered by two older children) and the emergence of 'ram-raiding'[1] (Beck, 1997). The then Home Secretary, as part of a visit to the US, inspected the 'shock incarceration' regime in Texas. A short time later HM Prison Service was commissioned to develop similar intensive regimes for YOs drawing on the positive elements of American approaches (Farrington et al., 2002).

A steering group was put in place to develop the regimes in line with the terms of reference set out. The characteristics of HIT are as follows:

- vigorous and demanding activities undertaken during a long, full and active day;
- sentence planning to determine the best use of time in custody and under supervision after release for each young offender;
- group work to address offending behaviour and encourage young offenders to think for themselves and others;
- use of group pressure to encourage conformity and positive attitude change;
- basic education for those with inadequate literacy and numeracy skills;
- NVQ-based vocational training;
- involvement of the home probation officer in throughcare to ensure a smooth transition from custody to supervision in the community (in Farrington et al., 2002a, p. 2–3).

Proposals for the HIT regime were submitted and agreed in 1995. The pilot site was to be Young Offender Institute (YOI) Thorn Cross. The new regime was implemented from July 1996. A second regime was agreed at around the same time, based at the Colchester Military Correction Training Centre (MCTC). This focussed more heavily on militaristic elements in the regime. For comparison purposes, the Thorn Cross and Colchester regimes outcomes were to be compared. Both intensive regimes targeted the young adult population, 18- to 21-year olds.

The high-intensity training programme

The HIT programme ran over 25 weeks, with five phases, each lasting five weeks. A maximum of 14 YOs joined every five weeks (Beck, 1997). The young people involved could progress through the phases independently of whether all goals were achieved. All were required to wear a standard uniform.

The five phases involved are as follows:

Phase 1: Initial assessment: During the first five weeks the individual's needs were assessed. This included assessment of educational and employment issues, offending-related needs as well as an assessment of physical health. Basic education and physical training were introduced and sentence-management plans completed. The initial phase ended with an outward bounds-type course in Snowdonia or the Lake District ('partnership and leadership skills').

Phase 2: Basic skills: Involved a series of classroom-based activities building on phase 1 and including progression towards educational qualifications, basic life and social skills, along with completion of an enhanced thinking skills[2] group work course.

Phase 3: Vocational training: The young people engaged in vocational training matched to the individual and the type of placement they would engage in during the final phase of the HIT. Vocational training included painting and decorating, plastering, welding, motor mechanics and catering and led to a nationally recognised qualification, the focus being to equip the young people with marketable skills. In this phase, HIT participants were mixed with others in the main site of Thorn Cross. Individual case conferences were held involving the young people, relevant staff and outside probation officers.

Phase 4: Pre-release: During this phase any outstanding work was completed, in education, vocational training, life and social skills training. In addition a further offending behaviour group work intervention was provided focussing on a number of issues. The psychological basis to this intervention is an approach based on the cognitive-behavioural group work intervention used earlier. It is based on the theory that much offending is driven by cognitive processes. It is argued that these serve to 'cognitively' permit and maintain criminal offending. The intervention therefore sought to analyse these underlying thoughts and encourage offenders to adopt more pro-social ways of thinking, which did not permit and maintain criminal behaviour. In addition, during these five weeks, interviews with prospective employer or training placements were arranged. Those who completed this phase were formally presented with a National Record of Achievement covering all qualifications achieved during time at the HIT centre, recognising their achievements. It is entirely possible that this would be potentially empowering for young people who had a history of exclusion from formal education in the past, although this is not referred to in the evaluation.

Phase 5: Community placement: The final five-week phase involved a work or training placement in the community, on temporary licence from Monday to Friday. Appropriate accommodation was arranged and approved by staff (modified from Farrington *et al.*, 2002a).

In line with the original brief of the project team the young people were involved in a very full day of activities. A typical weekday is outlined (modified from Farrington *et al.*, 2002a, p. 7) below.

06.00   Rise, clean room and unit
06.40   Room inspection

07.20   Drill
08.00   Breakfast
08.30   Skills training/education/offending behaviour group work
12.00   Lunch
13.00   Physical education
14.15   Skills training/education/offending behaviour group work
16.45   Personal hygiene
17.00   Evening meal
18.00   Evening class
20.00   Group meeting
20.30   Earned privileges
21.45   Personal hygiene
22.00   Lights out

The HIT regime was set up and delivered by multidisciplinary teams of staff which included prison officers, prison managers, psychologists and probation officers, who were specifically assessed for the role. They completed additional training to prepare for their HIT roles. In addition staff were engaged in the design and set-up at early stages. As with any new project or programme there were some early operational difficulties, which needed to be resolved by these teams of staff. The reported operational difficulties included that the first two intakes of YOs took advantage of the regime being new and therefore challenged all aspects of the regime; this is reported to have negatively affected later intakes. In addition, staff were in the early stages reluctant to impose disciplinary sanctions due to concerns about drop-outs and the high media interest in the regime (Farrington *et al.*, 2002a).

Colchester regime

In parallel with HIT being developed, a regime originally seen as likely to be more similar to the original American 'boot camp' approach was also planned and implemented. Plans to create a YOI at the Colchester MCTC[3] were announced in April 1996. The project during its creation and lifespan attracted both public praise and denouncement; this included criticisms that it was too army like and too costly. The experimental unit was closed in March 1998 at which point 66 young people had passed through the centre.

The Colchester approach differed from the HIT regime in that it was based in a military establishment. The regime was designed to match as closely as possible the experience of a military training regime (Farrington *et al.*, 2002b). The young people were housed in a separate building, with a capacity for 38 occupants, and had use of the MCTC facilities. All wore uniforms and staff were a combination of military and Prison Service staff (Farrington *et al.*, 2002b).

The programme had a total of three stages and participants gradually earned more freedom and better-quality living conditions as they progressed though each stage. Progression through stages was dependant on behaviour, specifically involving participants receiving weekly recommendations from staff. For example, marks were awarded for appearance, inspection, attitude to staff and others and effort (Farrington *et al.*, 2002a).

The stages are summarised below.

Stage one: (approximately six weeks long)

The participants

- had no access to television or a telephone;
- were escorted wherever they went;
- were locked in their rooms at night at 8.00 p.m.;
- undertook extended periods of military marching, drilling and physical training;
- had rigorous room and kit inspections;
- undertook basic literacy and numeracy education.

Stage two: (approximately eight weeks long)

The participants

- were no longer locked in their rooms at night;
- had access to a radio and a television;
- were escorted around the site;
- continued with extended period of military drill and physical training;
- undertook vocational training (e.g. painting and decorating, bricklaying);
- had career counselling (e.g. making job applications, money management).

Stage three: (approximately 12 weeks long)

The participants

- had regular access to television and a telephone;
- were trusted to make their own way round the site, and could work on the MCTC farm;
- could make supervised visits to town;
- could leave the site on community and conservation projects. (Modified from Farrington *et al.*, 2002b)

A typical day is outlined below.

06.00–07.00   Reveille; wash, shave, make beds
07.00–07.15   Unlock, stand by beds, roll call

07.15–08.00   Breakfast
08.00–08.40   Company administration and platoon officer's inspection
08.40–10.05   Parade followed by PT, sport, education, trade training
10.05–10.20   Tea break
10.20–12.30   PT, sport, education, trade training
12.30–13.30   Lunch
13.30–14.00   Company administration and platoon officer's inspection
14.00–16.15   Parade followed by PT, sport, education, trade training
16.15–17.00   Shower and company administration
17.00–17.30   Evening meal
17.30–18.30   Patrol on (room cleaning)
18.30–20.00   Daily debriefing, ironing and washing kit
20.00–20.15   Supper (tea and a chocolate bar)
20.15–22.00   Locked up/writing letters/board games
22.00   Lights out

Some of the included activities above were dependant on what regime stage the young person was in (modified from Farrington *et al.*, 2002a, p. 40–1).

Selection for intensive regimes and the design of the evaluation study

The criteria for selection for both the HIT and the Colchester regime were broadly similar. Young people were eligible if they were:

- male;
- aged 18–21 years;
- had approximately six months of their sentence left to serve;
- were suitable for open custodial conditions (e.g. no previous escape incidents or sexual offences);
- were mentally and physically able to engage with the regime (Farrington *et al.*, 2000a).

In practice, implementing the selection criteria was problematic, mainly as the condition to have at least six months to serve and being suitable for open conditions were largely incompatible.

The original evaluation design was based on the identification of 28 suitable young people every five weeks and randomly allocating half to the HIT centre and half to the control group. A total of 13 YOIs across England and Wales were targeted, yet very few young people were identified as suitable. The suitability pool was therefore increased by widening the selection criteria, in terms of the broader framework of YOs who represented a low risk to the public. As a result the main groups to be excluded were young people convicted of a sexual offence and those with convictions for large-scale serious drug dealing (Farrington *et al.*, 2000a).

In the main 'control groups' were young people who had less then six months of their sentence left to serve, lacked motivation to participate in the HIT regime or displayed unsuitable behaviour in their current YOI. As a result control groups tended to represent a higher risk group than those selected for HIT. To reduce the impact of these differences, control and experimental cases were matched on risk of reconviction on a case-by-case basis based on the Copas *et al.* (1994) risk of reconviction score. Control YOs were available for approximately two-thirds of experimental YOs (Farrington *et al.*, 2002a, p. 12).

Over the two-year evaluation period, there were 15 intakes, representing a total of 184 young people starting the HIT programme. Out of these a total of 106 completed the programme. The majority of young people who did not complete failed to complete phases 1–4 ($n = 43$), 35 more did not complete phase 5 (Farrington *et al.*, 2002a).

In addition, a series of psychological tests were administered to assess the impact of the regime on YO's attitudes and behaviour. Tests were administered at the beginning and end of the period of the custody in an effort to measure the degree of change in the following factors:

- control of emotion and aggression;
- ability to think before acting;
- attitudes to staff and inmates;
- anti-social behaviour;
- thinking styles relevant to criminal behaviour (in Farrington *et al.*, 2002b, p. 3).

Specifically, the tests used were the emotion control questionnaire (ECQ) (Roger and Najarian, 1989; Roger and Masters, 1997), the custodial adjustment questionnaire (CAQ) (Thornton, 1987) and the psychological inventory of criminal thinking styles (PICTS) (Walters, 1995a, 1995b, 1996).

Key findings – HIT regime

The young people from the first 15 intakes of HIT (July 1996–December 1997) were followed up over a two-year period.

An analysis of reconviction was derived by comparing predicted and actual reconviction rates for those completing HIT and a matched group of young people from YOIs, at one-year and two-year intervals after release. The control group was essentially those who were eligible according to the selection criteria but were not selected for either regime. Initially, Farrington and colleagues attempted to assign eligible YOs at random to the regime group or the control group, however, exceptions were made and the control group was

described as tending to be more 'criminogenic' than the experimental group
(Farrington *et al.*, 2002b). Therefore, the main comparison was between predicted and actual reconviction rates for experimental and control groups of
young people. Predicted reconviction scores were taken from the Offenders
Index[4] and actual reconviction data was derived from the Police National
Computer (PNC). Reconvictions for offences that were committed prior to the
current term of custody were omitted (Farrington *et al.*, 2002b).

Overall, the actual rate of reconviction versus predicted rate of reconviction
was lower in the first year for those completing HIT (47.2% predicted, 34.7%
actual). In comparison the control group were reconvicted, in the first year, as
often as predicted (56.1% predicted, 55.1% actual) (Farrington *et al.*, 2002a,
p. 16). However, this effect was not maintained over a two-year period, with
both experimental and control group's actual reconviction rates being almost
equal to predicted rates (experimental group predicted rate 66.4%, actual rate
65.1% and control group predicted rate 74.7%, actual rate 75.6%). However,
the early results were encouraging and there were some differential rates of
reconviction when the data is further disseminated. Furthermore, the fact that
the early reconviction rate data was not maintained is not surprising in that
support for this group of young people is likely to have been minimal at the
two-year follow-up stage.

Further analysis of the data showed that some of the variables studied had
differential results. For example, the youngest participants in the HIT programme (aged 18 or under) had a lower than predicted reconviction rate,
whereas comparison offenders in the control group did not. Conversely older
offenders had higher than predicted offending rate in both groups (Farrington
et al., 2002a). In addition, YOs with no adjudications in custody had a
considerably lower reconviction rate than predicted (51% predicted, 33%
actual).

Farrington *et al.* (2002a) also reported that those YOs with between
three and six previous convictions did 'considerably better than expected'
(predicted reconviction rate 77.3%, actual 60.4%). In contrast those who
had not been through HIT with three to six previous convictions had a predicted reconviction rate of 81.3% and an actual rate of 82.2%. The average
time between release from custody and reoffending was also assessed, and
it was concluded that the young people who had participated in the HIT
regime demonstrated a significantly longer average time period between release
and reoffending, approximately two months (Farrington *et al.*, 2002b). This
implies that completion of the HIT programme had a delayed impact on
reoffending.

The average number of offences committed in the two groups was assessed.
HIT programme participants committed an average of 3.5 offences each, compared to an average of 5.1 among the control group members. Widening

the impact of this to explore costs of crime to society, Farrington *et al.* (2002b) calculated, using Home Office figures on the average cost of each crime, the cost of crimes committed by the control group to be £9,903 per person on average. This figure was further adjusted to take into account the fact that HIT participants were initially at lower risk than the control group. After adjustments to account for differential risk levels, the cost of offences committed by the HIT group was reported as £7,423 per person (Farrington *et al.*, 2002b). Therefore, HIT participants cost society £2,480 less than the average control group offender. The additional cost per offender to participate in the HIT regime was calculated as £2,441, and therefore it was concluded that the HIT regime had 'recouped its costs' based on recorded convictions (Farrington, 2002b, p. 3). On average at least five indictable offences are committed for every one leading to a conviction. In view of this Farrington *et al.* (2002) note that a minimum of £5 was saved for every extra £1 spent of the HIT regime.

In addition psychological tests were completed on a relatively smaller number of YOs. The before and after comparison did not yield statistically significant data but indicated, post-participation in the regime, that:

- HIT programme participants displayed more positive attitudes towards staff;
- HIT programme participants had a higher degree of control of aggression;
- HIT programme participants showed some evidence of higher self-esteem ratings.

On the other hand, HIT programme participants showed increased pro-offending attitudes and did not appear to interact any better with other inmates. Furthermore, they did not appear to be 'more responsible', were not 'better behaved' and did not report to find the regime less stressful (Farrington *et al.*, 2002a, p. 13–14).

There are some limitations to such questionnaire data, specifically in that it measures what people say as opposed to their behaviour, and the link between such evaluations and reoffending is unclear. However, the positive views of staff reported is not surprising in light of the motivation and staff engagement reported. Additionally, a high proportion of young people in YOIs have experienced disrupted levels of care, and positive relationship development with significant adults could be hypothesized to have a positive impact on future pro-social behaviour. Again, it is likely that as this experience was limited to the short period of time young people were involved in the programme, it is unlikely to have longer-term impact. A potentially interesting study may be to recreate such positive relationships on release through community mentoring schemes and monitor the longer-term impact on behaviour.

Key findings – Colchester regime

Selection for the Colchester regime was broadly the same as for the HIT. A total of 61 young people completed the programme and 97 controls were followed up at 12- and 24-month periods.

Colchester participants also completed the three psychological tests that the HIT programme participants completed, detailed above (see Farrington *et al.*, 2002). On evaluation there was minimal difference between the Colchester participants and the control group. However, results indicated that the Colchester participants tended to have more positive attitudes towards staff and other inmates, were happier and less depressed, expressed higher levels of hope for the future and felt in better physical health than the control group (Farrington *et al.*, 2002b).

The actual rate of reconviction was approximately 6% lower than predicted for both groups. Similarly the average time between release from custody and reoffending was similar for both groups (Farrington *et al.*, 2002b). Although the average number of offences committed by the Colchester group, over a two-year follow-up period, was slightly lower than the average committed by the control group, the difference was not reported as being cost effective. That is the average cost to the state per person was higher for YOs in the Colchester group (£3,963 compared with £3,811) (Farrington *et al.*, 2002b). This was in the main as they committed more costly offences, primarily violent offences. As with the HIT programme costs, the control group were at a higher risk of reconviction than the experimental group. After adjustments had been made to account for differential risk between groups the average cost per YO in the experimental group rose to £4,650 (Farrington *et al.*, 2002b).

The Colchester regime was reported to have cost £4,711 per head in addition to the average cost of a standard regime. Applying the assumption, as before, that at least five offences are committed for every one leading to a conviction, at least 89p was lost for every extra £1 spent on the Colchester regime (Farrington *et al.*, 2002b). The authors concluded that the Colchester reconviction data suggests that the drilling and physical training elements of the HIT regime were not essential to its success.

Policy and practice implications

The HIT regime was successful in reducing reoffending, particularly in terms of the societal cost of offending. In contrast the Colchester regime had no impact on future reoffending at the two-year follow-up point but indicated some positive attitudinal change effects. It would be potentially interesting to have followed up the Colchester regime participants in the community with additional support services to ascertain whether the reported changes to self-esteem could be maintained.

The situation is further complicated by the recent Home Office evaluation, which reports no difference between the two-year reconviction rates for a large sample of adult male prisoners who had participated in a 'cognitive skills' group work intervention between 1996 and 1998 (Falshaw *et al.*, 2003). This calls into question whether the enhanced thinking skills element of the HIT regime was effective. If not this leaves us with focussing mainly on the potential positive effects of intensive resettlement and positive relationships developed with staff.

The evaluation data to date offers some potentially interesting avenues for future policy and practice. The initial results of the HIT programme showed some very promising results which declined over time. Some of the positive aspects to the approach included the intensive focus on the young people involved, a broad-based and multidisciplinary approach, high levels of ownership and engagement among staff, and intense focus on education and employment. Perhaps some of the broader weaknesses of the approach could be given additional focus in future interventions, such as increased focus on resettlement issues. This could include community-based follow-ups such as mentoring for young people, focus on familial issues and the development of pro-social support networks. In addition, as such high percentages of young adults involved with the criminal justice system have disrupted care histories, it may be beneficial to include approaches which address childhood experiences and attachment issues.

Furthermore, some of the limitations in the HIT approach were that it excluded large groups of YOs, such as young people displaying sexually harmful behaviour, young people with mental health issues and young people demonstrating low motivation to change. Perhaps one of the most interesting of these is the exclusion of young people with low motivation to change. This raises some difficult evaluation issues. For example, high motivation to change may have been the ingredient to positive change and not necessarily the particular therapeutic approach. As referred to earlier, approaches which target the individual needs of the young person have been reported to be most effective in terms of reducing reoffending. It could be argued that exclusion on the grounds of mental health issues potentially excludes a very large number of YOs, particularly in light of recent Youth Justice Board research suggesting that 31% of YOs had a mental health need, 18% had problems with depression, 10% reported experiencing anxiety issues and 9% met the criteria for post-traumatic stress disorder (YJB, 2005). In addition, YOs from minority ethnic backgrounds were reported to display higher levels of post-traumatic stress and female YOs had more mental health needs than males (YJB, 2005). The participants of the HIT programme were all male and the majority of them were white offenders. Further thought needs to be given to the needs to female YOs and the needs of black and minority ethnic (BME) offenders. It could of course be argued that this also applies to some of the evidence for the efficacy of such cognitive-based interventions and not just these regime-based approaches.

Finally, further to the recent work of McNeill *et al.* (2005), referred to earlier, focussing on the available research from the desistance from crime and psychotherapy literature, it would seem paramount to our interventions with young people that we do not lose sight of the diversity among this group. Important issues such as recognition of the lack of equal access to opportunity among this group must underpin interventions with young people, and a renewed focus on the quality of the relationship between workers/practitioners and young people. Any approach assuming homogeneity among groups of offenders is likely to reduce the probability of positive impact.

Notes

1. When a car, usually a stolen car, is driven through the front window of a shop so that the contents of the shop can be stolen.
2. Developed by the England and Wales Prison Service this is a cognitive-behavioural group work intervention that seeks to change offenders' thinking and behaviour through a structured and sequenced series of exercises designed to teach interpersonal problem-solving skills.
3. Colchester MCTC is the prison for the armed services and holds serving military personnel serving short sentences and personnel awaiting discharge from the military or transfer.
4. Large Home Office criminal database known as the Offenders Index.

Chapter 9

Military Corrective Training Centre: An Evaluation

David P. Farrington, Kate A. Painter and Darrick Jolliffe

Military Regimes

Boot camp prisons were first introduced in the US in 1983 in Georgia and Oklahoma. The focus of these early programmes was on creating a military atmosphere, with drilling, physical training, strict discipline and hard labour. Staff and inmates wore military uniforms and inmates entered in groups as squads or platoons. Later programmes added rehabilitative components such as counselling, academic education, cognitive-behavioural skills training and drug treatment. Boot camp prisons became more and more popular, and 36 states had them by 1994. Doris MacKenzie (1994; see also MacKenzie *et al.*, 1995) carried out the first large-scale evaluation of their use in eight states. Most were designed for young non-violent offenders without a previous extensive serious criminal history.

MacKenzie and her colleagues (1995) reported that inmates found the rules, discipline and activities stressful, especially in the first few weeks. They complained about verbal abuse and harsh treatment by staff. However, they also became physically fit and free from drugs. Compared with control inmates, boot camp inmates were more hopeful about the future, and especially hopeful about their chances of getting jobs. The boot camp staff were very enthusiastic about the programmes. They viewed their role as being supportive and helpful in enabling offenders to take responsibility for their actions and to change in positive ways. Probation and parole staff were generally more sceptical, but they reported that the improved appearance and training of offenders helped them to obtain employment. However, these staff emphasized how difficult it was for offenders when they returned home to face the influence of dysfunctional families, drug-using friends and poor employment opportunities.

MacKenzie and her colleagues (1995) found that recidivism rates of boot camp inmates (compared with controls in other prisons) were lower in three states, higher in one state, and no different in four states. The programmes with lower recidivism rates were those that devoted the most time during the boot camp to rehabilitative activities, and those with more intensive supervision after release. Hence, MacKenzie (1994) concluded that the military elements of boot camps did not reduce recidivism.

A recent exhaustive review of the effects of boot camp prisons on recidivism was completed by MacKenzie *et al.* (2001). They identified 44 controlled studies of the effects of boot camps on recidivism (i.e. comparing boot camp inmates with comparable control samples). Of the 44 studies, nine found that boot camps reduced recidivism, eight found that boot camps increased recidivism, and 27 found no effect on recidivism. The overall weighted average odds ratio was 1.02, not significantly different from the chance figure of 1.00. The only positive result was that boot camps for adults with aftercare treatment led to reduced recidivism (odds ratio = 1.46). Therefore, the existing literature does not suggest that the military elements of boot camp prisons are effective in reducing recidivism.

The Thorn Cross High-Intensity Training (HIT) Regime

In light of the widespread concern about crime committed by young offenders (YOs) that followed the James Bulger killing in 1993, Home Secretary Michael Howard visited the US in January 1994. During this visit, he inspected a shock incarceration programme (popularly known as a 'boot camp') in Texas. On his return, he commissioned the Prison Service to develop proposals for an intensive regime for YOs which drew on the positive elements of American boot camp programmes.

In November 1994, a Steering Group under the chairmanship of Ian Lockwood, North West Area Manager, was formed to oversee the introduction of an intensive regime into the Prison Service. A Project Group chaired by Iain Windebank, Governor of Thorn Cross Young Offender Institution (YOI), was formed to plan, prepare and implement such a regime under the guidance of the Steering Group. Thorn Cross YOI was chosen to pilot the regime because its regime and staff were perceived to be positive and because it had an unused residential unit available.

The terms of reference for the Project Group were agreed: to consider and make recommendations to the Steering Group on the setting up, monitoring and evaluation of a pilot regime which was to draw on the positive elements of American boot camp prisons. The terms of reference specified that the regime was to include:

- vigorous and demanding activities undertaken during a long, full and active day;
- sentence planning to determine the best use of time in custody and under supervision after release for each YO;

- group work to address offending behaviour and encourage YOs to think for themselves about how they behave and the effects on themselves and others;
- use of group pressure to encourage conformity and positive attitude change;
- basic education for those with inadequate literacy and numeracy skills;
- National Vocational Training (NVQ)-based vocational training;
- involvement of the home probation officer in throughcare to ensure a smooth transition from custody to supervision in the community.

The YOs who were to participate in this experiment were to be in the final stages of their sentences. It was thought that consideration should be given to including community work in the regime, as well as involving outside employers who might offer jobs on release.

The Project Group initially undertook a survey of available literature on the effectiveness of boot camps in the US, the 'what works' literature (e.g. McGuire, 1995; Vennard et al., 1997) and the lessons learned from the 'tough detention centres' or 'short sharp shock' initiative of the early 1980s (Thornton et al., 1984). Members of the Project Group paid visits to Colchester Military Corrective Training Centre (MCTC), the Airborne Initiative in Scotland (an outward bound initiative run by former members of the airborne regiments) and the US.

During the visit to the US, two members of the Project Group were able to visit four boot camp prisons in and around Washington (DC), Pennsylvania and New York City. They were also able to meet and discuss the available and emerging research literature on boot camps with several leading academics, including Doris MacKenzie of the University of Maryland and Thomas Castellano of the US National Institute of Justice.

Although the original boot camp prisons were based on basic military training with a strong emphasis on drill, hard physical labour and strict discipline, there was a clear move by the newer facilities towards a much greater emphasis on education and training, challenging offending behaviour, improving life and social skills, improving employability and using planned release back into the community through half-way houses. Members of the Project Group concluded that the military regime had little or no effect on reconviction rates.

The proposals for a new intensive regime for YOs were submitted to the Prisons Board on 15 May 1995 and to the Home Secretary and Minister of State for the Home Office on 22 May 1995. Approval to proceed with the programme was given on 18 September 1995 and announced by Home Secretary Michael Howard on 25 September 1995. The name High-Intensity Training (HIT) Programme was chosen for the project.

The HIT regime was described by Farrington *et al.* (2002). Briefly, there were five phases of five weeks each. The programme included physical training, drill, basic education, life-skills, social skills, enhanced thinking skills (a cognitive-behavioural intervention), and vocational training. During the last five weeks, the YOs were released on temporary licence from Monday to Friday each week to undertake work or training placement in the community. This placement aimed to provide the YOs with a permanent job or training opportunity following release. Hence, the military elements comprised only a small part of the HIT regime.

Evaluation of the HIT regime

Potential HIT YOs were identified by allocation unit staff in feeder YOIs (see Farrington *et al.*, 2002). A selection team from the HIT centre visited each of the feeder YOIs and interviewed all potential experimental YOs, administered psychological tests and checked records. Control YOs were identified from those who were deemed eligible for HIT but were not selected, because they lacked motivation for the HIT programme, or because their behaviour in their current YOI suggested that they were not suitable for the HIT programme. All control YOs were matched case-by-case with experimental YOs based on the Copas *et al.*'s (1994) risk of reconviction score. However, it was possible to obtain matched control YOs for only about 70% of experimental YOs. Hence, all experimental YOs were compared with all control YOs.

In the evaluation, predicted reconviction percentages were compared with actual reconviction percentages for experimental and control YOs. Two reconviction prediction scores were derived (by Chris Kershaw and Philip Howard of the Home Office) for open YOIs and were calculated for each YO. They were based on the same principles as the revised offender group reconviction scale (OGRS) score (Taylor, 1999). The first estimated the probability of a YO being reconvicted within one year of release, while the second estimated the probability of a YO being reconvicted within two years of release.

YOs in the first 15 intakes were released between February 1997 and December 1998. A one-year follow-up (Farrington *et al.*, 2000) showed that HIT YOs did significantly better than predicted: 35% of HIT YOs were reconvicted, compared with the prediction of 47%. In contrast, control YOs were reconvicted in one year about as often as predicted (actual 55%, predicted 56%).

A further analysis of one-year reconviction rates suggested that YOs in the earlier intakes (1–7) were relatively more successful than those in the later intakes (8–15). The HIT programme was most successful with medium- and high-risk YOs and least successful with low-risk YOs. It was successful with all types of offenders, but most successful with those convicted for offences other than burglary or violence. It was equally successful for YOs of all ages

(18, 19 or 20), and for YOs who had or had not previously been in prison. Its success did not vary according to the sentence length of the YOs (two years or more versus less than two years). However, it was more effective with YOs who had three or more previous convictions than with YOs who had two or fewer previous convictions.

About 40% of HIT YOs did not complete the programme successfully. However, non-completers who spent at least six weeks in the HIT centre did just as well as HIT successes. Non-completers who spent five weeks or less in the HIT centre did not do significantly better than predicted.

Two years after release, the actual percentage reconvicted had increased considerably and was similar to the predicted percentage reconvicted for HIT and control YOs: 66% predicted versus 65% actually reconvicted for HIT YOs, and 75% predicted versus 76% actually reconvicted for control YOs. There were now indications that the youngest offenders (those aged 18 or less on sentence) did better than expected in the HIT centre.

For those who were reconvicted, the average time between release and reoffending was 228 days for HIT YOs compared with 177 days for controls, a significant difference. Also, the average number of offences leading to reconvictions in the two-year follow-up period was significantly less for HIT YOs (3.5) than for controls (5.1). A cost–benefit analysis based on offences leading to reconvictions showed that the average HIT YO cost society £2,480 less than the average control YO during the two-year follow-up period. This was similar to the estimated additional cost per YO on the HIT regime of £2,441 (compared with a standard regime YOI).

However, offences leading to convictions represent only a small fraction of offences actually committed. Research is needed comparing self-reported offences with convictions of YOs to estimate how many offences are really committed per conviction. Based on past research, it is reasonable to speculate that at least five offences are actually committed per conviction. On this assumption, the average HIT YO would have cost society £12,400 less than the average control YO (£2,480 × 5). We concluded that, based on fewer crimes, at least £5 was saved for every extra £1 expended on the HIT regime.

The Colchester MCTC Regime

While the HIT regime was designed to be physically challenging, Home Secretary Michael Howard considered that there was still a need to establish a regime for YOs that more closely approximated American boot camps. In April 1995, he visited the Colchester MCTC and was impressed by the quality of training offered to the servicemen under sentence (Crowe, 1997). He also noted that MCTC had spare capacity, and considered that part of it could be used to accommodate YOs. He wrote to Defence Secretary Malcolm Rifkind and proposed a trial to compare the MCTC regime with the HIT regime.

Colchester MCTC began life in 1942 as a camp for 6,000 prisoners of war, mostly German, who built Nissen huts to live in. It became a military prison in 1946 and was renamed the MCTC in 1955. Between 1981 and 1984 the original Nissen huts were replaced by modern buildings. Nowadays it is the only military prison in England and houses detainees from the Royal Navy, Royal Marines and Royal Air Force as well as the Royal Army. It occupies a large, open, partly wooded site which includes an assault course and a pig farm. While there is no perimeter wall, armed soldiers patrol the grounds.

The plan to establish a YOI within the MCTC was announced on 17 April 1996 at the MCTC by Prisons Minister Ann Widdecombe and Armed Forces Minister Nicholas Soames. Ann Widdecombe said; 'The Home Secretary and I have been very impressed by what goes on at the MCTC. The sense of discipline, of smartness, of calm, and, most importantly, of achievement is clear as one walks around and talks to the detainees. We decided that if at all possible we would like to test whether the military approach to custody could benefit civilian YOs and be effective in reducing the level of reoffending among them'.

The first YOs were not received by Colchester YOI until February 1997, because of lengthy negotiations between the Prison Service and the Ministry of Defence. One contentious issue (raised by the Prison Governors' Association) was whether the Army Commandant was competent to be Governor of a YOI. Eventually, it was agreed that he was. Other issues centred on whether YOs could wear watches and wedding rings and have access to telephones in the MCTC. In general, conditions in the MCTC were more restrictive than in a normal YOI; for example, it was common for servicemen to have all their possessions taken away on entry to the MCTC. Eventually, the Prison Service signed an agreement with the Ministry of Defence for YOs to be accommodated at the MCTC, from February 1997 to March 1998 in the first instance.

The new Labour government which took office on 2 May 1997 were not committed to Colchester YOI, and its closure was announced by Prisons Minister Joyce Quin on 22 January 1998 in response to a parliamentary question. She said,

> The Government is determined to pursue an active regime in YOIs as part of its commitment to focus the youth justice system on the prevention of offending by young people. Statutory provision for this is contained in the Crime and Disorder Bill.

> We are therefore continuing the experimental 'high-intensity training' regime which the previous Administration established at Thorn Cross YOI. Although at £22,700 per place, this regime is more expensive than a typical YOI regime at

£17,300 per place, the Thorn Cross programme has been shown to have a more sharply focussed and better integrated set of activities. We believe therefore that Thorn Cross represents value for money.

However, we have been unable to reach the same conclusion with Colchester. Colchester YOI opened on 20 February 1997 initially for one year. The costs per place at Colchester, at £31,300, have been running at nearly twice those for a typical YOI and nearly £9,000 more than those at Thorn Cross. The Colchester regime has encouraged positive change in attitudes among YOs but the available evaluation has not supported the contention that it has been more effective in preventing reoffending than other initiatives. In view of this, and of the very high costs, we have concluded that Colchester YOI does not represent value for money. It will therefore close on March 31st, 1998.

Description of the Colchester regime

The Colchester YOI regime was a military regime with an emphasis on physical training, physical fitness and drilling. The military staff were at pains to point out that it was not a 'boot camp'. The regime was as similar as possible to that provided for detainees of 'D' company, but included some elements from the 'A' company regime. 'D' company comprises detainees who are being dismissed from the services; 'A' company comprises detainees who are returning to the services. The YOI regime was based on firmness tempered with understanding. YOs wore military uniforms with coloured tags signifying what stage they were in. YOs were required to march about the establishment at all times and to request permission from staff to speak or carry out any action. They had a haircut on reception and every two weeks thereafter. There was an emphasis on smartness and room and kit inspections. The idea was that imposed discipline would lead to self-discipline.

The regime was in three stages. The stage one regime was austere. YOs had almost all personal possessions (including cash) removed, although they were able to earn some of these (e.g. trainers, a personal stereo) later. All correspondence (except legal) in and out was screened and read. YOs had no access to television, were escorted wherever they went, and were locked in their rooms at night (8.00 p.m.–6.00 a.m.). They had a shower but not a bath and were allowed one telephone call a week. Those judged to have the best-kept room were allowed to listen to a radio from 8.00 p.m. to 10.00 p.m. when there was lights out.

YOs gradually earned more freedom and better living conditions as they progressed from stage one to stage three. Progression through the stages depended on getting recommendations in weekly reports by staff. Marks were given for such issues as appearance, inspection, attitude to staff and other YOs, effort and self-presentation.

In stage two, YOs could wear their own trainers and have a personal stereo, and they could watch a black-and-white television and videos. They were no longer locked in their rooms at night, although the living unit was locked. In stage three, YOs were no longer escorted everywhere around the site, and could watch a colour television and have a bath. They also had access to a telephone and were allowed out to the town (Colchester) in the company of a responsible adult. The telephone and town visits were the most sought after privileges.

The YOs were housed in eight rooms each holding four to five YOs. Because there were a maximum of eight places on stage three, YOs in stage two who were qualified for stage three but waiting to move up were placed on a 'special stage' where they had many of the privileges of stage three including unescorted movement around MCTC and accompanied town visits.

The content of the stages was as follows:

Stage one (four–six weeks)

- reception, medical, welfare, haircut;
- orientation/briefing, fire and emergency drills;
- regime conduct, standards, rules (e.g. on bullying and visits);
- room/kit layout and cleaning, wearing of uniform;
- room and kit inspections;
- basic foot drill and marching;
- physical training, assault course;
- interviews and sentence planning;
- life-skills;
- drugs, alcohol, anger management, offending, anti-bullying programmes;
- personal hygiene;
- literacy and numeracy;
- education and current affairs;
- first aid;
- map reading;
- rules of the game and leadership exercise.

Stage two (six–eight weeks)

- room and kit inspections;
- drill;
- physical training;
- career counselling, job search, employment applications;
- social security, welfare, assistance agencies;
- CVs and job interviews;
- education and training opportunities;
- money management;

- Rehabilitation of Offenders Act;
- literacy and numeracy;
- trade training: bricklaying, carpentry, motor mechanics, painting and decorating, information technology.

Stage three (eight–twelve weeks)

- room and kit inspections;
- PT and sport;
- community projects (e.g. painting an old people's home, building a new play area at a primary school);
- conservation projects (e.g. repairing paths in the Brecon Beacons National Park in South Wales);
- work on the MCTC farm with pigs and poultry;
- challenge pursuit expeditions in Snowdonia;
- day release for college courses;
- resettlement education (help with jobs after release).

A typical day was as follows:

06.00–07.00	Reveille; wash, shave, make beds
07.00–07.15	Unlock, stand by beds, roll call
07.15–08.00	Breakfast
08.00–08.40	Company administration and platoon officer's inspection
08.40–10.05	Parade followed by PT, sport, education, trade training*
10.05-10.20	Tea break
10.20–12.30	PT, sport, education, trade training[1]
12.30–13.30	Lunch
13.30–14.00	Company administration and platoon officer's inspection
14.00–16.15	Parade followed by drill, PT, sport, education, trade training[2]
16.15–17.00	Shower and company administration
17.00–17.30	Evening meal
17.30–18.30	Patrol (on room cleaning)
18.30–20.00	Daily debriefing, ironing and washing kit
20.00–20.15	Supper (tea and chocolate bar)
20.15–22.00	Locked up, writing letters, games
22.00	Lights out

There were some important differences between the regimes of YOs and military detainees. For example, YOs required an induction period into army life, including the development of physical fitness and training in drilling. Also, while military detainees typically served two-thirds of their sentences, the commandant could allow them to be released early (as early as half-way through their sentences) as a reward for good behaviour and progress. In contrast, YOs were normally released at the half-way point of their sentences (although they could have additional days awarded for misconduct), and they did not receive any further reduction in time served as a reward for good behaviour and progress in the YOI. YOs played football against military detainees and interacted with them during trade training and meal-times.

Operation of Colchester YOI

The rooms in which YOs lived in Colchester were spartan and they were deprived of many personal possessions, as explained. They were certainly shouted at and ordered around. However, the YOs thought that, in many ways, Colchester was better than other YOIs. The food was praised by the YOs for its quality and quantity. The army uniform and kit were of high quality, and YOs were measured carefully on reception so that they had well-fitting clothes. When offered the opportunity to keep their army boots and berets as souvenirs after leaving, all YOs kept these.

The drilling encouraged peer pressure and team spirit. The very high standards of cleanliness in Colchester compared favourably with other YOIs. The health, fitness and appearance of the YOs improved. Many YOs enjoyed the sport, physical training and the use of the gymnasium. Most also preferred the busy schedules in Colchester YOI to sitting on their beds all day doing nothing in other YOIs. They wore full military uniform for family visits, and many parents commented favourably on their smartness and bearing after seeing them on parade.

All Colchester YOI staff were volunteers and were drawn jointly from the military and from the Prison Service. In general they worked well together. Morale and optimism were very high at the start, but the delay in opening, the experience of dealing with YOs and the uncertainty of Colchester's future took its toll, and the morale of both staff and YOs plummeted after the closure decision was announced in January 1998. Military staff initially had some problems in dealing with YOs, who were not disciplined and did not obey orders like servicemen under sentence. In the early weeks, some military staff got angry with YOs who were abusive or swore at them and this led to a high rate of adjudications for prison offences.

The greatest bone of contention between the military and the Prison Service was the fact that there was hardly ever a full complement of prison officers, who were constantly being withdrawn from Colchester by the Area Manager to serve in other hard-pressed establishments. This meant that, in practice, the military staff were primarily responsible for running Colchester YOI. Unlike Thorn Cross, it seems that Colchester YOI never had the whole-hearted support of the Area Manager.

The YOs undoubtedly liked the military staff more than the prison officers. They said that the military staff treated them with respect and encouraged them a great deal (e.g. initially in drilling). The military staff would often sit down and chat with the YOs to give them paternalistic advice about their lives, and the staff had a strong interest in the YOs' personal development. The YOs admired some of the military staff (e.g. the PT instructor) as firm, but fair, masculine role models. Many YOs expressed the desire to join the army, but they were not eligible because of their serious criminal records.

In contrast, however much the prison officers tried to behave like the military staff, they were still viewed with suspicion and regarded as 'screws' by the YOs, who were less friendly with them. Many YOs spoke bitterly about their treatment by prison officers in other YOIs. They said that prison officers called them 'scum' and only spoke to them to give orders. It was difficult for the Colchester prison officers to break down this negative stereotype, however pleasant and considerate they were to the YOs.

The military operated a 'zero tolerance' policy to drugs and bullying, and impressionistically this seemed to be effective. YOs commented that bullying hardly ever occurred, despite the dormitory accommodation that was conducive to it (see e.g. McGurk and McDougall, 1991). Military staff believed that the removal of possessions prevented bullying connected with trafficking in possessions. The only positive drugs tests followed temporary release or resettlement leave, town visits or college attendance. The fact that no contact was allowed during visits from family and friends prevented drugs from being passed on these occasions. There were initial worries about absconding, but in the event this never happened. Of course, it must be remembered that the YOI unit was locked at night and that armed soldiers were patrolling the grounds.

Colchester YOI did not have many of the programmes of other YOIs, such as thinking skills or offending behaviour programmes. In addition, Colchester YOI Board of Visitors (1997) thought that a drug rehabilitation project was needed and that the Probation Service should provide aftercare or supervision after release: 'Without these issues being addressed the benefits of this project may soon be forgotten and inmates may return to their former criminal activities' (p. 10).

The main aims of the Colchester YOI regime were the following:

1   To reduce reoffending.
2   To give individuals self-confidence, self-esteem, self-discipline and self-pride.
3   To teach respect for individuals, authority, property and society.
4   To impart moral values.
5   To be physically demanding.
6   To teach life, educational and work skills.

7   To encourage personal and communal responsibility and self-reliance.
8   To provide rehabilitation training.

The mission statement was as follows:

> To develop a model establishment, the aim of which is to turn YOs into better citizens and prevent their return to crime. This is to be achieved through a demanding regime of training, rehabilitation and care intended to promote self-discipline, self-confidence, self-esteem, self-motivation and self-pride.

Qualitative evaluation: A view from the boys

We collected a great deal of qualitative data on the impact of the regime on the adjustments, perceptions, attitudes and behaviour of the YOs, from their perspective, based on interviews. Specifically, we were interested in their experiences of the regime internally with regard to impulsivity and self-control, social relationships and bonds within Colchester and externally with family and friends, and changes in anti-social attitudes. These factors are likely to be associated with criminal activity. The following extracts are based on a random sample of one-third of the Colchester YOs and hence are not specially selected in any way. They are taken verbatim from interviewer reports.

Self-esteem and personal confidence

Advocates of military-style programmes propose that the emphasis on structure, discipline and exercise enhances self-esteem and self-worth and provides an increased sense of responsibility. This is certainly borne out by the views of the Colchester YOs, as the following extracts illustrate:

> 'Before I came here, I had very low self-esteem. Now I feel much better about myself. My appearance, how others might view me, is now much more important to me. For example, I used to have two earrings in my left ear. I was made to remove these and I resented this. I put them back last week to see how they looked. I didn't like what I saw. I felt stupid with them in. They didn't go with my new appearance. Don't ever want to look that way again!' He said that at Warren Hill he had no pride. He would sit in his cell all day, bored. He said he had no confidence and looked scruffy. Since he has been at Colchester, his family has said he looks better.

> He said that MCTC had changed all of the inmates. They had 'more pride and care in what they do'. In addition he thought that the experience increased self-esteem and made people more positive towards the future. 'I have also been taught to take a more positive look at my future. I have had help to write my CV. I feel I have changed physically and mentally since I came here. I am more confident and more positive. I feel all this was there before, but it took being here to bring it out. It has given me a second chance.'

Phrases such as 'I've been given a second chance' or a 'real opportunity' were mentioned frequently. Nevertheless, it is clear that it was the educational and rehabilitative aspects of the programme that had most impact on self-esteem and self-confidence. The YO goes on, thus,

> 'All my future is decided and I have Colchester to thank for that. Without the help and guidance I received here, who knows what my future would have been. I know I have learned my lesson'. He is quite surprised that he does not feel as if he is being punished by being in Colchester. He said, 'I know it's intended to be a punishment. I realise that I am separated from my family and this is a punishment. Even so, Colchester is not punishment, it's rehabilitation. It's nothing like being in prison. I feel more determined, fitter, healthier than I have ever felt before. I hope others will receive the same benefit from Colchester that I have'.

Impulsivity, self-control and anti-social attitudes

It was striking that over the course of the programme the majority of inmates perceived that they had developed more self-control and that they had become less anti-social and had more respect for authority.

The following remarks are illustrative:

> He believes that Colchester has taught him to accept the reason for authority and he is less anti-authority and establishment. Before Colchester, he said that he was very anti-authority. He particularly disliked the police and felt that many of them were 'bent'. Colchester has taught him to control his temper. When he is released, they is 'no way' he is going to sort things out with his fists. This is not the way forward. 'Fighting only lands you back in prison' he said.

> 'Being at Colchester has taught me to control my temper and I feel I have been given a second chance'.

> 'Since I have been here, I have watched others who have arrived. Initially, they are aggressive and angry. Slowly they become able to take orders and become less aggressive. It is necessary to learn to take orders. When you go to work, there is always someone who will have to give you orders. You have to accept this and accept it without showing aggression. I believe I have learned this here.'

> While at Colchester, he has attended education and carpentry classes and has kept very busy. His opinion of Colchester is that it's 'not bad'. He said he has found it a worthwhile experience and it has taught him to control his temper and taught him more discipline.

> 'Colchester regime has taught me not to lose my temper. I now think before I speak. If a member of staff shouts at me, I don't shout back. I learned quickly that I couldn't behave like that at Colchester. Now I bite my tongue more. I am more polite and can accept and act on orders given'.

While it seems that inmates had developed more pro-social, positive attitudes within Colchester, any change in attitude did not necessarily enable them to surmount the difficulties they had to deal with on release. The following extract from an inmate who reoffended illustrates this. The YO was reinterviewed in a YOI, awaiting sentence for burglary. The purpose of the follow-up interview was to ask about the circumstances which led to his reoffending. While in Colchester, he gave every indication that he did not intend to reoffend. After leaving Colchester he reoffended within two days. This is his account:

> I went home. I hoped things would be different. Nothing was different. My mother is back with 'Him', my step-father. I fucking hate him. He's a bastard. He beats her up and she takes it. She stabbed him with a knife recently and then left him. Now he is back with her. She says she loves him. I don't understand. If I ever find any girl to love me I would never treat her like that. You can't imagine what it is like in that house. So much hate. I am just in the way. My brother has left. He is doing OK, he lives with my aunt. He has a job and is not on drugs. Doesn't even smoke! I had to get out. I left the house early morning and started to walk the streets. First, I wanted some drugs to help me 'get through'. I didn't have much money. I went to a gym and stole money from a wallet (£20). I bought drugs and alcohol. Went to a friend's flat and started to take the drugs with alcohol. Got totally 'spaced out'. At some point in time, can't remember when, I started to walk the streets. I didn't want to go home. Hate that place.

He then committed three burglaries to get money for his drug habit and was picked up by the police. He continued:

> When I left Colchester I felt as if I had been thrown out. I didn't want to go. I would have liked to stay. I even thought about doing something silly so I could get extra time there. I felt safe there. Like everyone was my brother and the staff were my friends. The padre was kind to me.

He commented that he felt 'very alone' when he left Colchester and the interviewer made the following observations:

> It would seem plausible that he feels safer in prison and that he may have purposely reoffended. This would also get him away from the intolerable situation at home. According to prison staff it was his mother who gave him drugs when he was released. It is also said that she introduced him to drugs at an early age in order to 'keep him quiet'.

Interviews with staff about the impact of the regime on future offending were also realistic. Some were hopeful that the regime would have instilled a sense of self-discipline, control and respect which might deter future offending. Others commented that some YOs had little chance of going straight if they returned to the same social and economic circumstances which prevailed at the time of their offence.

Impact on social bonds and social relationships

Aspects of the programme in Colchester also seemed to have a positive impact on improving social bonds and relationships within the institution and externally with inmates' families. The following extracts illustrates some of the inmates view:

> He said that he liked working in a team ('that's what the army is all about'), stating that he has become very close to the other inmates and predicted that he would keep in contact with them after release.

> Possibly the most important thing he has learned at Colchester is to communicate. He feels he will do better at job interviews as a result. He now knows that he can always find someone to help him if he needs it. He has also made a friend in Colchester. They intend to get a flat together when they leave. They believe that together they can support each other and keep away from those who influenced them before.

> He said that he has learned to relax and can have a laugh with the staff. There are some staff who he intends to keep in touch with on release.

> He said that the staff in MCTC were 'quite good and more like friends' that he could discuss personal issues with. He stated that this is very different to prison 'where the screws won't talk to you at all, where it's all one-way conversations. You can't talk to them in prison'. He claimed to get on well with the other YOs, who he felt were very similar to him, 'we all talk the same and understand each other.'

The experience of Colchester also seemed to improve relationships with family members. This appeared to be due to improved optimism concerning employment opportunities and perceived change in attitudes and behaviour. Thus according to one inmate:

> 'My parents are very pleased with my progress in Colchester. Even more than this, since I have been here, I have become closer to my grandfather. He has been in the army and knows Colchester. He runs an engineering firm. When he discovered I was doing the engineering course at Colchester, he was very pleased. He intends that, when I have my college course completed, I will go to work in his firm. He hopes I will eventually run it for him. This has brought us closer together and I am very pleased.

Another YO said;

> I do not intend to get into trouble with the law again. I used to go round in a gang and pick fights. My mother was very upset with me. She couldn't sleep at night knowing I was misbehaving. I love her but she couldn't make me stay at home. I don't ever intend to put her through all that worry again. Both my attitude and my behaviour has changed since I came to Colchester. I can now think straight. Being away from home has been very distressing. I remember how I used to behave and I am ashamed. Colchester has calmed me down a great deal.

I am less anti-everything. I look better and I am fitter. When my mother visits me, she says how well I look. She also tells me I don't shake anymore. I was not aware that I did. My mother is very pleased with the changes she has noticed in me. If she is pleased, so am I. When I leave here, I have a job to go to. My brother works in a shop in London and he has got me the job. I am looking forward to going to work; I will be a useful person. It will be a new start for me.

Similarly:

He felt that he has been 'learning how to work for things' and that this lesson will stay with him in the future. He now has better control of his anger and is 'generally grown-up.' All the changes that the regime invoked in him were 'for the better'. He said that he had previously 'been very rude and got on people's nerves.' He stated that 'my mum is proud of me and I'm proud of myself'.

It was apparent that there was family support for the Colchester programme. The majority of inmates said that parents and girlfriends approved of them being placed at Colchester. The following comments from three YOs are typical of many others:

'My mum always said I needed discipline and I've certainly had it in here.'

'They think it's much better than prison even though it takes longer to get here to visit.'

'They're proud of me being here but they take the rise a bit. Finishing letters with "left right, left right" '.

Positive aspects of the physical environment combined with positive relationships with staff appeared to enhance the impact of the therapeutic, educational programme. Offenders described Colchester as providing a cleaner, safer, drug-free environment and expressed relief at not being 'banged up 23 hours a day'. Many YOs said that prison atmosphere encouraged laziness, boredom and depression. They said that in prison other offenders spent much time boasting about their offences and trying to compete as to who could be hardest. In Colchester no one mentioned their offences. They trusted each other and there was no bullying because 'the military wouldn't stand for it'.

When asked whether the militaristic or educational training was more important, the majority of YOs thought that both the physical and rehabilitative aspects of the programme were important. For many offenders the military training had been the most fulfilling but improved education skills was mentioned by all. One offender said that for the first time in his life he had learned his 'times tables' and was able to do basic maths. They had all improved their letter writing skills. All mentioned, with pride, their ability to complete curriculum vitae which they had never heard of before. They all felt that they had improved their job prospects.

Many inmates said they did not actually like 'drill' but could see the point of it because everyone in the camp marched. In addition, many comments indicated that 'drill' instilled team spirit, self-confidence and a sense of achievement. Almost all commented positively on the fairness of the regime:

> He believes that the incentive and discipline scheme at Colchester is 'very fair and necessary. It is neither harsh nor soft. It's just right. It is necessary for YOs to recognise that once they work with the system, staff relate better to them and everything goes smoothly. It's the same as being at work. If the boss says "do this", you do it. Colchester is getting you ready for that'.

Likewise, with other household/hygiene chores, positive views were expressed:

> I know it sounds silly and everyone laughs about all the things we are made to do here: ironing, washing, cleaning, marching, P.E., etc., but all these things help. They are life skills, needed for our own survival. They teach you, at Colchester, to care for yourself and this experience is invaluable.

YOs also expressed gratitude at 'being kept busy' and not being 'banged up 23 hours a day'. On the contrary, 'you pray for bang-up here'.

YOs emphasized the attitude of and relationships with staff as being the main difference between Colchester and other YOIs. All said that they were treated as adults and were given respect by staff. Indeed, it was clear that relationships between staff and inmates were based on mutual respect and trust. Staff 'take a genuine interest in our care'. The staff at Colchester received great praise from all the inmates:

> 'They're great', one said. 'They help and advise wherever possible. In the evenings they come round to the rooms and we all sit and chat. They are like good acquaintances. We have constructive discussions. It's all very relaxed and natural. They do, of course, lay the law down when necessary. It's all part of their job'.

> Staff in prisons do not communicate with the prisoners, except to give orders. They certainly do not come to your cell and chat. To be fair to them, the inmates would not encourage this. If a prison officer was seen chatting to an inmate in his cell, it would look suspicious to other inmates. They might even give the inmate a bad time. It has to be a 'them and us' relationship. Whilst I was in Chelmsford, I did not speak personally to one prison officer.

> The staff are fine. They give us respect. We return it. That's the way it should be.

> Colchester staff are completely different to ordinary prison staff. They communicate with the inmates. It's an everyday occurrence to have conversations with staff. We have a laugh with them and they are always fair.

Negative aspects of Colchester

The most frequently cited negative features of the regime were the drill, rashes under arms caused by uniform fabric and lack of contact by telephone and visits. This is summed up by the following comments:

> No contact visits. I find these very difficult. I miss physical contact. When my girlfriend visits, I want to hold her hand. We are not permitted to do this because of the barrier. Visits are restricted here. Only every two weeks. If I was still at Onley, I would get four, every twenty-eight days. Phone calls are also restricted to one 10-minute call per week.

Another inmate echoed this disadvantage plus the early start to the day, which was also cited by others as a drawback, in comparison to other YOIs:

> In comparing the two regimes, he said that he had less money in MCTC than in normal prison as MCTC forbids detainees to spend their personal savings. This means that he cannot afford the toiletries and cigarettes that he wants. He stated that this 'is bad because I need fags when I get the hump'. A further disadvantage that he cited is the no contact in visits. He said that 'if I knew that I wouldn't have come'. He also disliked having to get up at 6.00 a.m. and having only 10 minutes phone time per week. He did not like 'not being able to disagree with people'.

Positive features of Colchester

The most frequently cited positive features were:

- self-confidence, independence;
- discipline;
- physical fitness;
- hygiene;
- healthier;
- improved education/vocational skills;
- teamwork;
- increased personal safety;
- positive relationships with staff.

When asked whether transference of the regime at Colchester to a prison setting would produce the same effects, all YOs said definitely not. YOs considered that what Colchester achieved was not simply a product of better facilities or more staff. It was the attitude of staff that mattered. Furthermore, the general view was that the physical and educational aspects of the Colchester programme would not work in prison without the type of military and prison personnel who would take an interest in each offender. It was also apparent that the inmates preferred military staff to prison officers who they still viewed as 'screws'.

Evaluating the MCTC Regime

YOs were eligible for allocation to Colchester YOI if they:

1   were male, aged 18–21;
2   had four to eight months to serve;
3   were suitable for open conditions;
4   were able, mentally and physically, to cope with the regime;
5   were considered likely to benefit from the regime.

Conditions 2 and 3 were inherently incompatible, leading to similar case flow problems to those experienced in Thorn Cross. In practice, allocation units in a number of YOIs were asked to identify possibly eligible YOs using a simple screening test (male, aged 18–21, four to eight months to serve, no current serious sexual offence, e.g. rape). Colchester YOI staff then visited these institutions to sift prison records to try to find YOs who met the criteria and to interview eligible candidates.

Regarding suitability for open conditions, the primary consideration was the risk to the public. Therefore, any YO who was likely to be dangerous if he absconded, based on available evidence, was not selected. Ideally, the military staff wanted YOs with no prior custodial experience. However, very few YOs who were allocated to Colchester were totally suitable for open conditions; the algorithm for selection to open conditions was often over-ridden, taking careful account of particular features of each individual case. Unfortunately, selection teams did not keep records of why they rejected YOs.

Ideally, YOs should have been allocated to Colchester soon after sentence. If a YO had already been in custody for some time and had conformed and progressed through a YOI incentive scheme, he would be dropping down to a more austere regime with fewer privileges if he were then transferred to Colchester. However, delays in the selection process meant that the typical experimental YO was serving a sentence of 18 months, had served three months in some other YOI and then served six months in Colchester. YOs serving sentences up to four years were considered eligible.

The aim was to have an intake of eight to 12 YOs every six weeks. Ideally, it was planned that 16 to 24 eligible YOs would be identified every six weeks and randomly allocated to experimental or control conditions. Efforts were made to assign YOs at random to experimental and control conditions for the first three intakes, but exceptions had to be made (e.g. to allow a YO to complete an educational course). For later intakes, the main criteria for allocating suitable YOs to experimental or control conditions were the distance of Colchester from the YO's home (because of visiting problems) and the need to allow YOs to complete educational courses that they had started (which meant that they were allocated to the control group).

There were great problems in identifying a sufficient number of suitable YOs. More suitable YOs were identified for intakes 6 and 7 because of the involvement of a senior research officer who assisted in the selection process, spending more time searching records in YOIs for potentially suitable candidates. Previous selection teams had given more priority to identifying experimental YOs than to identifying a sufficient number of eligible (experimental and control) YOs. The most efficient selection process was for intake 8 (34 eligible YOs were identified), which was then cancelled because of the closure of Colchester YOI.

Four experimental YOs refused to go to Colchester because they had been given misleading information in their YOI about the regime. Prison officers in some YOIs would tell YOs that, in Colchester, they would be cutting the colonel's lawn with nail scissors, painting coal white, polishing dustbins until they shone, or scrubbing floors all day. Efforts were made to dispel these false impressions by producing a folder with coloured photographs of Colchester YOI and a detailed prospectus of the training programme. This worked well but it mysteriously disappeared for long periods (possibly hidden by prison officers who were hostile to Colchester). Proposals were also made to take Colchester YOs as ambassadors on selection visits to other YOIs, but Colchester prison officers were reluctant to do this.

Two control YOs refused to be in the control group because they were suspicious that they might subsequently be allocated to Colchester. Only five experimental YOs did not complete the programme; two for bullying or assault, one for drug dealing, one for assault and drug use, and one for absconding on a town visit.

Analysis of reconvictions

The reconviction analysis was based on 66 experimental and 103 control YOs. The controls included 34 YOs who were screened as suitable for the planned intake of eight in January 1998 which was cancelled in the light of the closure decision on 22 January 1998. Of the 72 YOs originally allocated to the experimental condition, six did not go to Colchester because of outstanding charges or refusal. They were transferred to the control group. One YO was originally allocated to the control group but later went to Colchester, and he was counted as an experimental YO.

Previously, we analysed reconvictions in the first two years after release (Farrington *et al.*, 2002). We are now able to analyse reconvictions in the first four years after release. The Police National Computer was searched in June 2003 for reconvictions. In light of the delay of about two months between the occurrence of a conviction and its recording in the PNC, it is likely that reconvictions occurring up to April 2003 would be recorded. The present analysis is based on dates of offences, not dates of convictions. In light of the average delay of about four months between an offence and a conviction, it is likely that this analysis includes nearly all offences committed up to December 2002. The YOs' release dates ranged from 26 June 1997 to 16 September 1998, with a median of 1 April 1998. Therefore, all of the YOs had been at risk of reconviction for at least four years.

Reconviction prediction scores were calculated based on 13 variables: number of previous convictions, number of previous imprisonments, age at sentence, age at first sentence, sentence length, current offence type: violence, burglary, robbery, theft, fraud, criminal damage, drugs or others. Four scores were developed, predicting (1) percentage reconvicted in two years, (2) percentage reconvicted in four years, (3) number of offences leading to reconviction in two years, and (4) number of offences leading to reconviction in four years. The first and second scores were derived from logistic regressions and the third and fourth from ordinary least-squares multiple regressions, investigating the best predictors of reconvictions in the total sample of 166 experimental and control YOs who were found in the criminal records.

Table 9.1 shows that the predicted and actual percentages reconvicted after two years were very similar for both experimental and control YOs (49% predicted versus 50% actual for experimental YOs; 60% predicted versus 59% actual for control YOs). The same was true at the four-year follow-up, but the experimental YOs tended to be doing slightly worse than expected (66% predicted versus 70% actual for experimental YOs; 73% predicted versus 71% actual for control YOs). Logistic regression analyses showed that in neither case did experimental versus control condition influence the probability of reconviction after controlling for the prediction score.

Table 9.2 shows that the predicted and actual numbers of standard list offences leading to convictions after two years were very similar for both experimental and control YOs (1.8 predicted versus 1.6 actual for experimental YOs; 2.2 predicted versus 2.3 actual for control YOs). The same was true at the four-year follow-up (3.7 predicted versus 3.5 actual for experimental YOs; 4.6 predicted versus 4.8 actual for control YOs). On this measure, the experimental YOs were doing slightly better than expected.

Table 9.1   Predicted versus actual percent reconvicted

Follow-up period	Mean pred. score	Percent reconv.	Mean pred. score	Percent reconv.
Two years	48.7	50.0	59.7	58.8
Four years	65.8	70.3	73.3	70.6

Notes: Experimentals ($N = 64$); Controls ($N = 102$).

Table 9.2   Predicted versus actual number of offences

Follow-up period	Mean pred. score	Actual no. of offences	Mean pred. score	Actual no. of offences
Two years	1.8	1.6	2.2	2.3
Four years	3.7	3.5	4.6	4.8

Notes: Experimentals ($N = 64$); Control ($N = 102$).

However, multiple regressions showed that in neither case did experimental versus control condition influence the number of offences after controlling for the prediction score. Hence, Colchester YOI seemed to have no effect on reconvictions.

Conclusions

Why was the HIT regime more successful than Colchester YOI in reducing reoffending? In attempting to answer this question, it is important to focus on differences between the two regimes. The regimes were similar in many ways: in having austere conditions, a very disciplined approach, army-style drilling and physical training, vigorous and demanding physical activities, an emphasis on cleanliness and orderliness, attempts to inculcate team spirit and increase pride and self-confidence, basic education, trade training and outward bound courses.

There were two fundamental differences, however, between the regimes. First, the HIT centre focussed a great deal on offending behaviour programmes based on the 'What works' literature, and in particular on enhanced thinking skills. There is much empirical evidence (e.g. McGuire, 1995) suggesting that these programmes can be effective in reducing recidivism. Colchester YOI had no comparable programmes.

Second, the HIT centre put a great deal of effort into finding jobs or placements for experimental YOs and supervising them (using community mentors as well as personal officers) in their work activities in the last five weeks of their sentences. This should have helped YOs greatly in their transition from the YOI to the community. Many years ago, Margaret Shaw (1974) found that having prison welfare officers help inmates towards the end of their sentences with accommodation and employment problems after release led to a decrease in reconviction, and more recently Doris MacKenzie and her colleagues (2001) discovered that boot camps were only effective if they had aftercare resources. Colchester YOI Board of Visitors (1997) thought that the Probation Service should provide aftercare or supervision after release: 'Without these issues being addressed the benefits of this project may soon be forgotten and inmates may return to their former criminal activities' (p. 10).

In Colchester, many YOs liked being kept busy all day, liked an army-style regime and wearing army uniforms, liked sports and physical training, and became healthier, fitter and more self-confident. They also liked being treated with respect by the staff and enjoyed receiving paternalistic advice from masculine role models. However, these perceived benefits of the regime were not followed by decreased reconviction rates. Purely from the viewpoint of reducing offending, it seems likely that cognitive-behavioural skills training programmes and assistance in the transition from the YOI to the community (as provided in the HIT programme) were more important. Hence, this evaluation confirms that a military-style regime, without any offending behaviour or aftercare programmes, does not reduce recidivism.

Notes

1. These activities depended on the stage a YO was in. YOs in stage one could be in basic education or drilling, YOs in stage two could be in trade training, while YOs in stage three could be out at the MCTC farm or away from the site on community and conservation projects.
2. As in 1.

Chapter 10

Psychological Research into Life Sentence Offenders

David A. Crighton and Jo Bailey

Introduction

In recent years there has been a steady growth in the use of indeterminate prison sentences. This has been paralleled by growth in research in the use of life sentences. In this chapter the nature of indeterminate sentences in England and Wales and the key research available to date are outlined.

It is relatively common practice to use the term 'lifers' when referring to this group of offenders. While recognising that such jargon can be seen as questionable, the term is used here as an abbreviation for all those subject to life sentences. As such it covers both those life sentence offenders in prison custody and those in the community on life licence, whether or not under active supervision.

Definitional Issues

Prior to the twentieth century, capital punishment was used extensively in the UK for a wide range of crimes ranging from relatively minor thefts, through to murder (McCord, 1991). The nineteenth and early twentieth centuries saw the decreasing use of capital punishment as the primary means of managing crime. An example of this is the Infanticide Acts of 1938 and 1949 which were introduced primarily to end the practice of executing women suffering from what would now be recognised as post-natal depression, who had killed their infants.

The 1957 Homicide Act marked something of a sea change introducing categories of homicide for which the death penalty would be retained, while the mandatory life sentence was put in place for other categories. In England and Wales the death penalty for murder was suspended in 1965 and formally abolished in 1970. Throughout recent history though it had been relatively common for those sentenced to death to be reprieved, so that a system of detaining and managing life sentence prisoners had developed. The notion that such offenders would generally be released on licence was also established (Prison Reform Trust, 1993).

Slightly different provisions have been put in place for children (10–17 years) and young people (18–21 years). Children convicted of a murder committed when they were between the age of 10 and 17 are subject to the somewhat perversely named sentence of 'Detention at Her Majesty's Pleasure', following the abolition of the death penalty for children in 1933. Young people (aged 18–21) were until 2000 subject to the sentence of 'Custody for Life', when this sentence was effectively replaced by a similar sentence and procedures to those in place for adults.

Trial judges have, since at least 1861, been able to impose life sentences for a number of serious offences, where the judge feels that indeterminate imprisonment is warranted. Such sentences should only be imposed in exceptional circumstances primarily as a means of protecting the public from very 'high-risk' offenders (Cullen and Newell, 1999).

Current procedures for the release of life sentence prisoners are broadly founded on the Criminal Justice Act 1967, which created the Parole Board as an independent body to oversee arrangements for the release on licence of such offenders. The Parole Board also became the advisory body to assist the Secretary of State for the Home Office in exercising their discretion to release prisoners on licence. Recent legislative changes following from the impact of the European Convention on Human Rights have increased the role of quasi-judicial panels formed by the Parole Board, and decreased the role of elected politicians in deciding on release (Home Office, 2004).

Key Findings

Empirical findings

On 30 June 2000, there were 4,540 prisoners serving life sentences. The number of prisoners received into custody for life in 2000 was 492. This is a continuation of the increase in receptions since 1995, when there were 280. In June 1999, there were 4,206 prisoners serving life sentences, three-quarters of whom were serving a sentence for murder. Of these 96% were men. The number of life sentence prisoners first released on life licence rose from 85 in 1996 to over 120 in 1999. The average time served by these life sentence prisoners before being released on licence in 2000 was slightly more than 13 years. It is of course noted that such figures are based on an underestimate of the actual average time served in custody for lifers. There has not been much change in the average time served by lifers over the past decade: in 1990 the average time served was also 13 years (Bailey, 2006).

In 2000, there were around 26 men serving a life sentence for every woman serving a life sentence. This ratio approximates to the ratio of men to women in the general prison population (Home Office, 1997; Hudson, 2002). However, as Table 10.3 shows, the percentage increase over the last 10 years of women serving life is greater than the percentage increase of men serving life. This high rate of increase reflects the high rate of increase in the numbers of women serving sentences for other violent offences. However, what is not clear from published data (Home Office, 1997) is whether this reflects primarily a greater increase in the rate of receptions for women than for men, or a greater increase in the average time served by women compared with men.

Research into life sentence prisoners has looked at a range of factors. These have included studies looking at the socio-demographic characteristics of those subject to life sentences, through to supervision in the community and recall of those released on life licence (Tables 10.1 and 10.2).

Progress of Life Sentence Offenders Through the Prison System

In general, life sentence offenders are held in prison alongside, and sharing facilities with determinate sentence prisoners. This is the case for all women lifers, although for men serving life sentences there is an expectation that they will go through certain 'stages' of prison custody. They are always detained alongside determinate sentence prisoners. Men serving life sentences would normally spend a period in a 'local prison' immediately following conviction, awaiting allocation to a 'main centre'. They would then spend a phase in a 'main centre' (one of a small number of prisons nationally where all male life sentence prisoners formally begin their life sentence, and where their life sentence plan (LSP) is drafted) of approximately three years. At this stage a lifer is transferred either to a Category B training prison or to a dispersal prison[1] if they have been categorised as a Category A prisoner. Category A prisoners remain in dispersal prisons until their 'security risk'[2] is recategorised to Category B, at which point they should be transferred to a Category B training prison. Here it is expected that lifers will address those things felt to have led to their offence. Following this they should be transferred to a Category C (low security) training prison, not generally more than two years before the first formal review of their case by the Parole Board. Following a successful review they would then be transferred to a Category D (open) prison for two years and then, following another review, released.

For a woman serving a life sentence the 'system' is markedly different. As with men, following conviction women will generally be held in a local prison awaiting allocation to a 'first-stage prison', the female equivalent of 'main centres'. Women are allocated to one of the two such prisons, of which there

Table 10.1 Serious violent offences committed while on licence (Coker and Martin, 1985, p. 98) (Reproduced with permission)

	Offence	Penalty
Case 1	Buggery with a boy	5 years prison
Case 2	Buggery with a boy	3 years prison
Case 3	Assaulting a woman	6 months prison
Case 4	Fighting outside a pub	1 month prison
Same man (4)	Robbery	5 years prison
Case 5	Unlawful sexual intercourse	2.5 years prison
Case 6	Unlawful entry and threat with a gun	3 years prison
Case 7	Unlawful wounding	10 days prison
Case 8	Assault on wife	Recalled before criminal proceedings initiated
Case 9	Manslaughter	Life
Case 10	Manslaughter of mistress	Life
Case 11	Knife threat to wife	Recalled before criminal proceedings initiated
Case 12	Assault on wife	3 months prison
Case 13	Assault on wife	3 months prison
Case 14	Wounding woman with hammer	3 months prison
Case 15	Assault	3 months prison

Table 10.2 Serious non-violent offences committed while on licence (Coker and Martin, 1985, p. 99) (Reproduced with permission)

	Offence	Penalty
Case 1	Stealing cigarettes	12 months prison
Case 2	Indecent assault on a boy	9 months prison
Case 3	Housebreaking	2 years prison
Case 4	Storebreaking	18 months prison (suspended)
Case 5	Burglary	6 months prison
Case 6	Burglary/theft	6 months prison
Case 7	Theft	18 months prison
Case 8	Burglary	18 months prison
Case 9	False Pretences	6 months prison
Case 10		14 days. This man had eight further convictions after release

Table 10.3 Population serving life sentences in prison custody in England and Wales (Home Office, 1997)

	Men serving life			Women serving life			Ratio of men to women serving life in 1997
	1987	1997	% increase 1987–97	1987	1997	% increase 1987–97	
Young offenders	106	100	−0.5	8	9	12	8:1
Adults	2,159	3,484	60	66	128	94	37:1
Total	2,265	3,584	60	74	137	85	26:1

is currently one in the north of England and one in the south. Following a period in one of the first-stage prisons they would generally be transferred to one of four 'second-stage' prisons. Following a successful formal review of her case she would then be transferred to one of the three open prisons which hold women lifers (Home Office, 1995).

This process was formally set out by the Prison Service in 1993 when it introduced the LSP. It has been noted that this aimed to replace existing 'career plans' with a more structured and extensive planning process for life sentence prisoners (Cullen and Newell, 1999).

Lifers have been one group for which structured risk-assessment and risk-management work had been undertaken for some time within prisons, for the simple reason that their release was largely determined by the risk of grave reoffending that they were considered to represent. Risk assessments and reported evidence of risk reduction were therefore central to the process of managing life sentence prisoners in custody and through to release.

The life sentence plan

The LSP runs from remand to release and is also used in cases in which life sentence offenders are recalled to prison. The document is sectional in nature and different sections are opened at various stages of the life sentence prisoner's time in custody.

The LSP begins with an analysis of the index offence and other offences and a summary of 'risk factors' derived from these, with input from various assessment systems. The aim is for an integrated planning system that links to clearly defined targets and progress reviews in which staff can report in detail on contact with the life sentence prisoner. As such individuals should have in place a detailed programme of work made up of a series of specific interventions aimed at addressing a range of areas such as basic education, employment skills, drug abuse, alcohol abuse, mental health, physical health, accommodation issues and individual- and group-based work addressing aspects of their criminal behaviour (Brady and Crighton, 2003). A record of accomplishments is completed, which provides chronological information that the Parole Board and ministers can draw on in making decisions about release. The LSP system was being actively revised in the late 1990s.

In structuring thinking about 'risk', the LSP is designed to consider risk of harm to others (a known adult(s), children, staff, prisoners), risk of harm to self (lifers are at significantly increased risk of suicide (Crighton, 2000)), risk from others because of vulnerability and risk of escape or absconding.

The research undertaken for the Inspectorates review suggested that staff working with life sentence prisoners had come to view the LSP as nothing more than a 'bureaucratic necessity' with 'little relevance to their management of the lifer'. They noted that staff used and valued the F75 reporting[3] procedure much more than they valued the LSP (HM Chief Inspector of Prisons and Inspector of Probation, 1999).

Review of mandatory life sentenced offenders by the Parole Board

The date of the first review by the Parole Board (formal review) of a mandatory lifer takes place three years prior to the expiry of their 'tariff'.[4] This is the first occasion when the lifer can be considered for a transfer to open conditions. If the individual's tariff is equal to, or less than, three years, the first formal review takes place as soon as the arrangements can be made after sentencing (Home Office, 1995). Progress is then reviewed formally by the Parole Board at regular intervals (usually once every two years) until they are released into the community. The second formal review should take place on or near the date of expiry of the life sentence prisoner's tariff. This is the first occasion they can be considered for release on licence. A recommendation for release is, in the vast majority of cases, only actually given to a prisoner who has already served two years in open prison conditions, that is a prisoner who has already had at least one formal review of their case (Home Office, 1995).

For each formal review, staff at the prison and the community probation officer responsible for supervision, should the lifer be released, prepare reports. In 1995 reports were required from a prison manager (usually the 'lifer liaison officer'[5]); a prison officer; a prison-based probation officer; a community-based probation officer; medical practitioner[6] and prison chaplain. Reports could also be submitted by specialist staff with 'special knowledge' of the prisoner, for example, psychologists, psychiatrists, nurses,[7] education, PE and employment training staff (Home Office, 1995).

The Criminal Justice Act 2003 introduced a number of changes to the working of the Parole Board (Home Office, 2004). These have included a streamlining of processes, particularly in relation to preliminary decision making about hearings. The Stafford Judgement of 2002 is also likely to mean an increase in the number of oral hearings, since the continued detention of mandatory lifers beyond their tariff period will require an oral hearing. The Parole Board's work is also likely to become more focussed on those prisoners who constitute the greatest risk to the public. As such, considerable efforts have been made to improve approaches to assessing risk more effectively. There have also been efforts to improve the balance of specialist input available as Parole Board members, in particular with efforts to increase numbers of psychologists and psychiatrists (Home Office, 2004).

Research into the Parole Board has highlighted a number of significant findings. A review of 60 mandatory lifers released for the first time in 1995 reported that only 13% were released on or within one month of tariff expiry, and 43% were released over two years after their tariff expiry (Stone, 1997). Even these figures are likely to present a skewed picture, given that it does not include those prisoners who do not make significant progress towards release. These figures represent the situation for all women and men serving life sentences. Given the high ratio of men to women serving life sentences, the figures probably closely approximate to the figures for men. Similar calculations broken down for women and for men are unfortunately not published by the Parole Board, due presumably to the small numbers of women. Hence it is not clear from the research whether women also tend to be released some years after the expiry of their tariff.

In the late 1990s research by Stone (1997) and Cullen and Newell (1999) reported that mandatory life sentence prisoners when compared with discretionary life sentence prisoners remained at a disadvantage when it comes to their review and release. For example, mandatory lifers only received their 'Parole Board answer' some months after the Home Secretary has considered the case. Discretionary lifers received the answer from the Discretionary Lifer Panel (DLP) within seven days of the panel sitting.

Historically, mandatory and discretionary lifers were treated differently. Recent legal changes though, put in place to achieve compliance with European and Human Rights law, have had the effect of bringing the treatment of mandatory prisoners in line with the systems for discretionary prisoners.

Reviewing discretionary lifers

Under Section 34 of the Criminal Justice Act 1991, a review system was set up for discretionary lifers that was quite different from that for mandatory life sentence prisoners. The Parole Board has sole responsibility for directing release and the Home Secretary was not involved in the decision.

Release from custody

Until the introduction of the DLP in 1992, all life sentence prisoners had been dealt with in a similar manner. Since that time and until the Stafford Judgement, the Home Secretary retained the right to decide on the release of mandatory lifers. Until 1983, the Home Secretary also decided on the release or otherwise parole of mentally abnormal offenders. This power was transferred to mental health review tribunals (MHRT) by the Mental Health Act 1983. In many respects the oral hearings established by the Parole Board are similar to the tribunals established under the Mental Health Act.

A study of decision making at oral hearings has been reported (Hood and Shute, unpublished).[8] The study observed through 1992–4 a number of Parole Board panels reviewing life sentence cases. They examined 122 cases, 63 of which were pre-tariff with positive recommendations from the panel. Of these, 54 could hope for release very close to tariff expiry if the Home Secretary accepted the Parole Board recommendation. A minority (9) could not realistically have achieved release within a year of tariff expiry. Another 22 were three years or more past tariff expiry. The researchers concluded that if this was representative, then a majority of lifers could expect to be released at or near tariff.

Licence and recall

A system for release on licence and recall of life sentence offenders existed before the introduction of the Murder Act, with the Home Secretary's power to release lifers and recall them first given statutory form in the Criminal Justice Act 1948. This in part derived from the belief that life sentence prisoners should generally be released on licence after serving a finite time in prison (Machin et al., 1999).

The relationship between those released on life licence and the supervising officer was initially unclear. As a result, the National Probation Service (NPS) has developed and implemented national standards in this area of work. Initial standards were set out in National Standards for the Supervision of Offenders in the Community (Home Office, 1995).

The Probation Service has throughout its history had a complex role to perform, mixing elements of legal control, with elements of social care and support. During the 1990s and after there was a marked shift in the policy approach of the Probation Service. This resulted in it moving away from its traditional base in social work, with a key role of providing social support, towards a model of law enforcement (Shaw, 1996; Mantle and Moore, 2004).

The tension between these roles is especially marked when supervising life sentence offenders, where supervising officers must manage a marked 'control/treatment' dichotomy. Although the views of offenders will be taken into consideration regarding their wishes for issues such as employment and housing, ultimate decision making about their aftercare is necessarily dictated by the terms of their licence and enforced by the supervising officer. The range of problems facing ex-offenders in general though have been well documented and go beyond simple enforcement models. They may relate to a range of social-care problems including finding appropriate accommodation, employment, financial problems and lack of familial and social supports. In turn they are regarded as crucial in contributing to significantly reducing the risk of further offending (McNeill *et al.*, 2005).

Preparation for release

Thorough preparation for release is particularly important for lifers. They will generally have spent longer in prison than determinate sentence prisoners and as a result of this may have more problems adjusting to life in the community. They may also have restricted opportunities in terms of social support, employment and housing in the community as a result of the nature and seriousness of the original offence.

On release, the difficulties facing ex-prisoners are often exacerbated for lifers due to their length of imprisonment, potential loss of family or social network, and potential loss of job skills (Mitchell, 1989). In a detailed study of lifers under supervision in the community it was found that, on the whole, lifers chose not to talk about such difficulties with their supervising officers because of mistrust in the system and concerns about the results of such disclosures. Despite this, however, probation staff interviewed by the same researchers saw the power to recall as a vital sanction (Coker and Martin, 1985).

On release from open conditions, lifers are subject to supervision by the NPS on life licence. Under the terms of the Victims Charter (Home Office, 1990), victims or their surviving relatives are required to be consulted about the conditions of the licence and many life licences contain a condition preventing offenders from going to particular areas or approaching victims or their families.

When release seems likely, the holding prison requests the chief officer of the receiving probation area to appoint a supervising officer. This officer may be the existing home area officer who is already fully acquainted with the case and has dealt with the pre-release phase of the life sentence. The prison must send a pre-release report containing full information about the life sentence prisoner and their progress in relation to the LSP, along with a copy of the risk assessment, to assist in appointing and supporting a supervising probation officer. In parallel, the police (the National Identification Bureau (NIB) and the relevant chief constable) will be informed of the address the lifer intends to reside at. The supervising officer, via the chief officer, should report any changes of address to the NIB/chief constable. For lifers convicted of offences against children or persons under the age of 18, the procedures specified in IG 54/1994 and PC 73/1994[9] should be followed to alert social services to consider appropriate steps to safeguard any children or young persons who may be at risk. Notification should take place at least six weeks before release.

Additional conditions can be added to these standard licence conditions. Typically these might relate to continuation of medical treatment, specific employment restrictions or residence restrictions. The conditions must be enforceable; hence apparently attractive conditions such as abstinence from alcohol are avoided as being impossible to police effectively (Coker and Martin, 1985). Unfortunately there has been no good-quality published research on licence conditions to date although it has been argued that in most cases Parole Board panels impose the standard licence conditions with a few other requirements added (Padfield, 2002). The difficulties in enforcing certain conditions and also how conditions such as avoiding certain geographical areas infringe the licencee's liberty have also been noted, although little discussion of the rights of the victim or their family and friends seems to have occurred (Padfield, 2002). The Parole Board has no power to provide an unconditional licence. It has been convincingly argued that there is a clear need for further research into licence conditions, in particular what conditions are being set and to what extent these can be met by the offender, and also enforced by the supervising staff (Hood and Shute, 2000).

Supervision on licence

Supervising probation officers are required to submit reports on the lifer's progress to lifer unit[10] (Stone, 1997). The reports influence modification of the licence, either adding or taking away conditions over time. The licence applies for the remainder of the offender's life, although the conditions are likely to change with time and the level of supervision is generally reduced and in most cases ultimately suspended. Research suggests that five years after release 75% of those on life licence were no longer under any supervision (Coker and Martin, 1985).

Supervising officers are required to submit specific reports where they lose contact with the lifer. They also need to report when the lifer breaches licence conditions, the safety of the public appears to be at risk, the licencee is charged with any offence or there are any significant changes to the lifer's personal relationships (Coker and Martin, 1985).

In order to fulfil this role, the supervising officer should be an experienced practitioner who should be able to cope with the pressures and anxieties which working with life sentence prisoners can generate. On 31 December 1995, 700 life sentence offenders under licence (provisional figures) were supervised by the Probation Service representing a steady increase from 430 in 1984 (Stone, 1997).

Levels of supervision should be consistent with the National Standards for Supervision Before and After Release from Custody (Home Office, 1995) and should include contact with the offender at the relevant probation office and also at their home. The lifer manual also specifies the frequency and nature of supervision contacts as initially being at least weekly for the first four weeks, with a visit to the home address within the first 10 working days. Thereafter contact is fortnightly for the next two months and from then not less than monthly. Significant changes in the release supervision plan need to be agreed with a probation officer of at least assistant chief officer grade, prior to implementation (HM Prison Service, 2004a).

Guidelines indicate that a life sentence offender can have their supervision suspended following a period of satisfactory progress. This is a minimum of four years, with each case being considered on its own merits. The decision to suspend supervision lies with the Home Office and not with the NPS. Licence conditions can also be re-imposed. Any incident that comes to the notice of the Probation Service that gives rise for concern should be immediately notified to PLRG. PLRG will also contact the Probation Service about cases that come to their notice, normally from police information or further conviction.

The Experience of Life on Licence

Authority is at the core of the relationship between the licencee and the supervising officer. Probation supervisors have also shown remarkable variation in their approach to this area of practice (Coker and Martin, 1985).

The role of the supervising officer is worthy of more detailed consideration. Research has suggested that in terms of public protection they are 'the key figure' due to their particular knowledge of the offender and events relating to concern (Coker and Martin, 1985).

Recall

The executive power to recall life licencees is invested in the Secretary of State who may act on the recommendation of the Parole Board or on their own initiative. This power has been responsible for much of the criticism of recall decisions. Another concern has related to the dual role of the Parole Board who:

> will be fulfilling a dual function of recommending the initial recall and then reviewing their own decision.
>
> (Creighton and King, 1996)

The revocation of life licence applies in the same way for each category of life sentence prisoner/licencee, although there is a procedural difference when representations are heard (Stone, 1997).

Between October 1992 and October 1998, the Parole Board conducted 1,091 DLPs. Release was directed following 186 hearings (17%), 69 of these offenders had been in closed prison conditions when they were released. Of those released, 52 (28%) had been recalled to prison at the time of the study. This compared with a rate of 10% recall for those discretionary lifers who were released and recalled under the previous system (Cullen and Newell, 1999).

One reason suggested for the high rates of recall among discretionary lifers released following DLPs (particularly those who are released from closed conditions) is the loss of a period in open prison conditions, felt to be of value in 'testing' the life sentence offender and aiding the lifer's reintegration into society (Bailey, 1996).

In deciding whether to recommend the recall of a mandatory lifer released on life licence, the Parole Board should consider issues if there is risk, failures to co-operate with the supervising office and future compliance with supervision. Before deciding to recall a life sentence offender released on licence, the Parole Board must take into account the supervising officer's recommendation as to whether the licencee should remain on licence and take into account all of the papers submitted to it.

Reasons for recall

In the past, probation officers have found little guidance from instructions regarding recall distributed by the Home Office (Coker and Martin, 1985). Notes on supervision, including advice about recall, were part of the Home Office's initial explanation of the parole system when it originated in 1968 (Home Office Circular 46, 1968). There are a number of points germane to life sentence prisoners, but the key point is that there is a reliance on the supervising officer's discretion and judgement. Guidance to supervising officers does not provide a consistent message regarding decision making, which is likely to create inconsistency across cases (Coker and Martin, 1985).

In some cases, an individual may be given a determinate prison sentence but not have their life licence revoked. This occurs where the new offence is judged to be unrelated to previous offence-related behaviour or where it is considered by the staff involved in the case that a determinate sentence would be appropriate in terms of retribution and deterrence. In a sample of life licencees, 13% were recalled for offences of serious violence and 50% of those committing serious non-violent offences had their licence revoked. Those who committed non-serious offences were generally not recalled, and where the licence was revoked it appeared to be linked more with previous expressions of concern from the supervising officer than with the new offence (Coker and Martin, 1985).

Where 'concern' reports were submitted, the Home Office recalled life licencees in 29% of cases, compared with an 88% recall rate for those who were reported for licence violations[11] (Coker and Martin, 1985).

Supervising officers identifying cause for concern has proved a difficult area to classify. It is likely to be the result of a decision taken by an individual supervising officer and so it is reasonable to assume considerable variation in how 'cause for concern' may be interpreted. The Home Office has made attempts to reduce such differences of interpretation when it considers the case for recall, but must also place a degree of trust in the judgement of supervising officers.

Recent Research

The most recent analysis of the characteristics of those subject to life sentences is the study by Bailey (2006), which looked at a sample of 6,191 life sentence offenders on whom the Home Office had recorded information.

In line with the prison population more generally it has been noted that the vast majority of this group were men, with 269 (4%) of her sample being women. She also noted that 85% were from the UK. The majority had committed offences as an adult and, following from this, 83% had been sentenced to life imprisonment, compared with 17% who had committed offences aged under 21 years (Bailey, 2006).

A breakdown of the gender of life sentence offenders is given in Table 10.3 and a breakdown on the basis of index offence is given in Table 10.4. From this it is clear that around three-quarters of the population of life sentence offenders have been convicted of murder. Around a quarter are convicted of other serious offences and are therefore subject to discretionary life sentences. It is also notable that arson, a relatively low-frequency offence, results in a relatively high number of life sentences. One possible explanation of this is the potential for death and injury represented by the offence of arson.

In this study, a sample of 3,054 life sentence prisoners who had been discharged[12] from prison and 1,664 released on licence who had been at liberty was analysed. As outlined in Table 10.5, she found that just over 28% of these had been subject to a recall to prison. Just over half the life sentence

Table 10.4 Number of cases by index offence type (Bailey, unpublished)

Index offence	Number of cases	Percentage[a]
Murder	4,778	77
Manslaughter	427	7
Attempted murder	145	2
Wounding	149	2
Sexual offences	366	6
Aggravated burglary or robbery	47	1
Arson	210	3
Other	69	1

[a] All percentages rounded to the nearest %. The totals may therefore not be 100.

Table 10.5 Number of recalls to prison (Bailey, unpublished)

Number of recalls	Number of cases	Percentage
No recalls	2,895	95
1	119	4
2	27	1
3	9	<1
4	4	<1

population of 6,191 studied had not been discharged at all and it is argued that this group is likely to include an increased proportion of those considered as too high a risk to release (Bailey, 2006).

An additional complicating factor is the nature of supervision and the process of recall under licence (Bailey, 1996, 2006) where wide variations were found. A number of offenders may therefore have been engaged in high-risk behaviour but have simply not been recalled due to poor supervision and recall practices in some areas of the Probation Service.

Further detail was provided in relation to a sub-sample of 159 discharged life sentence prisoners (Bailey, 2006). As might be expected a statistically significant correlation of +0.25 between date of birth and date of discharge from prison was found. This suggests that older prisoners were more likely to be discharged (Bailey, 2006). The extent of this correlation is perhaps lower than might be anticipated given the length of sentences served and the fact that risk of many forms of offending decreases with age (Towl and Crighton, 1996; Crighton, 2004). This finding was to some extent confirmed by a finding of a statistically significant negative correlation (−0.22) between recalls and age suggesting that younger offenders were more likely to be recalled under licence (Bailey, 2006).

The rates of recalled offenders by country of birth were found to differ, with the main difference noted being an over-representation of offenders born in Jamaica (5.7% compared to 1.7% of the life sentence population) (Bailey, 2006). She noted that the numbers were small so any conclusions were necessarily tentative and for other Caribbean islands the numbers were too small to draw meaningful conclusions about what may seem like real differences. She posited a number of potential explanations for this finding. First she suggests that this predominantly black group of offenders may be subject to a range of social and economic factors that make them more likely to reoffend and/or breach their licence conditions. For example, they may be more likely to be unemployed, live in poor housing areas, mix with anti-social groups and so on. Such social exclusion factors though seem likely to apply similarly to life licencees born in Asia and Africa. It is also possible that Jamaican offenders may be subject to biases in the recall process itself; they may have been subject to less effective assessment and intervention work in custody, or they may engage in behaviours that make recall more likely. It seems that further research is warranted into this area. It is also important to be mindful that such apparent differences may simply be the product of normal variations which may occur across and within groups.

Table 10.6 summarises recalls to prison by type of sentence for a sub-set of 159 recalled offenders. It can be seen that those detained at Her Majesty's Pleasure are significantly over-represented in this group, comprising 12% of recalls against 7% of the life sentence population. In contrast those convicted as adults were under-represented. This difference was found to be statistically significant at the 5% level of probability ($\chi^2 = 4.941$, $p > 0.05$ d.f. 1) (Bailey, 2006). A number of possible explanations for this finding occur. These would include the possibility that those convicted at a younger age tend to be released at a younger age. In turn younger offenders tend to offend at higher

Table 10.6 Recalls by type of indeterminate sentence (Bailey, 2006)

Sentence type	Number of recalls	Percentage of recalls	Percentage of life sentence population
Her Majesty's Pleasure	19	12	7
Detention for life	4	3	1
Custody for life	18	11	9
Life imprisonment	118	74	83

rates (Farrington and Coid, 2003). It is also possible that those convicted of such serious offences as children may represent a group with more serious psychological and social difficulties.

In an analysis of recall by gender, it was found that there was only one case of a woman life sentence offender being recalled. This is a much lower level of recall 0.6% than the percentage of women life sentence offenders 5% (Bailey, 2006). Analyses of women lifers present a number of methodological issues, and caution is needed when assessing data on this group often due to the small numbers involved (Hudson, 2002).

In looking at the reasons for recalls of mandatory life sentence offenders, just over half (56%) were recalled following incidents of further criminal offending, while the remainder were recalled for breach of other licence conditions. A similar pattern was reported for discretionary life sentence offenders (Bailey, 2006).

Models of Assessing and Managing Risk

There is a significant and growing evidence base that can be drawn upon to inform the process of assessing and managing risk that is central to work with life sentence prisoners (Towl and Crighton, 1999; Monahan *et al.*, 2001; Prins, 2002; Crighton, 2004).

This evidence base suggests that unstructured approaches to risk assessment and management, whether or not conducted by experts, will tend to be poor in terms of accuracy. However, the use of more structured approaches to risk assessment and management can lead to marked gains in effectiveness.

Two particular models are advocated as being particularly helpful in effectively managing risk. These are the Cambridge model of risk assessment (CAMRA) and the use of iterative classification tree (ICT) approaches (Towl and Crighton, 1997; Crighton, 2004).

CAMRA provides an overall framework within which to consider risk and the model is outlined in Figure 10.1.

As can be seen, CAMRA provides a systemic framework within which to understand risk management. It also makes clear that effectively assessing and managing risk is an ongoing process, where new risks may arise and need to be responded to.

ICT approaches are relatively common in developed areas of risk assessment and management and, in particular, public health and physical medicine. They have the major advantage of fitting with approaches that effective clinicians are inclined to adopt: namely analysing the problem and identifying what can be done to address it almost in parallel (Monahan *et al.*, 2001). As such they can be seen as a fundamental part of the effective application of stage 3 within CAMRA.

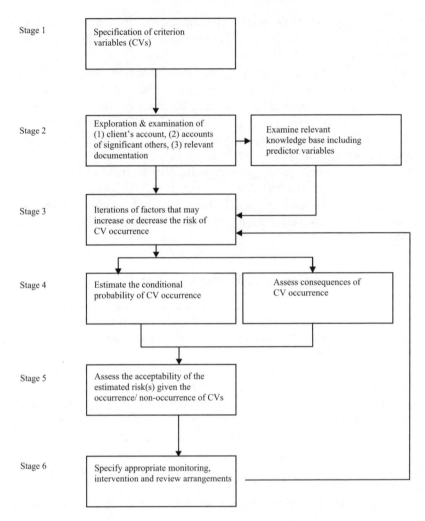

Figure 10.1   Cambridge risk assessment framework (CAMRA)

The approach diverges from what clinicians routinely do by imposing an evidence-based structure at each level of iteration of risk. A single example from the MacArthur risk-assessment study (Monahan *et al.*, 2001) is given in Table 10.7 below.

From this table it can be seen that at the first level of iteration, race appears to be a good predictor of violence among this sample of mentally disordered people, with 19.8% of African Americans showing violence, compared to 8.4% of white Americans. The next level of iteration however gives useful additional information here suggesting that African Americans living in areas rated as

Table 10.7 Post-discharge levels of violence by race and neighbourhood disadvantage

Neighbourhood description	Patient race	Percentage of violence
A. All neighbourhoods (33.7% African American)	African American ($n = 91$) White ($n = 179$)	19.8** 8.4
B. Low disadvantage neighbourhoods (4.4% African American)	African American ($n = 4$) White ($n = 86$)	0.0 3.5
C. Medium disadvantage neighbourhoods (27.2% African American)	African American ($n = 31$) White ($n = 83$)	12.9 12.0
D. High disadvantage neighbourhoods (84.8% African American)	African American ($n = 56$) White ($n = 10$)	25.0 20.0

Notes: **$p < 0.01$.

Source: Reproduced from Monahan *et al.* (2001, p. 58) by permission of Oxford University Press

low or medium in terms of social disadvantage are not at increased risk of violence. The overall difference appears to be based on a slightly higher rate of violence among African Americans living in highly disadvantaged areas and also the higher rates of African Americans living in such areas. Clearly the implications of this are quite different in terms of assessing and managing risk.

CAMRA and ICT approaches are mutually compatible and are supported by the developing evidence base in risk assessment. However, they do have drawbacks. They are both dependent on body of skilled and trained practitioners to use them. They are also heavily dependent on the quality of the evidence base available and for many areas of risk assessment and management this is poor or even non-existent. Without such data the power of such approaches to guide practitioners away from systematic errors is reduced.

Policy and Practice Implications

From this review it is evident that the evidence base on lifers is limited. Recently though there have been significant developments in the form of large-scale research studies (Bailey, 2006). There is though a need for the continued development of good-quality research and evaluation as a central part of the process of risk assessment and management with lifers. Such research is fundamental to the avoiding of poor judgements through want of the necessary data needed to make better judgements.

As noted above, risk is a complex and fluid notion (Towl, 2005). Largely as a response to this a range of simple 'quick fix' models have recently become fashionable. These tend to be based on cross-sectional correlational approaches. Such approaches might at best be seen as a short-term stopgap. At worst they might be seen as a serious diversion from developing the necessary effective and systemic models of risk assessment and management (Wald and Woolverton, 1991). However, with a growing recognition of the need to embrace – rather than avoid – complexity the field is ripe for further development.

Notes

1. 'Dispersal' prisons were put in place following the recommendations of the Advisory Council on the Penal System (1968) chaired by the distinguished criminologist Leon Radzinowicz. This body was established to consider the regime for those to be held under maximum security conditions (Advisory Council on the Penal System, 1968). It recommended that those prisoners classified as Category A (high-security risk) should be dispersed around a number of prisons and mixed in with the general establishment population rather than concentrated in only one prison. This ran counter to the earlier recommendation of the Mountbatten Report (Home Office, 1966) which recommended the concentration of such prisoners in a single establishment.
2. 'Security risk' refers to a number of issues including risk of escape, the means to effect an escape, and the level of potential harm to the public and political embarrassment to the government.
3. The term F75 refers to the Prison Service form on which reports on life sentence prisoners were written. These have since been replaced by LSP forms, which serve the same ostensible purpose.
4. The term tariff has now been replaced by minimum term/relevant part.
5. Lifer liaison officers are normally generic middle managers in prisons, responsible for the management and co-ordination of the system for life sentence prisoners.
6. Reports are completed by primary care doctors (general practitioners).
7. In 2005 these reports tend to be completed by a mix of forensic and general psychiatrists, mental health nurses, forensic and other specialists within applied psychology. Given the focus on the assessment and management of risk it is perhaps surprising that such reports were defined by prisons as optional, whereas reports from a GP, generic prison manager and prison officer were defined as essential.
8. Unpublished. Referenced in Padfield (2002).
9. Both IG 52/1994 and PC 73/1994 have now been superseded but are included here to give an historical picture of policy and practice development.
10. This unit was previously based within HM Prison Service. It is now based within the National Offender Management Service.
11. This applied to just eight individuals.
12. These discharges contained, amongst others, those released on licence, on appeal and those who died.

Chapter 11

Psychological Research into Sexual Offenders

David Crighton

Introduction

Sexual offending represents a significant social problem and one that causes a great deal of psychological and physical injury. There is little reliable data on the prevalence of sexual offending and the area also faces a number of challenging definitional issues. However, survey data does suggest high rates of such assaults. In one early study it was reported that in a sample of 521 people in the Boston area of the US 15% of women and 6% of men reported being sexually assaulted at some point in their lives (Finkelhor, 1984). Other researchers have estimated rates at much higher levels. For example, Marshall (1999) claims that the figure is up to about 50% for adult women and a similar figure for children who have suffered from sexual abuse.

Good-quality research in this area is predominantly from the US where in 1994 on any single day around 234,000 convicted sexual offenders were under care, custody or control (White *et al.*, 1998). The management of those who sexually assault others is also a long-term issue. It has been reported that just under a quarter of rapists were reconvicted towards the end of a 10-year follow-up period (Soothill, 1976).

Below are outlined some of the definitional issues that arise in this area of research. This is followed by a review of the evidence base to date in terms of randomised, non-randomised and qualitative studies. A number of implications are considered arising from the current and developing state of the literature in this area.

Definitional Issues

Sexual offending covers a wide range of offences. Definitions have also varied across jurisdictions and across time. For example, the age of consent to sexual behaviour has varied across cultures and history. Even so there is general agreement that a number of actions related to sexual behaviour should be criminal.

The majority of the evidence base relating to sexual offenders addresses two main groups: those who sexually offend against children and those who sexually offend against adults. Within this chapter, the term sex offender against children has been used to refer to the former group and sex offender against adults to refer to the latter. In much of the evidence base the terms paedophile and child molester are used to refer to those who sexually offend against children. The term paedophile is not used here as it has frequently caused concern, given its literal and quite inappropriate meaning of lover of children. As a result a number of researchers have preferred the use of the term child molester, since this makes clearer the harmful and negative nature of the behaviour. The term is not used here since it potentially excludes a broad range of sexual offending that may not involve physical contact, which may be classified as sexual offences. Such offences may also be perpetrated against adults and would include such things as exhibitionism and making obscene telephone calls.

In addition there is a range of problem sexual behaviours sometimes termed paraphilias (American Psychiatric Association, 2003) that might not come to the attention of the legal system. These might include such things as fetishism (being sexually aroused by inanimate objects). Where they are causing distress or interfering with day-to-day life, such behaviours may bring individuals into contact with health and social care services. In some cases such paraphilias may bring individuals into contact with the criminal justice system where the behaviour itself is proscribed, or where it leads to related behaviours that are illegal.

A powerful and highly pertinent characteristic of sexual offending is the high levels of under-reporting, a methodological challenge that is common to the evaluation of interventions generally. Surveys such as the British Crime Survey, which have looked at reported rates of sexual offending, suggest a large degree of under-reporting of such offences (Dodd et al., 2004; Nicholas et al., 2005). It is evident that there are high levels of hidden victimisation (Hood et al., 2002). This is also supported by studies of sexual offenders receiving treatment who, when asked about their levels of previous offending, report large numbers of un-recorded offences (Abel et al., 1987). Sexual offenders report much higher levels of offending than they have been convicted of, or that have been reported: these self-report rates of previous offending also tend to increase where researchers offer a greater degree of confidentiality (Abel and Rouleau, 1990). It is evident that the conviction rates for sexual offences are much lower than the true rates of such behaviour and that convicted sexual offenders probably represent a small subset of sexual offenders (Abel and Rouleau, 1990; Hood et al., 2002). This clearly has implications for what some researchers claim that we 'know' about sex offenders.

Since the vast majority of research into sexual offenders has focussed on those convicted in criminal courts of sexual offences, this raises the likelihood of systematic biases in the evidence base. For example, finding that those with a learning disability are over-represented (Hawk *et al.*, 1993) may be explained as a function of those with learning disabilities offending at a higher rate, or it may be that as a group they are more likely to be apprehended and convicted. Certainly from the available evidence base it seems that those convicted of criminal sex offences are unlikely to be a representative cross-section of sexual offenders and this strong caveat needs to be borne in mind when looking at the evidence base on treatment outcomes. Indeed much of what is written about sex offenders fails to sufficiently acknowledge the impact of such potentially very significant sampling biases.

Key Findings

A thorough review of psychological interventions with sex offenders looking at randomised studies has been conducted and reported (Kenworthy *et al.*, 2003.[1] A subsequent detailed review expanded this to include an analysis of non-randomised and qualitative studies has also been reported (Brooks-Gordon *et al.*, 2004).

The use of randomised control trials (RCTs) in this area had been controversial due to often strongly held beliefs that psychological interventions work and that individuals should not be denied treatment. Such views, they note, are based on weak evidence, primarily based on meta-analysis of non-randomised studies that psychological interventions with sex offenders work (Quinsey *et al.*, 1998; Friendship *et al.*, 2002). It has been suggested that this is largely an ethical issue (Towl, 2005). In the case of a treatment that is known to be effective and is available, it is clearly unethical to deny that treatment. The extension of this argument to interventions with sex offenders is based on the misguided and unfounded assumption that we know what interventions are effective in reducing such offending. Therefore the argument that excluding individuals from treatment, or denying them access to treatment is unethical, does not stand up to scrutiny (Towl, 2005). Indeed pursuing the logic of this argument further, requiring individuals to undertake treatments of unknown efficacy could equally be called into question as being harmful (Stockton and Crighton, 2003).

Prevalence

In an effort to pull together the disparate literature in this field a review of research into the management of people with disorders of sexual preference and convicted sexual offenders was conducted (White *et al.*, 1998). The decision by the researchers in this review to look at these two areas together can be seen as somewhat contentious, since it can be argued that the links between these two areas are complex. The somewhat curious rationale given by the reviewers was a desire to focus on problematic behaviours, rather than the legal categories of offences that vary across jurisdictions and time.

Overall they reported that up to the date of completion of their review little reliable prevalence data existed. They identified victim survey data looking at incest. Quoted rates of prevalence for women ranged from 12% to 28% and for men from 3% to 8% (Finkelhor, 1979, 1984; Baker and Duncan, 1985; Furby *et al.*, 1989; Mullen *et al.*, 1994).

They also noted that the research base is largely North American and pre-dominantly from the US where the median age of victims of sexual assault has been reported as 13 years and the median age of rape victims is 22 years (Bureau of Justice, 1998).

Randomised Studies

There have been three recent and detailed reviews of the use of interventions with sexual offenders. The earlier of these looked at pharmacological, surgical and psychological approaches, and the latter two focussed on psychological interventions with adult sexual offenders (White *et al.*, 1998; Kenworthy *et al.*, 2003; Brooks-Gordon *et al.*, 2004).

In assessing pharmacological interventions these were subdivided into three types. The pharmacological interventions assessed were the use of sex hormones, the use of anti-psychotics and the use of bromide-related compounds. They then went on to look at surgical interventions, essentially the use of surgical castration with male sex offenders. In reviewing the evidence on psychological interventions, the 1998 review sub-divided these into behaviour therapy, relapse-prevention approaches and a category of others that included, for example, orgasmic reconditioning[2] (White *et al.*, 1998).

In reviewing, the evidence-based studies that compared interventions with either a placebo or a 'standard care' and provided outcome measures including recidivism and those 'lost to follow-up' were considered (White *et al.*, 1998). Where possible a number of other 'secondary' outcome measures were also assessed and these included death rates, other forms of criminal offending, measures of mental state, patient satisfaction, penile plethysmograph assessment, measures of resource use or cost–benefit and side-effects. Where the data was of adequate quality they divided the follow-up periods into short term zero to six months), medium-term (up to five years) and long-term (more than five years) follow-ups. Based on their review the researchers argued that only studies with long-term follow-up provided adequate measures of the true rearrest and reconviction rates. In support of this view it has previously been reported that a significant number of rapists studied were not reconvicted until late into a very lengthy follow-up period (Soothill, 1976).

An extensive search of published research was conducted and studies were rated into three bands (A, B or C) on the basis of their methodological adequacy (White *et al.*, 1998). Where a study was a randomised trial and the process of randomisation was described, the study would be rated as A. Where there was randomisation but the process for ensuring this in the study was not described, the study was rated B. Where no mention of randomisation was made, the study was rated C. All C-rated studies were excluded since, in the absence of any evidence of randomisation, these failed to meet the minimum standards of scientific quality set out by the authors in their review. There were no A-rated studies found. Very surprisingly this means that, at the time of the review, there had been no obtainable RCTs with a clear methodology set out in this area.

Studies in which more than 50% of participants were lost at follow-up were also excluded, on the basis that such studies are open to an unacceptable level of selection bias. As a result of this 58 of the identified studies were excluded. In fact it is striking that at this point only three studies were retained as meeting the basic scientific standards set out by the researchers.

A small-scale study looked at a sample of 31 sex offenders in which the use of medroxyprogesterone,[3] imaginal desensitisation and the use of both these interventions were studied (McConaghy *et al.*, 1988). Conclusions based on this study need to be tentative given the small numbers involved. However, the use of medroxyprogesterone combined with imaginal desensitisation was found to be no better than imaginal desensitisation alone, suggesting that the use of this anti-libinal treatment did not have a positive effect.

A larger scale study of 155 sexual offenders compared the use of a cognitive-behavioural group work intervention (based on relapse prevention principles) with no intervention (Marques *et al.*, 1994). The mean duration of follow-up for this study was three years. No difference was found between the two groups in terms of rates of sexual offending (OR 0.76 CI 0.26–2.28). The treatment group did though show lower rates for non-sexual violent offences (OR 0.3 CI 0.1–0.89, NNT 10 CI 5–85). The treatment group also showed lower rates of violent and sexual offences combined (OR 0.14 CI 0.02–0.98 NNT 20 CI 10–437).

In a comparison between cognitive-behavioural therapy (CBT) and trans-theoretical counselling group therapy, the CBT group was found to have poorer attitudes to treatment (corrected $n = 38$, RR poor attitude to treatment 2.8 CI 1.26–6.22, NNH 2 CI 1–5) (Marques *et al.*, 1994).

In a comparison of the use of broadly psychodynamic group therapy compared to a no-intervention group, a number of significant findings have been reported (Romero and Williams, 1983). This study is complicated by the inclusion of a small number of people being 'treated' for homosexuality, which makes aspects of the study difficult to compare with more recent studies. Indeed it is somewhat surprising and, perhaps also indicative of the somewhat static state of this area of practice, that as late as 1983 such 'treatment' was being reported. Overall the authors found no significant difference between the treated and untreated groups (OR 1.87 CI 0.8–4.37) (Romero and Williams, 1983). The study was though weakened by a relatively short follow-up period of two to three years and a relatively high exclusion rate of over 10%.

In summarising the findings of this systematic review, the authors noted that an adequate evidence base in this area was lacking (White *et al.*, 1998). They also noted there was no evident reason why this could not take place, that the need to undertake such work was pressing, and that well-conducted and reported RCT studies were essential. They argued that less methodologically adequate studies are sufficient in this area (Marshall *et al.*, 1991b). In common with other researchers they rejected this implausible argument, noting ways in which RCT crossover trials could be used as one way to address any ethical concerns that had been detailed (Quinsey *et al.*, 1993; McConaghy, 1995; Begg *et al.*, 1996). A detailed discussion of these methodological issues is beyond the scope of this chapter. In essence though an RCT can be said to have a crossover design where the participants are given all the study interventions in successive periods. The order in which the participants receive each of the interventions is randomised. Such trials produce *within* participant comparisons, whereas parallel designs produce *between* participant comparisons. In such designs each participant acts as their own control for comparison purposes and this method can produce statistically and clinically valid results with fewer participants than would be required with a parallel RCT design (Jadad, 1998). In many respects sexual offending fits well with such designs since they are especially suited to 'chronic' and 'incurable' disorders and it is perhaps surprising and disappointing that such approaches have not been attempted.

In a review undertaken in 2003 the researchers looked for randomised studies with or without blinding[4] (Kenworthy *et al.*, 2003). A full range of psychological interventions was included in the initial review search, although studies of those aged under 18 years were excluded. The review criteria were similar to those used by White *et al.* (1998) although the search process was more extensive. As a result of this they identified a small number of studies for inclusion that met basic scientific criteria and had follow-up periods ranging from 1 to 10 years, where the drop-out rates were less than 50%. They identified two high-quality studies – Romero and Williams (1983) and Marques *et al.* (1994) – as well as a number of smaller-scale studies. The study by Marques is outlined above and in summary found no difference between those treated using cognitive-behavioural group work and no treatment in terms of rates of sexual offending. The treatment group did though show lower rates for non-sexual violent offences and also showed lower rates of violent and sexual offences combined.

The findings of a study that compared cognitive group-therapy treatment with counselling group therapy have been reported (Ryan, 1977). Unfortunately the methodology and reporting of this study makes many of its aspects opaque. However, some surprising results were reported. The cognitive therapy treatment was reported to be less effective at tackling poor attitudes (NNH2 CI 1–5). Cognitive distortions, sexual knowledge and sexual obsessions were similar for both approaches. The Ryan study is worthy of further consideration because it, quite unusually, notes a number of adverse treatment effects. Such effects tend to be poorly reported across most studies of treatment effects, an effect which may be part of a wider research bias to report 'positive' results and under-report 'negative' results (Towl and Crighton, 2005)

A methodologically rigorous study with an impressive 10-year follow-up of 231 sexual offenders was reported in the late 1970s (Romero and Williams, 1983). This study compared psychotherapy, group psychotherapy and no psychotherapy with a cohort of sexual offenders, going on to look at rearrest rates within 10 years. The researchers noted that 11% of the cohort had reoffended within 10 years and that group psychotherapy did not have a clear effect on this rate. Of the group that received no treatment, 7% were rearrested within 10 years, compared to 14% of the group that received therapy, a statistically non-significant result (RR 1.87 CI 0.78–4.47). They stressed the importance of very long follow-up periods in assessing treatment effects with sexual offenders, due in large part to the relatively low detection and conviction rates for such offences.

The implications of these findings have been considered in some detail as part of a broader review of the evidence base (Kenworthy et al., 2003). In comparison to the review by White et al. (1998) it is notable that the evidence base had improved. In particular the studies by Marques et al. (1994) and Romero and Williams (1983) are highlighted as good-quality studies on which practice might be based. The study by Romero and Williams (1978) in particular suggests that the follow-up periods in this area of research have been unduly short for this group of offenders. They also note that with very few exceptions the quality of the evidence base in this area remains poor. They are generally very critical of the frequent use of various self-report scales to measure change, given the lack of evidence to support a link between these and subsequent sexual offending. While recognising the potential for these to generate research hypotheses they suggest that such scales are often of 'little clinical utility'. They note that binary outcomes in terms of improved/not improved are possible to collect in this field and would be of greater utility.

They also note that the evidence base suggests that cognitive-behavioural group work treatment with sex offenders led to a reduction in violent offending, but no reduction in sexual offending (Marques *et al.*, 1994). The report of longer-term follow-up suggests no effects of treatment over a 10-year follow-up period and suggests the possibility of negative effect following treatment (Romero and Williams, 1978).

The overall conclusion from the current evidence base of randomised studies is that psychological interventions with sexual offenders are largely unproven and therefore represent experimental interventions. Such interventions may be helpful, neutral or harmful (Kenworthy *et al.*, 2003). The researchers went on to note the clear need for a large and well-designed RCT comparing a range of experimental treatments for sexual offenders.

Non-randomised studies

An extensive and high-quality review of the efficacy of sex offender interventions was undertaken in 2004 (Brooks-Gordon, *et al.*, 2004). This review identified 81 non-randomised studies, of which 21 met basic minimum standards in terms of sample size and methodological adequacy based on ratings by two assessors.

Seven studies reported a statistically significant effect on the treatment group: Aytes *et al.*, 2001 ($\chi^2 = 25.12$, d.f. $= 3$, $p < 0.01$); Berliner *et al.*, 1995 ($\chi^2 = 4.474$, $p < 0.05$); Henning and Freuh, 1996 (χ^2 (1, N $= 124) = 4.2$, $p < 0.05$; Looman *et al.*, 2000 ($\chi^2 = 14.7$, d.f. $= 1$, $p < 0.001$); Nicholaichuk *et al.*, 2000 (F(1, 162) $= 46.39$, $p < 0.001$); Turner *et al.*, 2000 ($\chi^2 = 6.12$, $p < 0.05$); Watson and Stermac, 1994 (F(1, 25) $= 7.32$, $p < 0.02$).[5] Four studies (Meyer *et al.*, 1992; Fisher, 1995; Shaw *et al.*, 1995; McGuire, 2000) did not report their data in ways that were usable by the reviewers (Brooks-Gordon *et al.*, 2004). Ten studies reported that intervention had no statistically significant effect on the attitudes or behaviour of sexual offenders (Rice *et al.*, 1991; Marshall *et al.*, 1991a, b; Hanson *et al.*, 1993, 2004; Proctor, 1996; McGrath *et al.*, 1998, 2003; Craissati and McClurg, 2000; DiFazio *et al.*, 2001).

There has been a growth in literature suggesting that psychological interventions with sex offenders work despite a paucity of relevant evaluative evidence (Brooks-Gordon *et al.*, 2004). It has been argued that no positive treatment effects can be found from quasi-experimental (non-randomised) studies (Quinsey *et al.*, 1993). The use of meta-analysis[6] in this area is contentious and has yielded limited results. One such analysis suggests that a failure to complete an intervention is a moderate predictor of recidivism. The researchers here though concluded that this was probably due to closer monitoring of those who failed to complete, rather than treatment efficacy (Hanson and Bussiere, 1998) In a 12-year follow-up study of those who had volunteered and those who had refused treatment no differences were found (Hanson *et al.*, 2004).

A large-scale study was conducted of public sector prisons in England and Wales (Friendship *et al.*, 2003b) looking at a sample of 647 sexual offenders. The study did not appear to have met the methodological standards set for inclusion in the review by Brooks-Gordon *et al.* (2004). It is included here for completeness, despite its lack of methodological sophistication, and because of the scale of the study.

All those studied had been volunteer participants during the period 1992–4 in the Prison Service's sex offender group work treatment intervention, involving between 80 and 170 hours of treatment. All had been discharged from prison and a minimum of two-year follow-up data was available on all. This group was compared with a matched control group of 1,910 sexual offenders who had not gone through this treatment. All controls had been serving a prison sentence of four years or more and were matched with the treated group on the year of discharge from prison. Both groups were also rated and matched on an assessment schedule called the Static 99 (Hanson and Thornton, 2000) which rated them in terms of risk. All life sentence offenders were excluded from the study. The authors also note that the control group may have included a number of prisoners who had begun but failed to complete treatment, potentially introducing a sampling bias.

In a reported study, the two-year sexual reconviction rates for a sample of offenders were calculated and compared using the χ^2 statistic for non-parametric data (Friendship *et al.*, 2003b). They reported no significant difference in reconvictions between the treated and untreated groups (treated 2.6% versus untreated 2.8%). They did, though, find a statistically significant difference between the groups when violent and sexual offences were combined (treated 4.6% versus untreated 8.1%, $p < 0.01$). Finally the authors looked at levels of 'global' reoffending and found no significant difference between the treated and untreated groups (treated 13.3% versus untreated 16.5% p n.s.). The authors do optimistically note that the trend was in the anticipated direction, but it may be argued that this reflects a lack of a basic understanding about the nature of statistical testing, where non-significant trends are generally attributed to random fluctuations (Howell, 1999).

Meta-analysis of non-randomised studies

Meta-analysis involves statistically pooling data from a number of different studies. Using this method some have reported that, when using matched longitudinal follow-up studies of sexual offenders, failure to complete treatment was a moderate predictor of reoffending. However, further analysis suggests that this finding is more likely to be due to monitoring of risk than treatment efficacy (Hanson and Bussiere, 1998).

Some evidence suggestive of positive treatment effects has emerged from the use of meta-analytic techniques. A reported analysis of 79 treatment studies found that those who completed relapse prevention treatment had a 7.2% re-arrest rate compared to 13.2% for all treatment interventions and 17.6% for those who had not been treated (Alexander, 1999). Similarly in England and Wales, small treatment effects have been reported, but were curiously only found when reconviction data for violent offences and for sexual offences was pooled (Friendship *et al.*, 2003a,b). When either group of offences were looked at separately no treatment effects were found. The authors do not give a detailed account of how the data was combined to yield this curious finding.

Qualitative studies

As with quantitative studies of interventions with sexual offending the majority of the literature is of poor quality. In reviewing this area Brooks-Gordon *et al.* (2004) identified 81 potentially sound studies. Of these, 31 could be located within the timescale set by the researchers. Using a series of exclusion criteria that focussed on the quality and relevance of the literature, four studies were found to meet the criteria used to assess 'soundness' (Brooks-Gordon, *et al.*, 2004).

Three of these studies were process evaluations. One of these looked at two cognitive-behavioural group interventions in local prisons in England and Wales (Houston *et al.*, 1995). This study was marked out by the use of a strong theoretical base that was made clear in the write-up of the study. The researchers looked at the emergent patterns of group behaviour and how these interacted to influence the intervention. The researchers noted that, as with other forms of psychological therapy, these interactions were complex. In the case of sexual offenders they also noted as particularly important the complex interaction between the roles of victim and victimiser and noted that many group members had been both at differing times. The authors suggested that the use by tutors of constructive peer challenging was an important part of addressing issues such as responsibility. The research did though have a num-ber of weaknesses. Most importantly no detail was given as to how the themes that were drawn out were identified by the researchers.

Two other process studies were reported based on a study of a sample of 20 male incest offenders (Scheela, 1992, 2001). These studies focussed largely on therapist experiences and perceptions of work with these offenders and how this interacted with therapeutic work. They noted a range of factors that seemed to be of marked importance. These included frustration among ther-apists at the perceived negative effects of mandatory requirements. Also noted were issues of desensitisation as a result of repeated exposure to the detail of sexual offending, issues of counter-transference, the need to develop realistic expectations about interventions with sex offenders and the need to effectively separate the person from the offence as part of effective working.

The final study included in the review explored the view of staff undertaking psychological interventions with sexual offenders in the UK (Lea *et al.,* 1999). Here the researchers conducted semi-structured interviews with 23 practitioners and used triangulation of data.[7]

The researchers found that the use of reflective and self-critical practice tended to increase in relation to the experience and length of training of the practitioner. More surprisingly perhaps they also reported that 30% of their sample defined sexual offenders in terms of some form of biological abnormality. It has been argued that such views may serve to help to abrogate some of the responsibility of sex offenders for their actions (Brooks-Gordon *et al.,* 2004).

Mentally Disordered Sex Offenders

There has to date been very little good-quality research published in relation to mentally disordered sex offenders. There has though been a limited amount of research looking at treatment interventions with learning disabled sex offenders.

A review of this area has been conducted (Ashman and Duggan, 2002). The authors noted that there had been no RCTs that met basic criteria of methodological adequacy. Overall they concluded that there was no adequate evidence base for the effectiveness or ineffectiveness of treatment interventions with this group. As a result practitioners currently need to base their practice on an inadequate evidence base drawn from methodologically inadequate studies, or extrapolated from the evidence base for non-mentally disordered offenders.

This finding is at best disappointing given the evidence in relation to rates of conviction for sexual offences among the learning disabled. In a study of 47 sexual offenders with learning disability it was reported that higher rates of recidivism were seen than in those without learning disability (Day, 1994). In a similar study of defendants at court, it was found the point prevalence rate (where a single point in time is used to identify when all individuals in a cohort show a particular characteristic at that time) for sexual offending among learning disabled offenders to be nearly twice that for non-learning disabled defendants (Hawk, 1993). Another reported study found a prevalence rate of 9% in a general population of learning disabled offenders and reported that between 10% and 15% of convictions for sexual offences are against those with learning disability, compared to prevalence rates in the community of learning disability of around 5% (Cooper, 1995).

Such findings raise a number of possibilities. Ashman and Duggan (2002) note that these prevalence rates may represent a marked underestimate of true rates, noting a high degree of tolerance for sexually inappropriate behaviours by people with learning disability. Another view might be that people with learning disability are far less able to avoid detection and, in turn, conviction, than are non-learning disabled sex offenders. Further research is required to interpret these prevalence findings. It does though remain questionable that those with learning disabilities have often been excluded from psychological interventions aimed at reducing sexual offending.

The evidence base in relation to other forms of mental disorder is even weaker than that for learning disability. There have been no RCTs looking at treatment effects for other groups of mentally disordered sex offenders. As with a number of other areas of clinical practice, this leaves practitioners in the position of making decisions about treatment in the absence of an adequate evidence base (Crighton, 1999).

Models

Approaches to work with sexual offenders have generally been only weakly grounded in theory. Despite this, there have been a number of attempts to provide a theoretical grounding for this area of research.

Where models have been used these have tended to be similar to those used in the area of substance abuse, seeing sexual offending as a cyclic and self-reinforcing behaviour (Finkelhor, 1979, 1984). Associations with models of drug addiction have an intuitive appeal and parallels can be drawn. For example, it is not uncommon for sexual offenders' behaviour to escalate in terms of frequency and/or severity. It can be argued by analogy that this is similar to substance abusers who take larger dosages of a substance in order to gain a similar effect. The analogy though is incomplete. There is no comparable physiological basis to that seen in substance abuse. Therefore this analogy can only ever be partial.

A better approach might be to adopt models used in public health contexts. Such models are concerned with the events associated with and leading up to an outcome of disease or injury as a process. Figure 11.1 illustrates a simplified example of a physical injury.

From this outline it is clear that different chains of events can result in the same outcome. The implications of this are that such chains can be broken at different points for different people. In addition one break is likely to be sufficient and such breaks may be easiest to achieve at less obvious points. In this example the chain of events might be broken by the intuitively obvious act of salting the pathway. In the second example the chain of events might be broken by the not necessarily obvious options of treating the ear infection. Equally the event might be averted by installing a handrail or by treating the brittle bone problem.

A—>B—>C—>Event

Where A is an icy path

B is a person hurrying to work

C is a slip and fall

And the event is a broken hip

G—>H—>I—>J—>K—>Event

G is a person with balance problems secondary to an ear infection

H is a set of stairs

I is the absence of a hand rail

J is a slip

K is the presence of brittle bones

And the event is a broken hip

Figure 11.1   Pathways to similar health outcomes

This example serves to illustrate an alternative to the addiction analogy commonly used when looking at sexual offenders, which tends to address the problem of sexual offending primarily at the level of physiological drives and supporting cognitions.

Policy and Practice Implications

In a 2004 review of this area it was noted as follows:

> 'Psychological treatments for people who have committed a sex offence is often recommended or mandated as part of a sentencing decision. The effectiveness of such treatments is debated and robust literature on this topic is minimal.'
>
> (Brooks-Gordon *et al.*, 2004).

The evidence base in relation to the treatment of sexual offenders suggests that there is a clear need to take stock of the research and to take on board some of the findings from the existing evidence base, as well as undertaking effective research into this area. Some authors have, albeit wholly unconvincingly, argued that lower levels of proof are appropriate in this area of work (Marshall *et al.*, 1991b), but this is not a widely accepted view (Brooks-Gordon *et al.*, 2004).

In recent years a small number of randomised trials of acceptable standard have been undertaken and these have suggested that current treatment approaches have no effect in reducing sexual offending (Romero and Williams, 1983; Marques *et al.*, 1994).

It is notable that some studies have found reductions in violent offending among those treated, suggesting that current treatments may be having some positive effects, but that these are poorly understood (Marques *et al.*, 1994, Friendship *et al.*, 2003a). Likewise non-randomised studies have yielded a pattern of findings suggesting no positive effects in reducing levels of sexual reconviction. Methodological limitations with such studies though add to the difficulty in interpretation.[8] Some have speculated that current approaches have not involved enough treatment (Friendship *et al.*, 2003b); others question the logic of this position (Towl, 2005). Evidence to support such post-hoc explanation is absent and, logically, many alternative post-hoc explanations could be generated.

The improved yet very limited evidence base in this area makes it clear that treatments for sexual offenders are experimental. It has been noted that:

> 'most is known about the use of cognitive behavioural techniques and general psychotherapeutic groups. Cognitive behavioural approaches may decrease recidivism at a year, compared to standard care, yet the general approach could even promote re-arrest (up to ten years). Sound qualitative research in this area is also minimal. The only recommendation that can be made is that both outcome and process evaluation in this area is possible and urgently required.'
>
> (Brooks-Gordon *et al.*, 2004).

Two main implications derive from an assessment of current psychological research in this area. First, that we need to treat any claims of best practice in the treatment of sexual offenders with some degree of caution. Following on from this there is therefore a need to develop a range of responses, to see which, if any, are effective. In seeking to do this, area of work would benefit from drawing from the broader evidence base on process and outcome research (McNeill *et al.*, 2004). Such research highlights the importance of therapist characteristics and the constructive engagement with clients as central to effective working to reduce reoffending.

In relation to severe and long term difficulties, public health models appear especially salient. It has been noted as follows:

> 'There has never been a public health problem successfully reduced by treating individuals after they have developed the problem, and we can expect that sexual assaults in our culture will not significantly decrease by treating the victimized. Ultimately, we must aim our scientific investigations at the primary, secondary, and tertiary prevention of the development of these paraphilic interests and paraphilic behaviors.'
>
> (Abel and Rouleau, 1990)

It is worth highlighting here that convicted sexual offenders represent only a small proportion of those who sexually assault others with high levels of hidden victimisation (Hood *et al.*, 2002). As such there is a risk of developing and testing approaches aimed at this subsample while failing to address broader issues of sexual assault in society. An effective public health approach would need to focus on broader and challenging issues of prevention and intervention with those not convicted of criminal offences. In line with this there is a pressing need to conduct high-quality RCTs to provide adequate outcome data on a broad range of approaches to intervention.

Notes

1. This review is cited as 2003 but was made widely available in 2005.
2. The authors' division of psychological interventions is open to some question here since techniques such as orgasmic reconditioning are arguably behavioural approaches. Some relapse prevention approaches might also be described as cognitive-behavioural approaches.
3. Medroxyprogesterone acetate is a derivative of progesterone and is active by the parenteral and oral routes of administration. It is believed to have anti-libinal effects and is in use as a contraceptive in women.
4. Blinding refers to whether the researcher and/or the participant in a study knows which intervention they are subject to. Clearly where researchers and/or participants in a study are aware of who is in the treatment group the potential for unintentional biases in the results is markedly increased.
5. A more detailed analysis of each of these studies is provided in Brooks-Gordon *et al.* (2004).
6. Meta-analysis is developed as a means of pooling data from multiple RCTs. The extension of this methodology to non-randomised studies is contentious. Given the limitations of the research base in this area meta-analysis simply pools poor-quality data. It can be argued that this raises more questions than it answers.
7. Triangulation of data refers essentially to the systematic use of multiple sources of information. Where such sources tend to converge greater confidence may be placed in the results than where the results are divergent.
8. As an example here non-randomised studies have used matched control groups. However, since it is not clear which variables are relevant in intervention work with sex offenders, it is not possible to be confident about such matched subjects designs. Positive and negative results of such studies may be explained as being due to differences between the groups or to the effects or non-effects of interventions.

Bibliography

Abel, G.G. and Rouleau, J.-L. (1990). The nature and extent of sexual assault. In W.L. Marshall, D.R. Laws and H.E. Barbaree (Eds), *Handbook of Sexual Assault*. New York: Plenum Press.

Abel, G.G., Becker, J.V., Mittleman, M.S., Cunningham-Rathner, J., Rouleau, J.-L. and Murphy, W.D. (1987). Self-reported sex crimes of nonincarcerated paraphiliacs. *Journal of Interpersonal Violence* **2(6)**, 3–25.

Advisory Council on the Penal System (1968). *The Regime for Long-Term Prisoners in Conditions of Maximum Security (The Radzinowicz Report)*. London: HMSO.

AIC (2002). What works in reducing young peoples involvement in crime? A review of current literature on youth crime prevention, Australian Institute of Criminology, Canberra.

Alexander, M.A. (1999). Sexual offender treatment efficacy revisited, sexual abuse. *A Journal of Research and Treatment* **11(2)**, 101–17.

Allan, S. and Gilbert, P. (2002). Anger and anger expression in relation to perceptions of social rank, entrapment and depressive symptoms. *Personality and Individual Differences* **32(3)**, 551–5.

American Psychiatric Association (2003). *Diagnostic and Statistical Manual of Mental Disorders (fourth edition)*. Washington: APA.

Anderson-Varney, T.J. (1991). An evaluation of a treatment programme for imprisoned child sex offenders. Unpublished dissertation. Michigan State University.

Andrews, D.A. and Bonta, J. (1994). *The Psychology of Criminal Conduct*. Cincinnati, OH: Anderson.

Andrews, D.A., Zinger, I., Hoge, R.D., Bonta, J., Gendreau, P. and Anglin, M., Douglas and Yih-Ing Hser (1990). Treatment of drug abuse. In M. Tonry and J.Q. Wilson (Eds), *Drugs and Crime, Crime and Justice, Vol. 13*. Chicago: University of Chicago Press.

Aronson, J., Blanton, H. and Cooper, J. (1995). From dissonance to disidentification: Selectivity in the self-affirmation process. *Journal of Personality and Social Psychology* **68**, 986–96.

Arrindell, W.A., Steptoe, A. and Wardle, J. (2003). Higher levels of depression in masculine than in feminine nations. *Behaviour Research and Therapy* **41**, 809–17.

Ashman, L. and Duggan, L. (2002). Interventions for learning disabled sex offenders. *The Cochrane Database of Systematic Reviews 2002*, **2**. Art. No.: CD003682. DOI: 10.1002/14651858.CD003682.

Aytes, K.E., Olsen, S.S., Zakrajsek, T., Murray, P. and Ireson, R. (2001). Cognitive/ behavioural treatment for sexual offenders: An examination of recidivism. *Sexual Abuse: A Journal of Research and Treatment* **13**, 223–1.

Babiker, G. and Arnold, L. (1997). *The Language of Injury: Comprehending Self-Mutilation.* Leicester: The British Psychological Society.

Bailey, J. (1996). The supervision of life sentence prisoners. Unpublished MSc dissertation. University of London, UK.

Bailey, J.E. (2006). Life Sentence Prisoners an empirical and qualitative evaluation. Unpublished Ph.D. dissertation for submission March 2006. Anglia Ruskin University, Cambridge, UK.

Baker, A.W. and Duncan, S.P. (1985). Child sexual abuse: A study of prevalence in Great Britain. *Child Abuse and Neglect* **9**, 457–67.

Ball, J., Shaffer, J. and Nurco, D. (1983). Day-to day criminality of heroin addicts in Baltimore: A study in the continuity of offence rates. *Drug and Alcohol Dependence* **12**, 119–42.

Barrington, M.R. (1969). The case for rational suicide. In A.B. Downing and B. Smoker (Eds) (1986). *Voluntary Euthanasia: Experts Debate the Right to Die.* London: Peter Owen.

Beautrais, A.L., Joyce, P.R. and Mulder, R.T. (1998). Psychiatric illness in a New Zealand sample of young people making serious suicide attempts.*New Zealand Medical Journal* **111**, 44–8.

Beck, A.T., Weissman, A., Lester, D. and Trexler, L. (1974). The measurement of pessimism: The hopelessness scale. *Journal of Consulting and Clinical Psychology* **42(6)**, 861–5.

Beck, G. (1997). The development of a new regime for young offenders.*Inside Psychology* **3**, 96–9.

Beech, A. and Scott Fordham, A. (1997). Therapeutic climate of sex offender treatment programs. *Sexual Abuse: A Journal of Research and Treatment* **9(3)**, 219–37.

Begg, C., Cho, M., Eastwood, S. *et al.* (1996). Improving the quality of reporting of randomized controlled trails. The CONSORT statement. *JAMA* **276(8)**, 637–9.

Berkowitz, L. (1998). Affective aggression: The role of stress, pain and negative affect. In R. G. Geen and E. Donnerstein (Eds), *Human Aggression: Theories, Research, and Implications for Social Policy.* London: Academic Press.

Berliner, L., Schram, D., Miller, L.L. and Milloy, C.D. (1995). A sentencing alternative for sex offenders: A study of decision making and recidivism. *Journal of Interpersonal Violence* **10**, 487–502.

Bickley, J. and Beech, A. (2002). An investigation of the Ward and Hudson Pathways Model of the sexual offense process. *Journal of Interpersonal Violence* **17(4)**, 331–393.

Björkqvist, K. (1994). Sex differences in physical, verbal, and indirect aggression: A review of recent research. *Sex Roles* **30**, 177–88.

Björkqvist, K., Österman, K. and Kaukiainen, A. (1992). The development of direct and indirect aggressive strategies in males and females . In K. Björkqvist and P. Niemela (Eds), *Of Mice and Women: Aspects of Female Aggression.* San Diego, CA: Academic Press.

Blud, L. (2003). Accreditation of offender behaviour programmes and recent developments in What Works initiatives in HM Prison Service. *Legal and Criminological Psychology* **8**, 65–6.

Bogue, J. and Power, K. (1995). Suicide in Scottish prisons: 1976–1993. *The Journal of Forensic Psychiatry* **6(3)**, 527–40.

Bonta, J. and Andrews, D.A. (2003). A commentary on Ward and Stewart's model of human needs. *Psychology, Crime and Law* **9(2)** 215–18.

Borrill J., Snow, L., Medlicott, D., Teers, R. and Paton, J. (2005). Learning from 'Near Misses': Interviews with women who survived an incident of severe self-harm in prison.*The Howard Journal of Criminal Justice* **44(1)**, 57–69.

Boster, F. J. and Mongeau, P. (1984). Fear arousing persuasive messages. In Bostrom (Ed.), *Communication Yearbook*. Beverley Hills: Sage.

Brady, K.E. and Crighton, D.A. (2003). Violent-offender groupwork. In G.J. Towl (Ed.), *Psychology in Prisons*. Oxford: Blackwell.

Brawley, O.W. (1999). The study of untreated syphilis in the Negro male. *International Journal of Radiation Oncology, Biology, Physics* **40(1)**, 5–8.

Brehm, J.W. (1966). *A Theory of Psychological Reactants*. Academic Press: San Diego.

Brooks-Gordon, B., Bilby, C., Kenworthy, T. *et al.* (2004). *A Systematic Review of Psychological Treatments for Adults Who have Sexually Offended or are at Risk of Sexually Offending*. Liverpool, UK: NHS National R&D Programme on Forensic Mental Health.

Brown, B., Crawford, P. and Hicks, C. (2003). *Evidence-Based Research: Dilemmas and Debates in Health Care*. Maidenhead: Open University Press.

Bureau of Justice (1998). Bureau of Justice Statistics. US Department of Justice Criminal Offender Statistics. http://www.ojp.usdoj.gov/bjs/crimoff.htm#sex1998

Calder, M.C. (1999). *Assessing Risk in Adult Males Who Sexually Abuse Children: A Practitioner's Guide*. Dorset: Russell House Publishing.

Campbell, D.T. and Fiske, D.W. (1959). Convergent and discriminant validation by the multitrait-multimethod matrix. *Psychological Bulletin* **56**, 81–105.

Chaikin, S. (1980). Puristic versus systemic information processing in the use of source versus message cues in persuasion. *Journal of Personality and Social Psychology* **39**,752–66.

Charlton, J. (1995). Trends and patterns in suicide in England and Wales. *International Journal of Epidemiology* **24**, 42–5.

Chen, S., Shechter, D. and Chaikin, S. (1996). Getting at the truth or getting along: Accuracy versus impression motivated heuristic and systemic processing. *Journal of Personality and Social Psychology* **71**, 262–75.

Cialdini, R.B. and Petty, R.E. (1981). Anticipatory opinion effects. In Petty, Ostrom and Brock (Eds), *Cognitive Responses in Persuasion*. Hillsdale: Erlbaum.

Cinamon, H. and Bradshaw, R. (2005). Prison health in England. *British Journal of Forensic Practice* **7(4)**, 8–13.

Clarke, J., Gerwirtz, S. and McLaughlin, E. (2000). Reinventing the welfare state. In J. Clarke, S. Gerwirtz and E. McLaughlin (Eds), *New Managerialism, New Welfare?* London: Sage Publications.

Cohen, M.A. (1998). The monetary value of saving a high-risk youth. *Journal of Quantitative Criminology* **14**, 1.

Coid, J., Wilkins, J., Coid, B. and Everitt, B. (1992). Self-mutilation in female remanded prisoners II: A cluster analytic approach towards identification of a behavioural syndrome. *Criminal Behaviour and Mental Health* **2**, 1–14.

Coker, J.B. and Martin, J.P. (1985*). Licensed to Live*. Oxford: Blackwell.

Colchester YOI Board of Visitors (1997). *Annual Report, 1997*. Colchester: Colchester YOI.

Connolly, T. Arkes, H.R. and Hammond, K.R. (2000). *Judgement and Decision Making (second edition)*. Cambridge: Cambridge University Press.

Cookson, H.M. (1977). A survey of self-injury in a closed prison for women. *British Journal of Criminology* **17(4)**, 332–47.

Cooper, A. (1995). Review of the role of antilibinal drugs in the treatment of sex offenders with mental retardation. *Mental Retardation* **33(1)**, 42–8.

Cooper, J., Fazio, R.H. and Rhodewalt, F. (1978). Dissonance and humour: Evidence for the undifferentiated nature of dissonance arousal. *Journal of Personality and Social Psychology* **36**,280–5.

Copas, J., Ditchfield, J. and Marshall, P. (1994). Development of a new risk prediction score. *Home Office RSD Research Bulletin* **36**, 23–9.

Craissati, J. (2004). *Managing High Risk Sex Offenders in the Community: A Psychological Approach*. Hove: Brunner-Routledge.

Craissati, J. and McClurg, G. (1997). The Challenge Project: A treatment programme evaluation for perpetrators of child sexual abuse. *Child Abuse and Neglect* **21**, 637–48.

Creighton, S. and King, V. (1996). *Prisoners and the Law*. London: Butterworths.

Crick, N.R. and Dodge, K.A. (1994). A review and reformulation of social information-processing mechanisms in children's social adjustment. *Psychological Bulletin* **115(1)**, 74–101.

Crighton, D. and Towl, G. (1997). Self-inflicted deaths in prison in England and Wales: An analysis of the data for 1988–90 and 1994–5. In G. Towl (Ed.), *Suicide and Self-Injury in Prisons, Issues in Criminological and Legal Psychology*. Leicester: The British Psychological Society.

Crighton, D.A. (1997). The psychology of suicide. In G.J. Towl (Ed.), *Suicide and Self-Injury in Prisons, Issues in Criminological and Legal Psychology*. Leicester: The British Psychological Society.

Crighton, D.A. (1999). Risk assessment in forensic mental health. *British Journal of Forensic Practice* **1(1)**, 16–18.

Crighton, D.A. (2000a). Suicide in prisons: A critique of UK research. In G.J. Towl, L. Snow and M.J. McHugh (Eds), *Suicide in Prisons*. Leicester: BPS Books.

Crighton, D.A. (2000b). Suicide in prisons in England and Wales 1988–1998: An Empirical Study. Unpublished Ph.D. dissertation. Anglia Ruskin University, Cambridge, UK.

Crighton, D.A. (2004). Risk assessment. In A.P.C. Needs and G.J. Towl (Eds), *Applying Psychology to Forensic Practice*. Oxford: Blackwell.

Crighton, D.A. and Towl, G.J. (2002). Intentional self-injury. In G.J. Towl, L. Snow and M.J. McHugh (Eds), *Suicide in Prisons*. Leicester: BPS Books.

Cronbach, L.J. (1951). Coefficient alpha and the internal structure of tests. *Psychometrika* **16**, 297–334.

Crowe, J.E.M. (1997). HMYOI Colchester: 'Marching toward better citizenship'. *Journal of the Military Provost Staff and the Military Provost Staff Corps Association* **99**, 18–22.

Cullen, E. and Newell, T. (1999). *Murderers and Life Imprisonment*. Winchester: Waterside Press.

Cullen, F.T. (1990). Does correctional treatment work? A clinically relevant and psychologically informed meta-analysis. *Criminology* **28**, 369–404.

Cullen, J.E. (1985). Prediction and treatment of self-injury by female young offenders. In D.P. Farrington and R. Tarling (Eds), *Prediction in Criminology*. Albany: State University of New York Press.

Davanloo, H. (1978). *Basic Principles and Techniques in Short-Term Dynamic Psychotherapy*. New York: Spectrum.

DaVinchi, L. (1998). *The Notebooks of Leonardo Da Vinci: Selections (Oxford World's Classics)*. Oxford: Oxford Paperbacks.

Day, K.(1994). Male mentally handicapped sex offenders. *British Journal of Psychiatry* **165**, 630–9.

Department of Health (2004). *The Organisation and Delivery of Psychological Therapies*. London: DOH.

Dexter, P. and Towl, G.J. (1995). An investigation into suicidal behaviours in prison. *Issues in Criminological and Legal Psychology* **22**, 45–53.

DiFazio, R., Abracen, J. and Looman, J. (2001). Group versus individual treatment of sexual offenders: A comparison. *Forum on Corrections Research* **13**, 56–9.

Dodd, T., Nicholas, S., Povey, D. and Walker, A. (2004). *Crime in England and Wales 2003/2004*. London: Home Office.

Dodge, K.A. (1986). A social information-processing model of social competence in children. In M. Perlmutter (Ed.), *Eighteenth Annual Minnesota Symposium on Child Psychology. Cognitive Perspectives on Children's Social and Behavioural Development*. Hillsdale, NJ: Erlbaum.

Donald, I. and Cooper, S.R. (2001). A facet approach to extending the normative component of the theory of reasoned action. *British Journal of Social Psychology* **40**, 500–621.

Dooley, E. (1990a). Prison Suicide in England and Wales, 1972–87. *The British Journal of Psychiatry* **156**, 40–45.

Dooley, E. (1990b). Non-natural deaths in prison. *British Journal of Criminology* **30(2)**, 229–34.

Dorries, C. (1999). *Coroners' Courts: A Guide to Law and Practice*. Chichester: John Wiley and Sons.

Drake, C. R. and Ward, T. (2003). Practical and theoretical roles for the formulation based treatment of sexual offenders. *International Journal of Forensic Psychology* **1(1)**, 71–84.

Driescher, K.H., Lammers, S.M. and van der Staak, C.P. (2004). Treatment motivation: An attempt for clarification of an ambiguous concept. *Clinical Psychology Review* **23(8)**, 1115–37.

D'Silva, K., Duggan, C. and McCarthy, L. (2004). does treatment really make psychopaths worse? A review of the evidence. *Journal of Personality Disorders* **18**, 2.

Dumond, R. W. (1992). The sexual assault of male prisoners in incarcerated settings *International Journal of the Sociology of Law* **20**, 135–57.

Duncan, B.L. and Miller, S.D. (2000). *The Heroic Client*. San Francisco: Jossey Bass.

Durkheim, E. (1887). *Suicide: A Study in Sociology*. Translated by J.A. Spaulding and G. Simpson (1952). London: Routledge and Kegan Paul.

Durkheim, E. (1952). *Suicide*. London: Routledge and Kegan Paul.

Durkheim, E. (1953). *Sociology and Philosophy*. New York: Free Press.

Fairbairn, G.J. (1995). *Contemplating Suicide: The Language and Ethics of Self-Harm.* London: Routledge.

Falshaw, L. (1993). Why Me? Can incarcerated young offenders be identified as potential victims of bullying by their behaviour within the penal environment? Unpublished BSc thesis. Aston University, UK.

Falshaw, L., Friendship, C. and Bates, A. (2003a). Sexual offenders – measuring reconviction, reoffending and recidivism. *Home Office Research Findings 183.* London: Home Office.

Falshaw, L., Friendship, C., Travers, R. and Nugent, F. (2003b). Searching for 'What Works': An evaluation of cognitive skills programmes. *Home Office Research Findings 206.* London: Home Office.

Farrington, D.P. (1993). Understanding and preventing bullying. In M. Tonry (Ed.), *Crime and Justice: A Review of Research.* Chicago: University of Chicago Press.

Farrington, D.P. (2003). British Randomized Experiments on Crime and Justice, Paper given at Symposium on 'Randomized Experiments in the Social Sciences' in Oxford, June, 2002, To be Published in: *Annals of the American Academy of Political and Social Science.*

Farrington, D.P. and Coid, J. (2003). *Early Prevention of Adult Antisocial Behaviour.* Cambridge: Cambridge University Press.

Farrington, D.P. and Jolliffe, D. (2002). *A Feasibility Study into Using a Randomised Controlled Trial to Evaluate Treatment Pilots at HMP Whitemoor (RDS/01/250).* Cambridge: Institute of Criminology, University of Cambridge.

Farrington, D.P, Hancock, G., Livingston, M., Painter, K. and Towl, G.J. (2000). Evaluation of intensive regimes for young offenders. *Home Office Research Findings 121.* London: Development and Statistics Directorate.

Farrington, D.P., Ditchfield, J., Hancock, G. *et al.* (2002a). *Evaluation of Two Intensive Regimes for Young Offenders.* London: Home Office (Research Study No. 239).

Farrington, D.P., Ditchfield, J., Howard, P. and Jolliffe, D. (2002b). Two intensive regimes for young offenders: A follow-up evaluation. *Home Office Research Findings 163.* London: Home Office.

Favazza, A.R. (1996). *Bodies under Siege: Self-Mutilation and Body Modification in Culture and Psychiatry (second edition).* Baltimore: The Johns Hopkins University Press.

Festinger, L. (1957). *A Theory of Cognitive Dissonance.* Evanston: Rowe, Peterson.

Festinger, L. and Carlsmith, J.M. (1959). Cognitive consequences of forced compliance. *Journal of Abnormal and Social Psychology* **58**, 203–10.

Feyerabend, P. (1999). Knowledge, science and relativism. In J. Preston (Ed.), *Philosophical Papers Volume 3.* Cambridge: Cambridge University Press.

Finkelhor, D. (1979). *Sexually Victimised Children.* New York: Free Press.

Finkelhor, D. (1984). *Child Sexual Abuse: New Theory and Research.* New York: Free Press.

Fisher, D. (1995). The therapeutic impact of sex offender treatment programmes. *Probation Journal* **42**, 2–7.

Flowers, G.T, Carr, T.S. and Ruback, R.B. (1991). *Special Alternative Incarceration Evaluation.* Georgia: Georgia Department of Corrections.

Freidman, J. and Sears, D. (1965). Warning, distraction and resistance to influence. *Journal of Personality and Social Psychology* **1**, 262–6.

Friendship, C., Beech, A. and Browne, K.D. (2002). Reconviction as an outcome measure in research. A methodological note. *British Journal of Criminology* **42**, 442–4.

Friendship, C., Falshaw, L. and Beech, A. (2003a). Measuring the real impact of accredited offending behaviour programmes. *Legal and Criminological Psychology* **8**, 115–7.

Friendship, C., Mann, R. and Beech, A. (2003b). The prison-based Sex Offender Treatment Programme – an evaluation. *Home Office Research Findings 205*. London: Home Office.

Friendship, L., Mann, R. and Beech, A. (2003c). Evaluation of a national prison-based treatment program for sexual offenders in England and Wales. *Journal of Interpersonal Violence* **18(7)**, 744–59.

Frisher, M., Heatlie, H. and Hickman, M. (2004). *Estimating the Prevalence of Problematic and Injecting Drug Use for Drug Action Team Areas in England: A Feasibility study using the Multiple Indicator Method.* London: Home Office London, online report.

Furby, L., Weintrott, M. and Blackshaw, L. (1989). Sex offender recidivism: A review. *Psychological Bulletin* **105**, 3–30.

Geddes, J.R. and Juszczak, E. (1995). Period trends in the rate of suicide in the first 28 days after discharge from psychiatric hospital in Scotland, 1968–92. *British Medical Journal* **311**, 357–60.

Geddes, J.R., Juszczak, E., O'Brien, F. *et al.* (1997). Suicide in the 12 months after discharge from psychiatric inpatient care, Scotland 1968–92. *Journal of Epidemiology and Community Health* **51**, 430–34.

Gendreau, P., Goggin, C. and Smith, P. (2000). Generating rational correctional policies: An introduction to advances in cumulating knowledge. *Corrections Management Quarterly* **4**, 52–60.

Gendreau, P., Goggin, C., Cullen, F.T. and Paparozzi, P. (2002). The common-sense revolution and correctional policy. In J. McGuire (Ed.), *Offender Rehabilitation and Treatment: Effective Programmes and Policies to Reduce Re-Offending.* Chichester: John Wiley and Sons.

Gilbert, D., Fiske, S. and Lindzey, G. (Eds) (1998). *The Handbook of Social Psychology (fourth edition, vol. 1).* Boston: McGraw Hill.

Gilbert, P. (2005a). Bullying in prisons: An evolutionary and biopsychosocial approach'. In J.L. Ireland (Ed.), *Bullying Among Prisoners: Innovations in Theory and Research.* Devon, UK: Willan.

Gilbert, P. (2005b). Compassion and cruelty: A biopsychosocial approach. In P. Gilbert (Ed.), *Compassion: Conceptualisations, Research and Use in Psychotherapy.* London: Brunner-Routledge.

Gilbert, P. and Miles, J.N.V. (2000). Sensitivity to social put-down: It's relationship to perceptions of social rank, shame, social anxiety, depression, anger and self-other blame. *Personality and Individual Differences* **29**, 757–74.

Glasser, W. (1965). *Reality Therapy.* New York: Harper Row.

Good, D.A. and Watts, F.N. (1989). Qualitative research. In G. Parry and F.N. Watts (Eds), *Behavioural And Mental Health Research: A Handbook Of Skills And Methods.* Hove: Lawrence Erlbaum Associates.

Goring, C. (1913). *The English Convict.* London: HMSO.

Gossop, M. (2005). *Drug Misuse Treatment and Reductions In Crime: Findings from the National Treatment Outcome Research Study (NTORS), National Treatment Agency for Substance Misuse, NHS, Research Briefing 8.* London: DOH.

Gossop, M., Marsden, J. and Stewart, D. (1998). *NTORS at One Year: Changes in Substance Use, Health and Criminal Behaviour One Year After Intake*. London: DOH.

Gunn, J. (2000). Future directions for treatment in forensic psychiatry. *British Journal of Psychiatry* **176**, 332–8.

Gunnell, D. and Frankel, S. (1994). Prevention of suicide: Aspirations and evidence. *British Medical Journal* **308**, 1227–33.

Guttman, L. (1968). A general nonmetric technique for finding the smallest coordinate space for a configuration of points. *Psychometrika* **33**, 469–506.

Hafiz, N. and Ireland, J.L. (2005). Psychological health, social self-esteem and bullying behaviour among prisoners: A study of young, adult and juvenile offenders. *Submitted manuscript*.

Hall, D. (2001). Reflecting on Redfern: What can we learn from the Alder Hey story? *Archives of Disease in Childhood* **84**, 455–6.

Hallsworth, S. (2005). In J. Pratt, D. Brown, M. Brown, S. Hallworth, and W. Morrison (Eds), The *New Punitiveness; Trends, Theories, Perspectives*. Devon, UK: Willan.

Hankoff, L.D. (1980). Prisoner suicide. *International Journal of Offender Therapy and Comparative Criminology* **24(2)**, 162–6.

Hanson, R.K. and Bussiere, M.T. (1998). Predicting relapse: A meta-analysis of sexual offender recidivism studies. *Journal of Consulting and Clinical Psychology* **66**, 348–62.

Hanson, R.K. and Thornton, D. (2000). Improving risk assessments for sexual offenders: A comparison of three actuarial scales. *Law and Human Behaviour* **24**, 119–36.

Hanson, R.K., Steffy, R.A. and Gauthier, R. (1993). Long term recidivism of child molesters. *Journal of Consulting and Clinical Psychology* **61**, 646–52.

Hanson, R.K., Gordon, A., Harris, A.J.R. *et al.* (2002). First report on the collaborative outcome data project on the effectiveness of psychological treatment for sex offenders. *Sexual Abuse: A Journal of Research and Treatment* **14**, 169–94.

Hanson, R.K., Broom, I. and Stephenson, M. (2004). Evaluating community sex offender programmes: A 12-year follow-up of 724 offenders. *Canadian Journal of Behavioural Science* **36(2)**, 85–94.

Harper, G. and Chitty, C. (2005). The impact of corrections on re-offending: A review of 'What Works' (second edition). *Home Office Research Study 291*. London: Home Office.

Hatty, S. and Walker, J. (1986). A National Study of Deaths in Australian Prisons. Canberra: Australian Institute of Criminology.

Hawk, G., Rosefield, B. and Warren, J. (1993). Prevalence of sexual offences amongst mentally retarded criminal defendants. *Hospital and Community Psychiatry* **44(8)**, 784–6.

Hawton, K. and Van Heeringen, K. (2000). Future perspectives. In K. Hawton and K. Van Heeringen (Eds), *The International Handbook of Suicide and Attempted Suicide*. Chichester: John Wiley and Sons.

Hayes, R.A. (2004). Introduction to evidence-based practices. In C.E. Stout and R.A. Haynes (Eds), *The Evidence-Based Practice: Methods, Models and Tools for Mental Health Professionals*. Hoboken, NJ: John Wiley and Sons.

Henning, K.R. and Freuh, B.C. (1996). Cognitive-behavioural treatment of incarcerated offenders: An evaluation of the Vermont Department of Corrections' cognitive self-change programme. *Criminal Justice and Behaviour* **23**, 523–41.

Henry, J. (2001). *The Scientific Revolution and the Origins of Modern Science (Studies in European History)*. Basingstoke, UK: Palgrave Macmillan.

HM Chief Inspector of Prisons and Inspector of Probation (1999). *Lifers: A Joint Thematic Review By Her Majesty's Inspectorates of Prisons and Probation*. London: Home Office.

HM Inspectorate of Prisons (1999). *Suicide in Prisons – Thematic Review*. London: Home Office.

HM Prison Service (2002). *Counselling, Assessment, Referral, Advice and Throughcare Services. Prison Service Order 3630*. London: HMPS.

HM Prison Service (2004a). *Lifer Manual PSI 28/2004*. London: HMPS.

HM Prison Service (2004b). *Prison Service Order (7035) Research Applications and Ethics Panel*. London: HMPS.

HM Prison Service and the National Probation Service (2003). *Driving Delivery; A Strategic Framework for Psychological Services in HM Prison Service and the National Probation Service*. London: Home Office.

Hodge, J. and Renwick, S.J. (2002). Motivating mentally abnormal offenders. In M. McMurran (Ed.), *Motivating Offenders To Change: A Guide To Engagement In Therapy*. Chichester: John Wiley and Sons.

Hollin. C.R. (2002). Risk-needs assessment and the allocation to offender programmes. In J. McGuire (Ed.), *Offender Rehabilitation and Treatment: Effective Programmes and Policies to Reduce Re-Offending*. Chichester: John Wiley and Sons.

Home Office (1966). *Report of the Inquiry Into Prison Escapes and Security by Admiral of the Fleet, the Earl Mountbatten of Burma*. Cmnd. 3175. London: HMSO.

Home Office (1990). *Victims Charter*. London: Home Office.

Home Office (1995). *National Standards for the Supervision of Offenders in the Community*. London: Home Office.

Home Office (1997). *Prison Population in 1997, England and Wales*. London: Home Office.

Home Office (2004). *Annual Report and Accounts of the Parole Board for England and Wales 2003–2004 (HC1100)*. London: The Stationery Office.

Hood, C. (1991). A public management for all seasons. *Public Administration* **69**, 1.

Hood, R. and Shute, S. (2000). The parole system as work: A study of risk based decision-making. Home Office Research Study No. 202, London, Home Office.

Hood, S.C. and Shute, R. Unpublished research paper. Quoted in Padfield (2002).

Hood, R, Shute, S, Feilzer, M, and Wilcox, A. (2002). Sex offenders emerging from long-term imprisonment: A study of their long-term reconviction rates and of parole boar members' judgements of their risk. *British Journal of Criminalogy* **42(2)**, 371–94.

Horvath, A.O. and Symonds, B.D. (1991). Relationship between working alliance and outcome in psychotherapy: A meta-analysis. *Journal of Counselling Psychology* **28**, 139–49.

Houston, J., Wrench, M. and Hosking, N. (1995). Group processes in the treatment of child sex offenders. *The Journal of Forensic Psychiatry* **6(2)**, 359–68.

Hovland, C.I. and Weiss, W. (1951). The influence of source credibility on communication effectiveness. *Public Opinion Quarterly* **15**, 635–50.

Howell, D.C. (1999). *Fundamental Statistics for the Behavioural Sciences (fourth edition)*. Pacific Grove, CA: Duxbury Press.

Howells, K. and Day, A. (2003). Readiness for anger management: Clinical and theoretical issues. *Clinical Psychology Review* **23**, 319–37.

Howells, K., Day, A. and Bryan, J. (2005). Readiness for treatment in high risk offenders with personality disorders. International Association of Forensic Mental Health Services, 5th Annual Conference, Melbourne, Australia, 18–21 April.

Howells, K., Day, A., Bubner, S. *et al.* (2002). Anger Management and violence prevention: Improving effectiveness. *Trends and Issues in Crime and Criminal Justice, 207.* Australian Institute of Criminology.

Hubbard, R., Craddock, S., Flynn, P., Anderson, J. and Etheridge, R. (1997). Overview of 1-year Outcomes in the Drug Abuse Outcome Study (DATOS). *Psychology of Addictive Behaviours* **11(4)**, 261–78.

Hudson, D.I. (2002). Women life sentence prisoners and the staff who work with them. Unpublished PhD dissertation. Anglia Ruskin University, Cambridge.

Hudson, K. (2005). *Offending Identities: Sex Offenders' Perspectives on their Treatment and Management.* Devon, UK: Willan.

Huesmann, L.R. (1998). The role of social information processing and cognitive schema in the acquisition and maintenance of habitual aggressive behaviour. In R.G. Geen and E. Donnerstein. *Human Aggression: Theories, Research, and Implications for Social Policy.* London: Academic Press.

Huesmann, L. R. and Podolski, C.L. (2003). Punishment: A psychological perspective. In S. McConville (Ed.), *The Use of Punishment.* Devon, UK: Willan.

Ireland, C. and Ireland, J.L. (2000). Descriptive analysis of the nature and extent of bullying behaviour in a maximum-security prison. *Aggressive Behavior* **26**, 213–33.

Ireland, J.L. (1999a). Bullying behaviours amongst male and female prisoners: A study of young offenders and adults. *Aggressive Behavior* **25**, 162–78.

Ireland, J.L. (1999b). Provictim attitudes and empathy in relation to bullying behaviour among prisoners. *Legal and Criminological Psychology* **4**, 51–66.

Ireland, J.L. (2001a). The relationship between social problem solving and bullying among male and female adult prisoners. *Aggressive Behaviour* **27**, 297–312.

Ireland, J.L. (2001b). Bullying behaviour among male and female adult prisoners: A study of perpetrator and victim characteristics. *Legal and Criminological Psychology* **6**, 229–46.

Ireland J.L. (2002a). Social self-esteem and self-reported bullying behaviour among adult prisoners. *Aggressive Behavior* **28(3)**, 184–97.

Ireland, J.L. (2002b). Do juveniles bully more than young offenders? A comparison of the perceived and actual bullying behaviour reported by juvenile and young offenders. *Journal of Adolescence* **25**, 155–168.

Ireland, J.L. (2002c). How does assertiveness relate to bullying behaviour among prisoners? *Legal and Criminological Psychology* **7**, 87–100.

Ireland, J.L. (2002d). *Bullying Among Prisoners: Evidence, Research and Intervention Strategies.* London: Brunner-Routledge.

Ireland, J.L. (Ed.) (2005a). *Bullying Among Prisoners: Innovations in Theory and Research.* Devon, UK: Willan.

Ireland, J.L. (2005b). Psychological health and bullying behaviour among adolescent prisoners; A study of young and juvenile offenders. *Journal of Adolescent Health.* In press.

Ireland, J.L. (2005c). Bullying among prisoners: The need for innovation. In J.L. Ireland (Ed.), *Bullying Among Prisoners: Innovations in Theory and Research*. Devon, UK: Willan.

Ireland, J.L. (2005d). Prison bullying and fear: Can fear assist with explanations of victim responses? In J.L. Ireland (Ed.), *Bullying Among Prisoners: Innovations in Theory and Research*. Devon, UK: Willan.

Ireland, J.L. (2005e). Patient-to-patient anti-bullying policy and procedures: Ashworth High Secure Hospital. Unpublished documentation.

Ireland, J.L. and Archer, J. (1996). Descriptive analysis of bullying in male and female adult prisoners. *Journal of Community and Applied Social Psychology* **6**, 35–47.

Ireland, J.L. and Archer, J. (2002). The perceived consequences of responding to bullying with aggression: A study of male and female adult prisoners. *Aggressive Behavior* **28**, 257–72.

Ireland, J.L. and Archer, J. (2004). The association between measures of aggression and bullying among juvenile and young offenders. *Aggressive Behavior* **30**, 29–42.

Ireland, J.L. and Ireland, C.A. (2003). How do offenders define bullying? A study of adult, young and juvenile male offenders. *Legal and Criminological Psychology* **8**, 159–73.

Ireland, J.L. and Monaghan, R. (2005). Behaviours indicative of bullying among young and juvenile male offenders: A study of perpetrator and victim characteristics, *Aggressive Behavior*, in press.

Ireland, J.L. and Murray, E. (2005). Social problem solving and bullying: Are prison bullies really impaired problem solvers? In J.L. Ireland (Ed.), *Bullying Among Prisoners: Innovations in Theory and Research*. Devon, UK: Willan.

Ireland, J.L. and Power, C.L. (2004). Attachment, emotional loneliness and bullying behaviour: A study of adult and young offenders. *Aggressive Behavior* **30**, 298–312.

Ireland, J.L. Archer, J. and Power, C.L. (2005). Nature and extent of behaviours indicative of bullying among male and female adult prisoners: A study of behavioural and descriptive predictors. *Submitted manuscript*.

Jadad, A.R. (1998). *Randomised Control Trials a User's Guide*. London: BMJ Books.

Jobes, D.A., Berman, A.L. and Josselon, A.R. (1986). The impact of psychological autopsies on medical examiners' determination of manner of death. *Journal of Forensic Sciences* **31**, 177–89.

John Howard Society of Alberta (1997). Alternative Custody Programs for Youth.

Jones, J.H. (1993). *Bad Blood: The Tuskegee Syphilis Experiment (new and expanded edition)*. New York: Free Press.

Jones, L. (2005). Notes from the chair. *Forensic Update* **83**, 3.

Kempinen, C. and Kurlychek, M.C. (2001). Pennsylvania's Motivational Boot Camp: Report to the Legislature.

Kenworthy, T., Adams, C.E., Bilby, C., Brooks-Gordon, B. and Fenton, M. (2003). Psychological interventions for those who have sexually offended or are at risk of offending. *The Cochrane Database of Systemic Reviews. Issue 4. Art. No.: CD004858. DOI: 10.1002/14651858.CD004858*.

Kershaw, C. (1999). Reconviction of offenders sentenced of released from prison in 1994. *Home Office Research Findings No. 90*. London: Development and Statistics Directorate.

Knight, R.A. and Prentky, R.A. (1990). Classifying sexual offenders: The development and corroboration of taxonomic models. In W.L. Marshall, D.R. Laws and H.E. Barbaree (Eds.), *Handbook Of Sexual Assault: Issues, Theories and Treatment of the Offender*. New York: Plenum Press.

Krietman, N. (1977). *Parasuicide*. Chichester: John Wiley and Sons.

Kuhn, T. (1996). *The Structure of Scientific Revolutions (third edition)*. Chicago: Chicago University Press.

Lambert, J.A., Cronin, S., Chasten, A.L. and Lickel, B. (1996). Private versus public expressions of racial prejudice. *Journal of Experimental Social Psychology* **32**, 437–59.

Lane-Morton, T. (2005). What health partnerships should seek to provide for offenders. *British Journal of Forensic Practice* **7(4)**, 3–7.

Latissa, E.J., Cullen, F.T. and Gendreau. P. (2002). beyond correctional quackery – professionalism and the possibility of effective treatment. *Federal Probation* **66**, 43–9.

Leddy, J. and O'Connell, M. (2002). The prevalence, nature and psychological correlates of bullying in Irish prisons. *Legal and Criminological Psychology* **7**, 131–40.

Lea, S., Auburn, T. and Kibblewhite, K. (1999). Working with sex offenders: The perceptions and experiences of professionals and paraprofessionals. *International Journal of Offender Therapy and Comparative Criminology* **43(1)**, 103–19.

Lee, M. and George, S. (2005). Drug strategy unit. *British Journal of Forensic Practice* **7(4)**, 39–48.

Lee-Evans, M. (1994). Behavioural assessment. In M. McMurran and J. Hodge (Ed.) *Assessment of Clients in Secure Settings*. UK: Jessica Kingsley Publishers.

Levant, R. (2004). The empirically-validated treatments movement: A practitioner/educator perspective. *Clinical Psychology Science and Practice*, **11**, 219–24.

Liebling, A. (1991). Suicide in prisons. Unpublished PhD dissertation. University of Cambridge, UK.

Liebling, A. (1992). *Suicides in Prison*. London: Routledge.

Liebling, A. and Krarup, H. (1993). *Suicide and Self-Injury in Male Prisons – A Summary*. London: Home Office.

Linehan, M.M., Armstrong, H.E., Suarez, A., Allmon, D. and Heard, H.L. (1991). Cognitive-behavioural treatment of chronically parasuicidal borderline patients. *Archives of General Psychiatry* **50**, 971–4.

Lingoes, J.C. (1973). *The Guttman-Lingoes Non-Metric Program Series*. Ann Arbor, MI: Mathesis.

Livingston, M., Jones, V. and Hussain, S. (1994). The extent of bullying amongst adult prisoners at HMP/YOI Moorlands. Unpublished Report, Psychology Research Report, 20, East Midlands, UK.

Livingston, M.S. and Chapman, A.J. (1997). Bullying and self-injurious behaviour in young offenders. *Journal of Prison Service Psychology* **3**, 78 - 81.

Looman, J., Abracen, J. and Nicholaichuk, T.P. (2000). Recidivism among treated sexual offenders and matched controls: Data from the regional treatment centre (Ontario). *Journal of Interpersonal Violence* **15**, 279–90.

Lösel, F. (1998). Treatment and management of psychopaths. In D. Cooke, A.E. Forth and Hare (Eds), *Psychopathy: Theory, Research and Implications for Society*. NATO Science Series, 88.

Machin, D., Coghill, N. and Levy, E. (1999). Life sentence prisoners in Scotland. Edinburgh, Stationary Office.

MacKenzie, D.L. (1990). Boot Camp prisons: Components, evaluations and empirical issues. *Federal Probation* **54**, 44–52.

MacKenzie, D.L. (1994). Results of a multi-site study of boot camp prisons. *Federal Probation* **58(2)**, 60–6.

MacKenzie, D.L., Brame, R., McDowall, D. and Souryal, C. (1995). Boot camp prisons and recidivism in eight states. *Criminology* **33**, 327–57.

MacKenzie, D.L., Wilson, D.B. and Kider, S.B. (2001). Effects of correctional boot camps on offending. *Annals of American Academy of Political and Social Science* **578**, 126–43.

Mann, R.E., Webster, S.D., Schofield, C. and Marshall, W.L. (2004). Approach verses avoidance goals in relapse prevention with sex offenders. *Sexual Abuse* **16(1)**, 65–75.

Mantle, G. and Moore, S. (2004). On probation: Pickled and nothing to say.*The Howard Journal of Criminal Justice* **43(3)**, 299–316.

Mark, P. (1992). Training staff to work with sex offenders. *Probation Journal* **30(l)**, 1–13.

Marques, J.K., Day, D.M., Nelson, C. and West, M.A. (1994). Effects of cognitive-behavioural treatment on sex offender recidivism. *Criminal Justice and Behaviour* **21**, 28–54.

Marshall, W.L. (1999). Diagnosis and treatment of sexual offenders. In I.B. Weiner and A.K. Hess (Eds), *The Handbook of Forensic Psychology (second edition)*. New York: Wiley.

Marshall, W.L. and Serran, G.A. (2004). The role of therapist in offender treatment. *Psychology, Crime and Law* **10(3)**, 309–20

Marshall, W.L., Eccles, A. and Barbaree, H.E. (1991a). The treatment of exhibitionists: A focus on sexual deviance versus cognitive relationship features. *Behaviour Research and Therapy* **29**, 129–35.

Marshall, W.L., Jones, R., Ward, A. *et al.* (1991b). Treatment outcome with sex offenders. *Clinical Psychology Review* **11**, 465–85.

Martin, C. and Player, E. (2000). *Drug Treatment in Prison; An Evaluation of the RAPt Treatment Programme*. Winchester: Waterside Press.

Martin, C., Player, E. and Liriano, S. (2003). Results of evaluations of the RAPt Drug treatment programme. In M. Ramsay (Ed.), *Prisoners' Drug Use and Treatment: Seven Research Studies, Home Office Research Study 267*. RDS, Home Office: London.

Maxwell P. and Mallon D. (1997). Discrimination against ex-offenders.*The Howard Journal* **36**, 352–66.

McCall, M. (2004). Deaths in Custody in Australia: 2003, National Deaths in Custody Program (NDICP) Annual Report, Canberra, Australian Institute of Criminology.

McConaghy, N. (1995). Are sex offenders ever 'cured'? Treatment options are limited by a lack of scientific evidence. *The Medical Journal of Australia* **162**, 397.

McConaghy N., Blasczynski, A. and Kidson, W. (1988). Treatment of sex offenders with imaginal desensitization and/or medroxyprogesterone. *Acta Psychiatricia Scandinavicia* **77**, 199–206.

McConaghy, N., Armstrong, M.S. and Blaszcynski, A. (1988). Expectancy, covert sensitisation and imaginal desesitization in compulsive sexuality. *Acta Psychiatrica Scandinavica* **72**, 176–87.

McCord, N. (1991). *British History, 1815–1906*. Oxford: Oxford University Press.

McCorkle, R.C. (1992). Personal precautions to violence in prison. *Criminal Justice and Behavior* **19**, 160–73.

McGrath, M., Cann, S. and Konopasky, R. (1998). New measures of defensiveness, empathy, and cognitive distortions for sexual offenders against children. *Sexual Abuse: A Journal of Research and Treatment* **10**, 25–36.

McGrath, R.J., Cumming, G., Livingstone, J. and Hoke, S. (2003). Outcome of a treatment programme for adult sex offenders: From prison to community. *Journal of Interpersonal Violence* **18**, 3–18.

McGuire, J. (Ed.) (1995). *What Works: Reducing Reoffending*. Chichester: John Wiley and Sons.

McGuire J. (1997). Plenary Sessions: Researching 'what works': Some implications for the use of imprisonment.*Inside Psychology* **3**, 1.

McGuire, J. (2000). Defining correctional programmes. *Forum on Correctional Research* **12**, 5–9.

McGuire, J. (2002). Integrating findings from research reviews. In J. McGuire (Ed.), *Offender Rehabilitation and Treatment; Effective Programme and Policies to Reduce Re-Offending*. Chichester: John Wiley and Sons.

McGuire, J. (2004). Commentary: Promising answers, and the next generation of questions.*Psychology, Crime and Law* **10(3)**, 335–45.

McGuire, J. and Priestly, P. (2000). Reviewing what works: Past, present and future. In J. McGuire (Ed.), *What Works: Reducing Reoffending, Guidelines from Research and Practice*. London: John Wiley and Sons.

McGurk, B.J. and McDougall, C. (1991). The prevention of bullying among incarcerated delinquents. In P.K. Smith and D. Thompson (Eds), *Practical Approaches to Bullying*. London: David Fulton.

McGurk, J. (2001). What works in correctional intervention? Evidence and practical implications. In G.A. Bernfeld, D.P. Farrington and A.W. Leschied (Eds), *Offender Rehabilitation in Practice: Implementing and Evaluating Effective Programmes*. Chichester: John Wiley and Sons.

McHugh, M.J. (2000). Suicide prevention in prisons: Policy and practice. *British Journal of Forensic Practice* **2(1)**, 12–16.

McMurran, M. and Theodosi, E. (2005). (In submission). Is offender treatment non-completion associated with increased reconviction over no treatment?

McNeill, F., Batchelor, S., Burnett, R. and Knox, J. (2005). 21st*Century Social Work, Reducing Re-Offending: Key Practice Skills*. Edinburgh: Scottish Executive.

Meltzer, H., Jenkins, R., Singleton, N., Charlton, J. and Yar, M. (1999). *Non-Fatal Suicidal Behaviour among Prisoners*. London: Office for National Statistics.

Menninger, K. (1935). A psychoanalytic study of the significance of self-mutilations. *Psychoanalytic Quarterly* **4**, 408–46.

Menninger, K. (1938). *Man against Himself*. London: Rupert Hart-Davis (Harvest Books).

Meyer, L.J., Cole, C. and Emroy, E. (1992). Treatment for sex offending behaviour: An evaluation of outcome. *Bulletin of the American Academy of Law* **20**, 249–53.

Michel, K. (2000). Suicide prevention and primary care. In K. Hawton and K. Van Heeringen (Eds), *The International Handbook of Suicide and Attempted Suicide*. Chichester: John Wiley and Sons.

Miller, G.A. (1967). *Psychology – The Science of Mental Life*. Harmondsworth: Pelican/ Penguin.

Miller, T., Gemmell, L., Hay, G. and Donnall, M. (2004). *The Dynamics of Drug Misuse: Assessing Changes in Prevalence*. Home Office: London.

Millon, T. (1999). *Personality-Guided Therapy*. Chichester: John Wiley and Sons.

Minichiello, V., Aroni, R., Timewell, E. and Alexander, L. (1990). *In-Depth Interviewing: Researching People*. Melbourne: Longman Cheshire.

Mitchell, B. (1989). A Report on the Nature of 250 Convictions for Murder Between 1978 and 1982. *In House of Lords (1989) Report of the Select Committee on Murder and Life Imprisonment. Volume III – Oral Evidence Part 2, and Written Evidence*. London: HMSO.

Monahan, J., Steadman, H., Silver, E. *et al.* (2001). *Rethinking Risk Assessment: The Macarthur Study of Mental Disorder and Violence*. New York: Oxford University Press.

Moore, D. and Hannah-Moffat, K. (2005). The liberal veil: Revisiting Canadian penality. In J. Pratt, D. Brown, M. Brown, S. Hallworth, and W. Morrison (Eds), *The New Punitiveness; Trends, Theories, Perspectives*. Devon, UK: Willan.

Morgan, H.G. (1979). *Death Wishes? The Understanding and Management of Deliberate Self-Harm*. Chichester: John Wiley and Sons.

Morrison, D. and Gilbert, P. (2001). Social rank, shame and anger in primary and secondary psychopaths. *The Journal of Forensic Psychiatry* **12(2)**, 330–56.

Mullen, P.E., Martin, J.L., Anderson, J.C., Romans, S.E. and Herbison, G.P. (1994). *British Journal of Psychiatry* **165**, 35–47.

Narey, M. (2005). The challenge of reducing offending behaviour – the English experience. Key note address. International Association of Forensic Mental Health Services, 5th Annual Conference, Melbourne, Australia, 18–21 April.

Neuringer, C. (1962). Methodological problems in suicide research. *Journal of Consultant Psychology* **26**, 273–8.

Nicholaichuk, T., Gordon, A., Gu, D. and Wong, S. (2000). Outcome of an institutional sexual offender treatment programme: A comparison between treated and matched untreated offenders. *Sexual Abuse: A Journal of Research and Treatment* **12**, 139–53.

Nicholas, S., Povey, D., Walker, A. and Kershaw, C. (2005).*Crime in England and Wales 2004/2005*. London: The Stationery Office.

NOMS (2005). *National and Offender Management Service Strategy for the Management and Treatment of Problematic Drug Users within the Correctional Services*. London: Home Office.

O'Carroll, P.W. (1993). Suicide causation: Pies, paths and pointless polemics. *Suicide Life Threatening Behaviour* **23**, 27–36.

O'Connor, R. and Sheehey, N. (2000). *Understanding Suicidal Behaviour*. Leicester: BPS Books.

O'Donnell, I. and Edgar, K. (1996). The extent and dynamics of victimization in prisons (revised report). Unpublished research paper. Centre for Criminological Research, University of Oxford, UK.

Olgloff, J.R.P. and Davies, M. R. (2004). Advances in offender assessment and rehabilitation: Contributions of the risk – needs – responsivity approach. *Psychology, Crime and Law* **10(3)**, 229–42.

Padfield, N. (2002). *Beyond the Tariff: Human Rights and the Release of Life Sentence Prisoners*. Devon, UK: Willan.

Petty, R.E. and Cacioppo, J.T. (1977). Forewarning, cognitive responding and resistance to persuasion. *Journal of Personality and Social Psychology*, **35**, 645–55.

Petty, R.E. and Cacioppo, J.T. (1979). Effects of forewarning of persuasive intent and involvement on cognitive responses. *Personality and Social Psychology Bulletin* **5**, 173–6.

Petty, R.E. and Wegener, D.T. (1998). Attitude change, multiple roles for persuasion variables. In Gilbert, Fiske and Lindzey (Eds), *The Handbook of Social Psychology (fourth edition, vol. 1)*. Boston: McGraw Hill.

Plutchick, R. and Conte, H. (1997). *Circumplex Models of Personality and Emotion*. Washington, DC: American Psychological Association.

Plutchik, R. (1980). *Emotion: A Psychoevolutionary Synthesis*. New York: Harper Row.

Plutchik, R. (1994). *The Psychology and Biology of Emotions*. New York: Harper Collins.

Plutchik, R. (1997). Suicide and Violence: The two stage model of countervailing forces. In A.J. Botsis, C.R. Soldatos and C.N. Stefanis (Eds), *Suicide: Biopsychosocial Approaches*. Amsterdam: Elsevier.

Plutchik, R. and Van Praag, H.M. (1990). A self-report measure of violence risk II. *Comprehensive Psychiatry* **30**, 1–7.

Polaschek, D.L. L. and Collie, R.M. (2004). Rehabilitating serious violent adult offenders: An empirical and theoretical stocktake. *Psychology, Crime and Law* **10(3)**, 321–34.

Popper, K.R. (1968). *The Logic of Scientific Discovery*. London: Hutchinson. Republished as Popper, K.R. (2003). *The Logic of Scientific Discovery*. London: Routledge Classics.

Power, K.G., Dyson, G.P. and Wozniak, E. (1997). Bullying among Scottish young offenders: Prisoners' self-reported attitudes and behaviour. *Journal of Community and Applied Social Psychology* **7**, 209–18.

Power, K., McElroy, J. and Swanson, V. (1997). Coping abilities and prisoners' perceptions of suicidal risk management. *The Howard Journal* **36(4)**, 378–92.

Pratt, J., Brown, D., Brown, M., Hallworth, S. and Morrison, W. (Eds) (2005). The *New Punitiveness; Trends, theories, perspectives*. Devon, UK: Willan.

Prins, H. (2002). Risk assessment: Still a risk business. *British Journal of Forensic Practice* **4(1)**, 3–8.

Prison Reform Trust (1993). *Committee on the Penalty for Homicide: Report*. Rochdale: RAP Ltd.

Prochaska, J.O. (1999). How do people change, and how can we change to help many more people? In M. Hubble, M.A., Duncan, D. Barry *et al.* (Eds), *The Heart and Soul of Change: What Works in Therapy*. Washington, DC. American Psychological Association.

Proctor, E. (1996). A five year outcome evaluation of a community based treatment programme for convicted sexual offenders run by the probation service. *Journal of Sexual Aggression* **2**, 3–16.

Proeve M. and Howells K. (2002). Shame and guilt in child sexual offenders. *International Journal of Offender Therapy and Comparative Criminology* **46(6)**, 657–67.

Qin, P. and Nordentoft, M. (2005). Suicide risk in relation to psychiatric hospitalisation: Evidence based on longitudinal registers. *Archives of General Psychiatry* **62**, 427–32.

Quinsey, V.L., Harris, G.T., Rice, M.E. and Lalumiere, M.L. (1993). Assessing treatment efficacy in outcome studies. *Journal of Interpersonal Violence* **8**, 512–23.

Randall, P. (1997).*Adult Bullying: Perpetrators and Victims*. London: Routledge.

Reinhardt (2002). Doctors are more interested in having high incomes than providing better health care. *BMJ*, **324**, 1335.

Reinhardt, U.E., Hussey, P.S. and Anderson, G.F. (2003). U.S. health care spending in an international context.*Health Affairs* **23(3)**, 10–25.

Rice, M.E., Harris, G.T. and Cormier, C.A. (1992). An evaluation of a maximum security therapeutic community for psychopaths and other mentally disordered offenders. *Law and Human Behaviour* **16(4)**, 399–412.

Rice, M.E., Quinsey, V.L. and Harris, G.T. (1991). Sexual recidivism among child molesters released from a maximum security institution. *Journal of Consulting and Clinical Psychology* **59**, 381–6.

Rigby, K. and Slee, P.T. (1991). Bullying among Australian school children: Repor-ted behaviour and attitudes towards victims. *Journal of Social Psychology* **131**, 615–27.

Roger, D. and Masters, R. (1997). The development and evaluation of an emotion control training programme for sex offenders. *Legal and Criminological Psychology* **2**, 51–64.

Roger, D. and Najarian, B. (1989). The construction and validation of a new scale for measuring emotion control. *Personality and Individual Differences* **8**, 845–53.

Rogers, R.W. (1983). Cognitive and physiological processes in fear appeals and attitude change: A revised theory of protection motivation. In Cacioppo and Petty (Eds), *Social Psychophysiology: A Sourcebook*. New York: Guilford.

Romero, J.J. and Williams, L.M. (1983). Group therapy and intensive probation supervision with sex offenders. *Federal Probation* **47**, 36–42.

Rooth, F.G. and Marks, I.M. (1974). Persistent exhibitionism: Short term response to aversion, self-regulation and relaxation treatments. *Archives of Sexual Behaviour* **3(3)**, 227–49.

Ross, R. and McKay, J. (1979). *Self-Mutilation*. Lexington, MA: Lexington Books.

Rothman, K.J. and Greenland, S. (Eds) (1998). *Modern Epidemiology*. Philadelphia, PA: Lippincott Williams and Wilkins.

Roy, A. (1982). Risk factors for suicide in psychiatric patients. *Archives of General Psychiatry* **39**, 1089–95.

Royal College of Psychiatrists (2002). *Suicide in Prisons*. London: Royal College of Psychiatrists.

Ryan, P.E. (1997). A study of the effect of the transtheoretical approach upon sex offenders. Unpublished dissertation, Southwestern Bapist Theological Seminary.

Salter A.C. (1988). *Treating Child Sex Offenders and Victims: Assessment and Treatment of Child Sex Offenders*. Beverly Hills: Sage publications.

Scheela, R.A. (2001). Sex Offender Treatment: Therapists' experiences and perceptions. *Issues in Mental Health and Nursing* **22(8)** 749–67.

Sex Offender Treatment Programme: Theory manual (January 2001). Offending Beha-viour Treatment Team. London: HM Prison Service.

Shaw, S. (1996). Prisoners serving life sentences. *The Times (London)*, 4 April.

Shaw, M. (1974). *Social Work in Prison*. London: HMSO.

Shaw, T.A., Herkov, M.J. and Greer, R.A. (1995). Examination of treatment completion and predicted outcome among incarcerated sex offenders. *Bulletin of the American Academy of Psychiatry and Law* **23**, 35–41.

Sheath, M. (1990). Confrontative work with sex offenders: Legitimised nonce-bashing? *Probation Journal* **37(4)**.

Shields, I.W. and Simourd, D.J. (1991). Predicting predatory behaviour in a population of incarcerated young offenders. *Criminal Justice and Behaviour* **18**, 180 - 94.

Shneidman, E.S. (1985). *Definition of Suicide*. New York: Wiley.

Shye, S., Elizur, D. and Hoffman, M. (1994). *Introduction to Facet Theory: Content Design and Intrinsic Data Analysis in Behavioural Research*. London: Sage.

Simon, L., Greenberg, J. and Brehm, J. (1995). Trivialisation: The forgotten mode of dissonance reduction. *Journal of Personality and Social Psychology*, **68**, 247–60.

Singleton, N., Meltzer, H., Gatward, R., with Coid, J. and Deasy, D. (1998). *Psychiatric Morbidity among Prisoners in England and Wales; Summary Report*. Office of National Statistics on behalf of the Department of Health. London: The Stationery Office.

Smalley, H. (1911). *Report by the Prison Commissioners*. London: HMSO.

Smith, P.K. and Brain, P. (2000). Bullying in schools: Lessons from two decades of research. *Aggressive Behavior* **26**, 1–9.

Snow, L. (1997). A pilot study of self-injury amongst women prisoners. In G.J. Towl (Ed.), *Suicide and Self-Injury in Prisons*. Leicester: British Psychological Society.

Snow, L. (2000). The role of formalised peer-group support in prisons. In G. Towl, L. Snow and M. McHugh (Eds), *Suicide in Prisons*. Oxford: Blackwell.

Snow, L. (2002). Prisoners' motives for self-injury and attempted suicide. *British Journal of Forensic Practice* **4(4)**, 18–29.

Soothill, K.L. (1976). Rape: A twenty two year cohort study. *Medicine, Science and the Law* **16(1)**, 62–9.

Steel, C.M., Southwick, L. and Crichlow, B. (1981). Dissonance and alcohol: Drinking your troubles away. *Journal of Personality and Social Psychology* **41**, 831–46.

Stockton, W. and Crighton, D.A. (2003). Sex-offender groupwork. In G.J. Towl (Ed.), *Psychology in Prisons*. Oxford: Blackwell.

Stone, N. (1997). *A Companion Guide to Life Sentences*. Berkeley: Owen Wells.

Stout, C.E. (2004). Controversies and Caveats. In C.E. Stout and R.A. Haynes (Eds), *The Evidence-Based Practice: Methods, Models and Tools for Mental Health Professionals*. New York: Wiley.

Sutton, J., Smith, P.K. and Swettenhem, J. (1999a). Social cognition and bullying: Social inadequates or skilled manipulators? *British Journal of Developmental Psychology* **17**, 435–50.

Tabachnick, B.G. and Fidell, L.S. (1996). *Using Multivariate Statistic (third edition)*. New York: Harper Collins.

Taylor, R. (1999). *Predicting Reconvictions for Sexual and Violent Offences using the Revised Offender Group Reconviction Scale*. London: Home Office (Research Findings No. 104).

Tetlock, P.E. (1992). The impact of accountability on judgment and choice: Towards a social contingency model. *Advances in Experimental Social Psychology* **25**, 361–76.

Tetlock, P.E., Skitka, L. and Boettger, R. (1989). Social and cognitive strategies of coping with accountability: Conformity, complexity and bolstering. *Journal of Personality and Social Psychology* **57**, 632–41.

Thornton, D. (1987). Assessing custodial adjustment. In B.J. McGurk, D.M. Thornton and M. Williams (Eds), *Applying Psychology to Imprisonment*. London: HMSO.

Thornton, D., Curran, L., Grayson, D. and Holloway, V. (1984). *Tougher Regimes in Detention Centres*. London: HMSO.

Tittle, C.R. (1969). Inmate organisation: Sex differentiation and the influence of criminal subcultures. *American Sociological Review* **34**, 492–505.

Toch, H. (1992). *Living In Prison: The Ecology of Survival*. Washington, DC: APA.

Toch, H., Adams, K. and Grant, J.D. (1989). *Coping: Maladaptation in Prisons*. New Brunswick: Transaction Publishers.

Tong, L.S. and Farrington, D.P. (2004). *How Effective is the 'Reasoning and Rehabilitation' Programme in Reducing Reoffending? A Meta-Analysis of Evaluations in Four Countries*. Cambridge: Institute of Criminology, University of Cambridge.

Topp, D.O. (1979). Suicide in Prison. *British Journal of Psychiatry* **134**, 24–7.

Towl, G.J. (1994). Ethical issues in forensic psychology. *Forensic Update* **39**, 23–6.

Towl, G.J. (2000). Suicide in prisons. In G.J. Towl, L. Snow and M.J. McHugh (Eds), *Suicide in Prisons*. Leicester: BPS Books.

Towl, G.J. (2003). Psychological Services in HM Prison Service, In G.J. Towl (Ed.), *Psychology in Prisons*. Oxford: Blackwell.

Towl, G.J. (2004a). Applied psychological services in HM Prison Service and the National Probation Service. In A.P.C. Needs and G.J. Towl (Eds), *Applying Psychology to Forensic Practice*. Oxford: Blackwell.

Towl, G.J. (2004b). Leadership of applied psychological services in prisons and probation. *British Journal of Forensic Practice* **6(3)**, 25–9.

Towl, G.J. (2005a). National Offender Management Services: Implications for applied psychologists in probation and prisons. *Forensic Update* **81**, 22–6.

Towl, G.J. (2005b). Risk assessment. *Evidence Based Mental Health* **8**, 91–3.

Towl, G.J. and Crighton, D.A. (1996). *The Handbook of Psychology for Forensic Practitioners*. London: Routledge.

Towl, G.J. and Crighton, D.A. (1997). Risk assessment with offenders. *International Review of Psychiatry* **9**, 187–93.

Towl, G.J. and Crighton, D.A. (1998). Suicide in prisons in England and Wales from 1988 to 1995. *Criminal Behaviour and Mental Health* **8**, 184–92.

Towl, G.J. And Crighton, D.A. (2002). Risk assessment and management. In G.J. Towl, L. Snow and M.J. McHugh (Eds), *Suicide in Prisons*. Oxford, Blackwell.

Towl, G.J. and Crighton, D.A. (2005). Distributed leadership for devolved services. *British Journal of Leadership in Public Services* **1(1)**.

Towl, G.J., Snow, L. and McHugh, M.J. (Eds) (2000). *Suicide in Prisons*. Oxford: Blackwell.

Townsend, P. Donaldson, N. and Whitehead, M. (1990). *Inequalities in Health: The Black Report and the Health Divide*. London: Penguin.

Tumim, S. (1990). *Report of A Review By Her Majesty's Chief Inspector of Prisons for England and Wales of Suicide and Self-Harm in Prison Service Establishments in England and Wales*. London: HMSO.

Turner, B.W., Bingham, J.E. and Andrasik, F. (2000). Short term community based treatment for sexual offenders: Enhancing effectiveness. *Sexual Addiction and Compulsivity* **7**, 211–24.

Turner, J.C. (1987). *Rediscovering the Social Group: A Self-Categorisation Theory*. Oxford: Blackwell.

Van Heeringen, K., Hawton, K. and Williams, J.M.G. (2000). Pathways to suicide: An integrative approach. In K. Hawton and K. van Heeringen (Eds), *The International Handbook of Suicide and Attempted Suicide*. Chichester: John Wiley and Sons.

Vennard, J., Sugg, D. and Hedderman, C. (1997). *Changing Offenders' Attitudes and Behaviour: What Works?* London: Home Office.

Wald, M.S. and Woolverton, M. (1991). Risk assessment: The emperor's new clothes? *Child Welfare* **70(3)**, 397–9.

Walsh, B.W. and Rosen, P.M. (1988). *Self-Mutilation: Theory, Research and Treatment*. New York: The Guildford Press.

Walters, G.D. (1995a). The psychological inventory of criminal thinking styles, Part I: Reliability and preliminary validity. *Criminal Justice and Behaviour* **22**, 307–25.

Walters, G.D. (1995b). The psychological inventory of criminal thinking styles, Part II. Identifying simulated response sets. *Criminal Justice and Behaviour* **22**, 437–45.

Walters, G.D. (1996). The psychological inventory of criminal thinking styles, Part III. Predictive validity. *International Journal of Offender Therapy and Comparative Criminology* **40**, 105–12.

Ward, T. and Hudson, S. (1998). A model of the relapse process in sexual offenders. *Journal of Interpersonal Violence* **13**, 700–25.

Ward, T. and Siegert, R.J. (2002). Toward a comprehensive theory of child sexual abuse: A theory knitting perspective.*Psychology, Crime, & Law* **8**, 319–51.

Ward, T. and Stewart, C. (2003a). Criminogenic needs and human needs: A theoretical model. *Psychology, Crime and Law.* **9(2)**, 125–43.

Ward, T. and Stewart, C. (2003b). The relationship between human needs and criminogenic needs. *Psychology, Crime and Law* **9(3)**, 219–24.

Ward, T., Nathan, P., Drake, C.R., Lee, J.K. and Pathe, M. (2000). The role of formulation based treatments for sex offenders. *Behaviour Change* **17**, 251–64.

Ward, T., Day, A., Howells, K. and Birgden, A. (2004). The multifactor offender readiness model. *Aggression and Violent Behavior* **9**, 645–73.

Watson, R. and Stermac, L. (1994). Cognitive group counselling for sexual offenders. *International Journal of Offender Therapy and Comparative Criminology* **38**, 259–70.

White, P., Bradley, C., Ferriter, M. and Hatzipetrou (1998). Managements of people with disorders of sexual preference and for convicted sexual offenders. *The Cochrane Database of Systematic Reviews, Issue 4. Art. No.: CD000251. DOI: 10.1002/14651858.CD000251*

Williams, J.M.G. (1997). *Cry of Pain: Understanding Suicide and Self-Harm*. London: Penguin.

Wool, R.J. and Dooley, E. (1987). A study of attempted suicides in prison. *Medical Science and the Law* **27(4)**, 297–301.

Youth Justice Board (2005). *Mental Health Needs and Provision*. London: Youth Justice Board.

Index